The Eagle Triumphant

How America Took Over
the British Empire

Robert Smith Thompson

John Wiley & Sons, Inc.

Published by John Wiley & Sons, Inc., Hoboken, New Jersey
Published simultaneously in Canada

For general information about our other products and services, please contact our Cus-tomer Care Department within the United States at (800) 762–2974, outside the United States at (317) 572–3993 or fax (317) 572–4002.

Wiley also publishes its books in a variety of electronic formats. Some content that appears in print may not be available in electronic books. For more information about Wiley products, visit our web site at www.wiley.com.

Library of Congress Cataloging-in-Publication Data

Thompson, Robert Smith.
   The eagle triumphant : how America took over the British empire / Robert Smith Thompson.
      p.   cm.
   ISBN 0-471-64665-2
   1. United States—Foreign relations—20th century. 2. World War, 1914–1918—Diplomatic history. 3. World War, 1939–1945—Diplomatic history.
   4. Imperialism—History—20th century. I. Title.
   E744.T495 2004
   327.73'009'041—dc22   2003025489

Printed in the United States of America
10 9 8 7 6 5 4 3 2 1

To Judy, as always

Contents

Acknowledgments

I give thanks to James Mannock, Brian Porter, and Brian Livesey, all once of the London School of Economics, for advice. My gratitude also to Russell Galen, my agent, who does wondrous things. And my appreciation to Stephen Power, an editor whose support has been invaluable.

Hail, Caesar!

Under the bright but chilly late winter Egyptian sunshine, an American vessel of war served as the stage for a show probably unique in the annals of the U.S. Navy. The Yalta Conference was just over and the USS *Quincy*, which had transported President Franklin D. Roosevelt as far as Malta (from where he had flown to the Soviet Union), had steamed to the Suez Canal and dropped anchor in the Great Bitter Lake, an inland sea about two-thirds of the distance down the waterway. There, on February 20, 1945, President Roosevelt came aboard again.

With the conference at Yalta concluded—Roosevelt, Churchill, and Stalin had met to determine the shape of the postwar world—FDR had ridden by car to Sevastopol and toured the battlefield where in the 1850s Great Britain and France had defeated czarist Russia in the Crimean War. Then he had flown to an Egyptian airfield near Ismailia, just west of the canal. Thereupon he had been carried aboard the *Quincy* and prepared to meet the local satraps.

The word *satrap* has a long and telling history. We find its origin in the Old Persian *khshathrapavan*, meaning "protector of the country." At some point, perhaps during the Athenian efforts to fend off the Persian Empire, the word entered into Greek. The imperial Romans picked it up, spelling it *satrapes*. Passing eventually into English, it signified a subordinate ruler. In the course of its evolution, "satrap" came to conjure up a picture of local leaders bowing, scraping, even performing the kowtow before the throne of the

1

emperor. So it was aboard the *Quincy* during the morning of February 20, 1945.

Draping a large black cape over Roosevelt's shoulders, naval aides wheeled him up to the forward gun deck. There he was lifted onto an ornate armchair, his throne.

The first of the satraps was the young Egyptian king Farouk. He had been a British creation, the puppet ruler of an Egypt that had long been a British protectorate (meaning an informal colony), and he had survived in his position for one reason: he had kept order on behalf of the British Empire. But now, his playboy's corpulence bulging against the brass buttons of his British-style admiral's uniform, he was paying homage to the new emperor, President Roosevelt. FDR gave him a twin-motored transport plane and urged him to plant more rice.

The next supplicant was Haile Selassie, the king of Ethiopia. Back in the 1930s, Italy's Benito Mussolini had shocked the world by invading the East African country, but the Ethiopians had fought his forces to a standstill; during World War II, the British had driven the Italians out altogether. Ethiopia thereafter had seemed on the verge of succumbing to British influence. Yet here was the Ethiopian monarch, a small, dignified, black-bearded man in a cap and an oversized British military-issue greatcoat, also placing himself at Roosevelt's disposal. He got four reconnaissance vehicles.

Finally came King Ibn Saud of Saudi Arabia: tall, with a dark goatee and flowing white robes. His was the best part of the pageant. From his palace in Riyadh, which contained both the traditional harem of Islam and the only electric elevator on the Arabian peninsula, he had traveled by motor convoy southwestward to Jidda, on the Red Sea. Once his yacht reached the Suez Canal, seamen aboard the *Quincy* had made special arrangements to keep him comfortable. Dozens of thick carpets had been spread on the foredeck and a royal tent had been set up for the king to sleep in.

The king showed up with a retinue of relatives, guards, valets, food tasters, and servers of ceremonial coffee. Soon he invited the officers of the *Quincy* to a banquet held in the approved Arab fashion, with all sitting cross-legged and eating rice pilaf and broiled lamb kebab with their fingers.

While Ibd Saud was on board the ship, Anna Roosevelt Boettiger, the president's daughter who had accompanied her father to Yalta, kept out of sight. The Saudi king, FDR had told her, on such occasions would not allow women in his presence. "By the way," he had added, "those women he does see, he confiscates."

What did Ibn Saud really want? After Farouk and Haile Selassie had backed away from Roosevelt's presence, the answer became clear. While Arab guards, colorfully garbed and armed with daggers and rifles, stood about the deck, the Saudi king approached the American president. To maintain his power on the Arabian peninsula, he explained, he needed modern weapons.

Roosevelt listened carefully, then proffered a deal. The United States would extend military aid to Saudi Arabia and even pay Ibn Saud's bills; the assistance would be part of the Lend-Lease program.

In return the United States, before the war only a minor presence along the Persian Gulf, would get full drilling rights in Saudi fields. America would replace Great Britain as the controller of Arabian oil.

Not until the last day of the Yalta Conference had Roosevelt said anything to Churchill about his impending visit with King Ibn Saud. According to Col. William Eddy, the American minister to Saudi Arabia and the official who had set up the meeting aboard the *Quincy*, Churchill was "thoroughly nettled" and "burned up the wires of all his diplomats" with orders to arrange a similar conference. Indeed, after a brief stopover in Greece, hoping to soothe anti-British sentiments there—Greece traditionally also had been a British protectorate—he hurried to meet with Ibn Saud. But Churchill had come too late and he had too little to offer: Britain was broke.

Churchill returned to London empty-handed. In one corner of the world, the *Pax Britannica* had been replaced by the *Pax Americana*.

I came across this episode, reported in the *New York Times* on February 21, 1945, while looking through old newspaper microfilms. At the time, I was doing research for a book on World War II in Asia and the Pacific, and my thoughts were far from any goings-on in the Middle East. But in the course of that work I came across evidence in the Public Record Office in London showing that at the end of the war the State Department went all out to keep British firms from returning to their prewar preeminence in the China market; that market, real or supposed, was to be an American preserve. (The Communists, of course, had other ideas.)

While in London, I also learned that in 1942 Churchill lashed out at Harry Hopkins, FDR's special emissary, with a "string of cuss words far into the early hours of the night." Hopkins's sin was that he was relaying Roosevelt's demand that the British leave India.

A kind review of my book in the *Toronto Globe and Mail* led to a visit to that city. After I gave a lecture, the reviewer (a historian at Trinity College of the University of Toronto), several of his colleagues, and I sat around a fire in the common room. The talk turned to FDR. Did you know, one asked me, that in 1939 the president extended the Monroe Doctrine to Canada? I checked: he did.

Enunciated by President James Monroe in 1823, the doctrine had stated that the "American continents are henceforth not to be considered as subjects for future colonization by any European power." The implication had been that the United States would protect Central and South America from European aggression. Now, in 1939, Roosevelt was assuming Great Britain's long-standing role as the protector of Canada.

A similar matter came to my attention. In 1941, the prime minister of Australia, like Canada a British dominion, encamped for six months not in London but rather in Washington, looking for protection against Japan.

So, almost by accident, I had a little list: Saudi Arabia, China, India, Canada, and Australia. A pattern was emerging. In each case, in the era of World War II, in theater after theater, Uncle Sam was replacing John Bull.

How far-reaching was this pattern? What were its origins? What were its consequences?

These questions led me back to the start of World War I, when Winston S. Churchill was the first lord of the admiralty and Franklin D. Roosevelt was assistant secretary of the navy; and they led me forward to the end of World War II, when Churchill was out of office and Roosevelt was dead. At the beginning of that period, when they first met in London, Churchill sneered at Roosevelt as an upstart and an underling (at least this was FDR's recollection, expressed in 1939 to Ambassador Joseph P. Kennedy); by its end, after a long series of wartime summit conferences, Churchill to all intents and purposes was Roosevelt's humble servant.

The turnabout in their personal roles, however, reflected something much broader, a great transformation of twentieth-century international relations. In 1914, at the beginning of World War I, the globe was Europe-centered, Britain-protected, and London-financed. In 1945, at the end of World War II, the globe was North America–centered, United States–protected, and New York–financed. The British Empire was in its death throes, and the American empire was very much alive.

The international changing of the guard, to be sure, was not just the result of the Roosevelt-Churchill story. Broad historical forces had been at work, and the British government in the two world wars had made decisions that had virtually eliminated its power abroad. Nevertheless, the emergence of the American empire has been the central feature of world affairs ever since 1945, and nothing illustrates that transference of power more vividly than the turbulent friendship of Roosevelt and Churchill.

Before we proceed, however, we need take up a crucial question: *is* there an American empire?

It is probably our most cherished item of national faith that the United States is not an imperial power. Empire, after all, is for those others, the French and the Belgians with their steaming tropical domains; the Axis powers and their brutal conquests; the Soviet Union imposing its system on a host of enslaved nations; and, above all, the British and the splotches of red that on old maps and globes used to highlight the colonies on which the sun never set. America, we are convinced, possesses no such empire.

Yet when we say "empire," the principal example we have in mind is the British, and the British Empire was always more than the sum of its formal colonies. It embraced also a host of protectorates, especially along the sealanes between India and Gibraltar; its investments underwrote the economies of Asia, Africa, and the Americas; the Royal Navy ruled the waves and, combined with the British army, carried out the highest goal of Victorian foreign policy, the containment of Russia.

And America? America most certainly possesses *de facto* colonies. What else are Puerto Rico, Guantánamo, Grenada, Guam, and Okinawa, and the military bases that encircle the globe from the North Pacific to the North Atlantic? In number, furthermore, America's protectorates—Japan, South Korea, Taiwan, the Philippines, Thailand, Pakistan, the emirates of the Persian Gulf, Kuwait, Saudi Arabia, Egypt, Bosnia, and all the members, old and new, of the North Atlantic Treaty Organization—far exceed those of the *Pax Britannica*. American investments, private and public, cover the earth. The American military rules not only the waves but also the rocks and rills, deserts and forests, and much of both hemispheres besides. In containing Russia (the British called it the Great Game; the Americans termed it the Cold War), the United States took up where Great Britain left off. America is the very model of a modern major empire.

But how did the American empire, a fait accompli if there ever was one, come to exist? The answer begins with the raising of the curtain on the drama that Churchill called the Thirty Years' War: the British decision, early in August 1914, to intervene in the war that was getting under way on the European continent and that would not end until the spring of 1945.

In *A Coffin for Dimitrios*, the English novelist Eric Ambler wrote: "The situation in which a person, imagining fondly that he is in charge of his own destiny, is, in fact, the sport of circumstances beyond his control, is always fascinating. It is the essential element in most good drama."

In early August 1914, the sea lords of Britannia succumbed to such an illusion of control. Three decades later, as Roosevelt had wanted, the United States of America stood in Great Britain's place.

Part I
The Great War

CHAPTER 1

The Waltz of War

1

Sarajevo was shaped like a bowl. Ringed by the mountains of Bosnia, the peaks around the town sloped down to orchards and outlying farms. Paths and then lanes twisted down farther yet, passing among whitewashed houses; a scattering of churches, mosques, and synagogues; and at last rows of shops and bazaars. At the bottom of the bowl lay the major thoroughfare. It was called the Appel Quay, for it ran alongside the Miljačka River, a stream that divided Sarajevo in two. Crossing the water was a series of stone bridges, one of which, at the end of the quay and at the base of Franz Josef Street, was the Lateiner Bridge. Later it took the name of the Princip Bridge.

For there, on the morning of June 28, 1914, Gavrilo Princip, a young Bosnian Serb, murdered Archduke Franz Ferdinand, the heir apparent to the throne of the Austro-Hungarian Empire, and his wife, Archduchess Sophie. The deaths set off the conflagration that engulfed the world.

The visit of the imperial couple to Sarajevo was the climax of their visit to Bosnia. Part of the Austro-Hungarian Empire since the late nineteenth century, the province had become turbulent. The region seeming on the verge of revolution, the archduke had gone to ascertain the readiness of the army. After two days of observing maneuvers, he and his wife on the sunny Sunday morning of June 28 took a train to Sarajevo; Franz Ferdinand was scheduled to give a speech from the steps of the town hall.

Waiting on the platform of the Sarajevo station was Oskar Potiorek, a lean, uniformed man in late middle age; he was the governor-general of Bosnia. After the train stopped, he held out a gloved hand to help Sophie step down from the carriage. In her forties, she was somewhat plump in a white silk dress. Aside from a red sash, the rest of her ensemble—the ermine tails over her shoulder and her wide, veiled hat—also was white. She was dressed in the fashionable manner for a late June morning.

Just behind her, the archduke carried her white parasol. A stout man with protruding blue eyes and a waxed, upturned mustache, he was decked out in black trousers with red stripes down the sides; a light blue tunic that bulged at his waistline; and a high, tight collar that bore three gold stars: the ceremonial uniform of an Austrian cavalry general. As he descended the steps, the green feathers that crowned his helmet brushed the top of the doorframe. He returned Potiorek's salute.

After an honor guard had presented arms, Potiorek directed his imperial guests and their aides to a row of six waiting automobiles. Police officers and security guards already occupied the first; in the second car, the mayor of Sarajevo, who was a Muslim wearing a fez, sat with the local chief of police. The next vehicle was reserved for Potiorek and the archducal couple. The aides and more guards went to the last three cars.

By modern standards, the third car was small, save for the height of the folded-down top behind the rear seat. A black Graf und Stift, made in Vienna, it boasted black leather seats and a high, wooden steering wheel. The archduke and archduchess took their seats in the back, facing the steering wheel; Potiorek then sat on the folding seat, looking back upon their royalties. The driver was a Czech named Leopold Sojka. Count Franz Harrach, an Austrian lieutenant colonel, mounted the running board on the left side of the car. With all the automobiles filled, the procession started forward.

One after another, the automobiles headed onto the Appel Quay. Off to the right, the river sparkled in the sunshine. On the left, where a row of apartment buildings ran parallel to the quay, Turkish rugs hung from balconies. Windows displayed the archduke's portrait, pictures cut from local newspapers. Flags and banners lined the street.

The Graf und Stift was midway along the quay. Governor-General Potiorek was pointing across the river, showing the archduke a dun-colored military barracks, just constructed. The time was 10:00 AM.

At that moment several things happened, almost at once. Over by the embankment wall, a tall young man in a black coat and hat made a motion. Sojka, the driver, saw a black object rise in the air and fall toward the car; he stepped on the accelerator hard. The archduke spotted the same object and raised a hand to protect his wife. Bouncing off his knuckles, the missile hit the pavement and exploded, damaging the grille and windshield of the car directly behind. Police officers wrestled the bomb thrower to the ground. The imperial car raced ahead to his destination, the Sarajevo town hall.

Once a badly shaken Franz Ferdinand had given his speech, he consulted with Governor-General Potiorek. The plan had been that the archduke and archduchess next would visit the provincial museum, up in the hills. But the streets there were narrow and full of alleyways where more potential assassins might hide. Assuming that the police had cleared the Appel Quay, therefore, Franz Ferdinand and Potiorek agreed that the couple should leave Sarajevo as soon as possible, returning to the station via the river road.

Upon leaving the municipal building, however, the lead driver made a mistake. Instead on going straight back, he turned at the corner of Franz Josef Street, steering uphill. The second car followed right behind. Leopold Sojka, the chauffeur of the archducal automobile, started to do the same.

Suddenly, though, Potiorek screamed: "What is this? Stop! You are going the wrong way! We ought to go along the Appel Quay!"

Slamming on the brake, Sojka brought the imperial car to a stop, yanking the gearshift into reverse. He did so right in front of the Schiller Delicatessen, a store that faced the Lateiner Bridge.

Then Potiorek saw him. Slipping between people gathered in front of the delicatessen, a young man, short and slight, with long dark hair and deep-set blue eyes, had come into view. He was wearing a tieless white shirt closed at the collar and an ill-fitting dark jacked buttoned down the front. His right hand was in a side pocket.

Then, as he stepped forth from the crowd, approaching the car from the right side, his hand came out of the pocket. It was holding a revolver.

The young man was Gavrilo Princip and he fired the revolver twice. An hour later, Archduke Franz Ferdinand and Archduchess Sophie were dead.

2

On the afternoon of June 28, the air in Vienna felt soft and the sky was a silken blue. The day was the eve of the feast of Sts. Peter and Paul, and in a holiday mood nearly all the people of the city seemed to be outdoors. Many took streetcars to Baden, a spa in the Vienna Woods, were vacationers sat in beer gardens and strolled along the paths that led among the chestnut trees of the Kurpark.

Seated on a bench at the edge of the park was the writer Stefan Zweig, reading a book and listening vaguely to the musicians in a bandstand nearby. Suddenly, he realized, the music had stopped. Looking up, Zweig saw that people were crowding around a placard just affixed to the bandstand. Putting his book down, Zweig walked over. On the placard was the text of a telegram already sent from Governor-General Potiorek in Sarajevo to Emperor Franz Josef at the Austrian resort of Bad Ischl. The cable stated that the archduke and archduchess had fallen victims to political assassinations.

At about noon the next day, June 29, the aged emperor reached the Hofburg Palace in Vienna. An immense mass of buildings, the Hofburg was a city within the city. Having been erected and expanded over the centuries, it was full of contrasts. A dark and dank medieval entryway opened onto a wide extent of carved stone walls and high, arched windows. Inside, the sunlight illuminated gilt and white paneling, damask walls, and stucco cherubs in the corners of the ceilings. Similarly baroque was the nearby Ballhaus Palace, home of the

Austro-Hungarian foreign ministry: there, immediately after the arrival of the emperor, the highest officials of the realm met to consider the Sarajevo assassinations.

They had little doubt who was responsible for the atrocities: Serbia. Count Leopold von Berchtold, the foreign minister, told the German ambassador, who was present, that Belgrade surely had been involved. In fact, the first reports from the police in Sarajevo indicated that Princip, along with half a dozen coconspirators, had confessed to having been trained, equipped, and financed by the Black Hand, a secret society with close ties to the Serbian government. For years, furthermore, that government had been putting out anti-Austrian propaganda and, Vienna suspected, supporting other acts of anti-Austrian terror.

What was to be done? The Austro-Hungarian authorities came to a quick decision: Serbia must be "eliminated as a factor of political power in the Balkans." The circumlocution meant war. A few days later, after securing the support of Austria's ally, Germany, in launching such a war, Count Berchtold laid his scheme. A balding, blue-eyed man with a square chin and a neat mustache, he authorized the drafting of an ultimatum to Serbia. Its language was to be so harsh that Serbia could not possibly accept it. Then Berchtold would have a pretext for an attack.

There was, however, a catch. Serbia was allied to Russia, and if Russia went to Serbia's defense, the czar's armies would pass close by the German frontier. Russia, furthermore, had another ally: France. Berchtold therefore wished to keep his plot a secret as long as possible.

3

On the afternoon of July 20, 1914, the battleship *France* dropped anchor in the bay at Kronstadt, the island fortress in the Gulf of Finland outside St. Petersburg. Aboard the battleship were France's President Raymond Poincaré and Premier René Viviani, arrived in Russia for a long-planned state visit. When the accompanying

French warships also came to rest, the Russian imperial yacht, already positioned in the harbor, put out a launch. It returned with the French leaders aboard. Amid the roar of salutes from shore batteries, Czar Nicholas II greeted them at the top of the gangplank. A band on the deck played the French and Russian national anthems. The formalities over, the yacht set sail for Peterhof, a czarist retreat on the Baltic coast.

Wrote Maurice Paléologue, France's ambassador to Russia,

[The] weather was cloudy. Suddenly a fresh breeze from the open sea brought us a heavy shower, but as suddenly the sun burst forth. . . . A few pearl-gray clouds through which the sun's rays darted, hung here and there in the sky like sashes shot with gold. . . . [I]n a limpid flood of light the estuary of the Neva spread the immense sheet of its greenish, changing waters which always remind me of Venice.

As the yacht crossed the estuary, Poincaré and Nicholas retired to the stern for serious talk. According to Paléologue, who apparently was standing or sitting nearby, the czar was afraid that leftists in the Chamber of Deputies would pull France out of the eighteen-year-old Franco-Russian alliance. Poincaré assured him that in France all political parties were patriotic.

France, he assured the czar, would maintain its alliance commitment. But would Russia, in case of war with Germany, reciprocate? On the afternoon of July 22, Poincaré had his answer. Leaving Peterhof by train, the French party rode to a great encampment outside St. Petersburg, witnessing there what purported to be a display of Russian military might.

Paléologue certainly was impressed. He wrote:

A blazing sun lit up the vast plain, a tawny and undulating plain bounded on the horizon by wooded hills. While . . . the tsaritsa, and president of the [French] Republic, the . . . grand duchesses, and the entire imperial staff were inspecting the cantonments of the troops, I waited for them [on a hill] on which

tents had been pitched. The elite of Petersburg society were . . .
crowded into the stands. The light toilettes of the women, their
white hats and parasols made the stands look like azalea beds.
Before long . . . the tsar was galloping by . . . , followed by a brilliant escort of the grand dukes and aides-de-camp. They all dis-
mounted and assembled on a low hill dominating the plain.
The troops, without arms, were drawn up in serried ranks . . .
below the row of tents. The first line ran along the very foot of
the hill. The sun was dropping . . . in a sky of purple and gold.
On a sign from the tsar an artillery salvo signaled evening
prayer. The bands played a hymn. Everyone uncovered. A non-
commissioned officer recited the *Pater* in a loud voice. All these
men, thousands upon thousands, prayed for the tsar and Holy
Russia. The silence and the composure of that multitude, the
vision of the alliance which sanctified everything, gave the ceremony a touching majesty.

The ceremony represented the solidity of the Franco-Russian
alliance. But it left unanswered the question of what, given a war in
the Balkans, Germany would do.

4

The next day, July 23, the *Hohenzollern*, the special steam yacht of
Kaiser Wilhelm II, put in at a fjord on the Norwegian coast. Accompanied by a protective squadron from the German High Seas Fleet,
the kaiser, he of the withered left arm, upturned mustaches, brilliant
mind, and mercurial temperament, was enjoying his annual summer
cruise.

With the yacht anchored in the fjord, Wilhelm and his guests
went ashore at the Norwegian village of Wik, where an old wooden
church stood on a promontory. An English parson happened to be
in the sanctuary, and the kaiser engaged him in a discussion of worship. Back on the yacht, the kaiser and his party gathered in the
smoking room.

There Wilhelm received a telegram from the Norddeutsch wire service: the message said that Austria-Hungary had sent its ultimatum to Serbia. In the account of Admiral Georg von Müller, a naval aide, the news "brought a flush to his cheeks." But he laid it aside and joined the others for a game of cards.

July 25 was more eventful. This time Norddeutsch carried the full text of the ultimatum. After breakfast, the kaiser walked the deck and, seeing that Admiral Müller was holding a copy of the report, remarked:

"*Was, das ist doch einmal eine forsche Note.*" (Well, for once that's a strong note.)

Müller replied: "*Ja, forsche ist die Note, aber sie bedeutet Krieg!*" (Yes, the note is strong, but it means war!)

The Austro-Hungarian ultimatum to Serbia was indeed strong. It demanded that Belgrade cease all its anti-Austrian activities, that it punish all officials guilty of anti-Austrian deeds, and that it accept the participation of Austrian police, on Serbian soil, in the identification, apprehension, and execution of all those involved in the Sarajevo assassinations.

Serbia had until 6:00 PM on July 25, 1914, to comply unconditionally with all these terms; otherwise Austria-Hungary would declare war. The government in Vienna the previous day had distributed copies of the ultimatum to the embassies of all the powers, including Great Britain.

5

Seated around the long, green-baize-covered table in the cabinet room at 10 Downing Street, with H. H. Asquith, the prime minister, positioned directly beneath the clock on the marble mantelpiece, the members of the British government on the afternoon of July 24 had been talking about the situation in Ireland. Catholics there wanted independence, Protestants demanded continued union with Great Britain, and the Emerald Isle was about to explode. No one in the cabinet room knew what to do.

Winston S. Churchill, then first lord of the Admiralty, wrote in his memoirs of World War I,

[The] discussion had reached its inconclusive end and the cabinet was about to separate, when the quiet grave tones of [Foreign Secretary] Sir Edward Grey's voice were heard reading from a document which had just been brought to him from the Foreign Office. It was the text of the Austrian note to Serbia. He had been reading or speaking for several minutes before I could disengage my mind from the tedious and bewildering debate which had just closed. We were all very tired, but gradually as the phrases and sentences followed one another, impressions of a wholly different character began to form in my mind. This note was clearly an ultimatum, but it was an ultimatum such as had never been penned in modern times. As the reading proceeded it seemed absolutely impossible that any state in the world could accept it, or that any acceptance, however abject, would satisfy the aggressor. The parishes of Fermanagh and Tyrone faded back into the mists and squalls of Ireland, and a strange light began immediately, but by perceptible gradations to fall upon the map of Europe. . . . I went back to the Admiralty at about 6 o'clock. I said to my friends . . . that there was real danger, and that it might be war.

At his desk that evening, Churchill wrote to Clementine, his wife: "My darling one, I . . . am coming to you and the kittens tomorrow by the 1 o'clock train. I will tell you all the news then. Europe is trembling on the verge of a general war. The Austrian ultimatum to Servia [sic] being the most insolent document of its kind ever devised."

The next morning, July 25, Sergei Sazonov, the Russian foreign minister, joined other high officials aboard a train for Tsarskoe Selo, known as the Czar's Village, by the shore of the Baltic. Inside the Catherine Palace, Czar Nicholas II, a small man with a mustache and pointed beard, greeted Sazonov and the others, leading them into a study that overlooked the blue of the sea.

Russia must support Serbia, Nicholas stated in his thin voice. After some discussion with the assembled ministers, he ordered the calling up of the reserves, the sending of officers' families to the safety of the Russian interior, and the holding of merchant ships in the ports for naval or military use. He also had the soldiers recalled to their barracks and cadets promoted to officers.

Then he read aloud from a document that, in the face of the Austro-Hungarian ultimatum to Serbia, Sazonov had prepared and brought to Tsarskoe Selo. It proclaimed that Russia's frontier districts in Poland and the Ukraine, the regions of the frontiers of Germany and Austria-Hungary, now existed in a "state of war."

That afternoon, Serbia accepted the Austrian demands. Austria-Hungary rejected the response out of hand.

6

At about nine o'clock on the morning of Sunday, July 26, a short, stoop-shouldered, rather pudgy man with thinning red hair walked out of his rented cottage at Cromer on the North Sea; his pugnacious lower jaw gave him the air of an English bulldog. He was, of course, Winston Churchill. As promised, he had joined his family for a weekend at the shore.

"I went down to the beach and played with the children," Churchill wrote. "We dammed the little rivulets which trickled down to the sea as the tide went out. It was a very beautiful day. The North Sea shone and sparkled to the far horizon." But, Churchill wondered, what "was there beyond that line where sea and sky melted into one another"? Had the whole of the German High Seas Fleet put out of its base at Kiel? Was it cruising off the Norwegian coast? Was it preparing to attack, perhaps right at the Cromer beach?

Alarmed, Churchill returned to London that night. In the morning, July 27, he went first to the Admiralty, where he consulted with First Sea Lord Prince Louis Battenberg, and then proceeded to 33 Eccleston Square, Sir Edward Grey's town house near Victoria Station. Prince Louis and Sir Edward both thought the European situation dangerous and urged Churchill to retain the British fleet in the English Channel, where it had been staging annual maneuvers. News of the retention, they believed, might deter Germany from war.

Churchill, however, wanted to do more. "As early as Tuesday, July 28," he wrote, "I felt that the fleet should go to its war station"—at Scapa Flow in the Orkney Islands above Scotland, from where it would have a straight shot at Germany. Churchill nonetheless feared to bring the matter before the cabinet (the majority of which wanted no part of war) "lest it should mistakenly be considered a provocative action likely to damage the chances of peace." Churchill therefore informed only one person, H. H. Asquith, the prime minister.

With baggy tweeds and his wavy gray hair needing a trim, Asquith looked like the university don he might have become; he had taken the highest possible honors at Oxford. But he had gone into the law and then, as the leader of the Liberal Party, he became the master of British politics. Squarish of face and placid of manner, he wasted no words.

Upon hearing the request to move the fleet to Scapa Flow, Churchill wrote, Asquith "looked at me with a hard stare and gave a sort of grunt. I did not require anything else."

Instead of returning to battle stations in the Mediterranean, the Red Sea, and even farther to the east, as they normally would have done, the greatest ships of the Royal Navy steamed northward. Churchill, Grey, and Asquith may have seen the move as deterrence. Berlin saw it as provocation.

Back in Germany from his cruise, Kaiser Wilhelm II was glowing with an idea: through the brilliance (as he saw it) of his diplomacy, he would confine the war to the Balkans. So on the morning of July 28, he sat at his desk in his country estate at Potsdam, just a few miles outside Berlin, and dictated a cable to Vienna. Austria-Hungary, he suggested, would occupy the Serbian capital—and stop there until Serbia had fulfilled the promises set forth in its reply to the ultimatum.

Such was Wilhelm's "Halt in Belgrade" scheme. Even though Vienna had no intention of complying, the kaiser did not sever the German–Austro-Hungarian alliance.

At 10:45 PM, also on July 28, he fired off another cable, this to his cousin Czar Nicholas II. The message began with "Dear Nicky." It went on to say that the kaiser was trying to get Austria-Hungary to communicate directly with Russia; he hoped that Russia would reciprocate. "Therefore," the kaiser concluded in English, "with regard to the hearty and tender friendship which binds us . . . I am exerting my utmost influence to arrive to a satisfactory understanding with you. I confidently hope you will help me in my efforts to smooth over difficulties that may arise. Your very sincere and devoted friend and cousin, Willy."

Kaiser Wilhelm may well have been the czar's "sincere and devoted friend," but as a diplomat, he was a failure. That very afternoon, July 28, Austria-Hungary had declared war on Serbia.

7

At eight o'clock in the morning of Wednesday, July 29, with President Poincaré and Premier Viviani aboard, the *France* neared the breakwaters at the Dunkirk harbor and dropped anchor. As the French leaders came ashore, thousands of onlookers cheered and waved little French tricolor flags.

"It was truly France herself that stood in greeting," Poincaré wrote in his memoirs. "We did not have to read a newspaper to follow the sentiments of the French people. If I understood the point of the acclaim, it meant: 'Finally, you are here! . . . Return to your post quickly. We have full confidence in you that you can keep us out of war. But if war comes, you can count on us!'"

Two hours later, Poincaré's train reached Paris. Stepping onto the platform, he mounted an open carriage and, surrounded by a squadron of equestrian guards, with plumed helmets, scarlet jackets, and glistening swords, started forth. All along the route to the Élysée Palace, the sidewalks were packed with enthusiastic crowds.

At the palace itself, the iron grille gate swung open and the presidential carriage crunched across the gravel of the courtyard. As he walked through the glass front door held open by a bemedaled usher, Poincaré had the sense that all French social classes were united in the common patriotic cause: war with Germany.

The French president, however, was a realist. Even joined by Russia, he realized, France could not defeat Germany. So the question of the hour was: would England come in?

Mounting the low stone stoop of 10 Downing Street, the nineteen members of the British cabinet late on the morning of July 29 filed into the cabinet room. All but four (including Churchill, Grey, and Asquith), it became plain, opposed intervention in a Continental war.

July 30. Germany sent an ultimatum to Russia, demanding an end to its mobilization. On that same day, France began to mobilize against Germany. Germany sent a similar ultimatum to Paris.

July 31, London. Sir Eyre Crowe, a high-ranking bureaucrat in the Foreign Office, was distraught. Fiercely opposed to the neutralism of the cabinet, he spent the morning composing a memorandum for Sir Edward Grey. In part it read: "The theory that England cannot engage in a big war means her abdication as an independent state. . . . A balance of power cannot be maintained by a state that is incapable of fighting and consequently carries no weight."

In the cabinet meeting later that morning, Churchill reiterated the Crowe position. "It is no exaggeration to say that Winston occupied at least half of the time," Asquith wrote to Venetia Stanley, his mistress. "Winston very bellicose and demanding immediate [naval] mobilization."

Churchill admitted his belligerence: "At the cabinet I demanded the immediate calling out of the fleet reserves and the completion of our naval preparations. . . . The cabinet . . . took the view . . . that this step was not necessary to our safety."

On August 1, 1914, Germany declared war on Russia and France. Germany would strike at France first, passing through Belgium.

8

Late the next morning, August 2, a Sunday, Margot Asquith, the tall, slender, sharp-faced wife of the prime minister, was driven to St. Paul's Cathedral to attend a communion service. Afterward she went to Carlton House Terrace to call on Prince Max von Lichnowsky, the German ambassador to Great Britain, and his wife, Princess Mechtilde. Both were immensely popular in London society.

Mrs. Asquith found the princess lying on a green sofa with a dachshund by her side; her eyes were swollen from crying. The ambassador, who had just returned from a breakfast conversation with the prime minister, was nearby, pacing up and down the living room. "Oh! Say there is surely not going to be a war!" he burst out. "Dear Mrs. Asquith, can nothing be done to prevent it?"

Having no answer to the question, she returned to 10 Downing Street. There the cabinet was meeting again.

Sir Edward Grey, tall, lanky, hawk-faced, the quintessential English aristocrat with an estate near the Scottish border, dominated the meeting. The Foreign Office that very morning had received news that the German army, heading for France, had entered Belgium. Ever since the 1830s, Great Britain had guaranteed Belgian neutrality.

Grey, however, concentrated on a different point. Two years before, he had sent to Paul Cambon, the French ambassador, a letter promising that if Germany attacked France, the Royal Navy would defend the French Channel ports. The letter had been kept secret, even from the cabinet. Now Grey showed a copy around and raised the question whether Great Britain could abandon such a commitment.

Combined with Germany's violation of Belgian neutrality, Grey's revelation won the support of most of the neutralists for an intervention in Europe. Grey now had authorization to raise the matter of that intervention with the full House of Commons.

9

On the afternoon of August 3, the House was crowded. The green benches on the floor reserved for the cabinet members and the leaders of the opposition were full; so were all the back benches, staircases, and passageways. Margot Asquith and others sat in the guest gallery, looking down on the floor through a latticework screen.

Below her, Grey walked to the end of the polished oak table, laid his papers across the dispatch box, and began to speak:

"Last week I stated that we were working for peace not only for this country, but to preserve the peace of Europe. Today . . . it is clear that the peace of Europe cannot be preserved."

Step by step, Grey revealed what he had not before disclosed to the House: 1912 Anglo-French military and naval conversations and his subsequent note of assurance to Ambassador Cambon. He held aloft a copy of that note.

Next he took up the issue of Belgian neutrality, contending that Great Britain should uphold that principle. Doing so, he held, was in Britain's interest, for Belgium had been the gateway of British commerce in Europe.

Finally, at the end of his nearly hour-long speech, Grey made his final appeal:

I ask the House from the point of view of British interests, to consider what may be at stake. If France is beaten in a struggle of life and death, beaten to her knees, loses her position as a world power, becomes subordinate to the will and power of one greater than herself . . . and if Belgium fell under the same dominating influence, and then Holland and Denmark, then would not Mr. Gladstone's words come true, that just opposite to us there would be . . . the unmeasured aggrandizement of a [single] power?

The ovation was loud. Grey continued,

It might be said, I suppose, that we might stand aside, husband our strength, and that whatever happened in the course of this war, at the end of it we could intervene to put things right, and to adjust them to our own point of view. But if in a crisis like this, we ran away [Cheers] from obligations of honour and interest, I doubt whether whatever material force we might have at the end of it would be of very much value.

In his oration, Grey had made no mention of a critical point: that if the Royal Navy could defend the French Channel ports, then surely it could defend the British home islands. His point, instead, was that if Britain failed to fight, it would lose influence not only with France and Russia but also with the vast external realm of its empire. For Sir Edward Grey, the fundamental point was the preservation of the *Pax Britannica*.

The House received Grey's appeal with thunderous applause. When it adjourned, Grey went out into the lobby. Churchill caught up and asked, "What happens now?"

Grey replied: "Now we sent them [the Germans] an ultimatum to stop the invasion of Belgium."

After the adjournment, Prime Minister and Mrs. Asquith rode back to 10 Downing Street. The crowds were so dense that extra police had to be brought in from Scotland Yard to clear the way for the automobile. Mrs. Asquith later commented:

I looked at the excited cheerers, and from the happy expression on their faces you might have supposed that they welcomed the war. I have met with men who loved stamps, and stones, and snakes, but I could not imagine any man loving war. Too exhausted to think I lay sleepless in bed. Bursts of cheering broke like rockets in a silent sky, and I listened to snatches of 'God Save the King' shouted in front of Buckingham Palace all through the night.

The evening found Grey in his rooms at the Foreign Office, talking with J. A. Spender, the editor of the *Westminster Gazette*. During a pause in the conversation, Grey rose from his desk and walked to a window. Looking out on St. James's Park and noticing the glow of the streetlights as they came on along the Mall, he remarked, "The lamps are going out all over Europe and we shall not see them lit again in our lifetime."

10

The morning of August 4, 1914, brought an end to the lovely weather that had prevailed for the previous month. Dark clouds scudded up from the Channel, spitting down flurries of rain and brushing in patches of fog. London was shrouded in gray, the atmosphere being, in the word of the *Westminster Gazette*, "unsettled." The term described the sky above as well as the mood below, at least with some members of the British cabinet.

While the elderly Lord John Morley, who was the lord president of the council (an advisory post) and an author of renown, was nibbling his dry toast at breakfast in his home at Wimbledon, by the southwestern corner of London, a messenger arrived from 10 Downing Street. Morley had made no secret of his intention to resign from the government in protest over the impending intervention. Morley was of the old school of British diplomacy: to him, not Germany but Russia was the great menace to British interests. To him, Germany posed no threat to Britain, at home or abroad; throughout most of the nineteenth century, however, Russia had had its designs on the Indian Raj.

Asquith had sent down a last-minute appeal. "Think twice and thrice, and as many times more as arithmetic can number," he had written, "before you take a step which impoverishes the government, and leaves me stranded and almost alone."

After pacing his library and garden, Morley had himself driven to Whitehall. On the way he passed Victoria Station. The walkways were jammed with people who to Morley looked like Germans and Austrians trying to get home.

Once in his office, Morley sat down at his desk and penned a reply to Asquith: "Your letter shakes me terribly," he wrote. "It goes to my very core." But in this, his formal letter of resignation, Lord Morley went on to draw one cardinal difference between himself and his cabinet colleagues: "To bind ourselves to France, and to whatever demands may be made by Russia on France [is only] playing Russia's game."

Throughout most of the nineteenth century, Great Britain's policy had been that of "splendid isolation," staying aloof from Continental commitments. Britannia, after all, had ruled the waves. Always the prescient intellectual, Lord Morley sensed that the days of the British imperium were fast coming to an end.

11

Shortly before three o'clock, Asquith went to the House of Commons to announce the sending of the ultimatum to Germany. It would expire that evening at eleven o'clock, Greenwich time.

Then the Speaker of the House read aloud a message from King George V:

> The present state of public affairs in Europe constituting in the opinion of His Majesty a case of great emergence . . . His Majesty deems it proper to provide additional means for the military service, and therefore . . . His Majesty has thought it right to . . . order that the Army reserve shall be called out on permanent service.

When the Speaker had finished reading the royal message and the members had left the chamber, Mrs. Asquith went downstairs to the prime minister's room.

"Henry looked grave," she wrote, "and gave me John Morley's letter of resignation, saying, 'I shall miss him very much; he is one of the most distinguished men living.'"

For some time they said nothing. She went to the window, standing behind Asquith's chair.

"Is it all up?" she asked.

He answered without looking at her.

"Yes, it's all up."

Shortly after the House adjourned, Walter Hines Page, the U.S. ambassador, called on Grey. Worn and pallid, the foreign secretary was standing against the mantelpiece in his office. He sat and then returned to the fireplace.

"England would be forever contemptible," Grey said, "if it should sit by and see this treaty [for Belgian neutrality] violated. Its position would be gone if Germany were thus permitted to dominate Europe. . . . We have told Germany that if this assault on Belgium's neutrality is not reversed, England will declare war."

"Do you expect Germany to accept it?" Page asked.

Grey shook his head.

"No, of course everybody knows that there will be war."

After a moment Grey spoke again, his eyes filling with tears. "Thus the efforts of a lifetime go for nothing," he said. "I feel like a man who has wasted his life."

12

That evening, as the rain stopped, a huge crowd filled the center of London. As the multitude surged forward and around the Victoria Memorial, King George V and his family appeared on a balcony of Buckingham Palace. As one, a million voices sang "God Save the King."

After dinner at 10 Downing Street, not far away, Margot Asquith joined her husband in the cabinet room. Grey was there already, seated at the baize-covered table. So were R. B. Haldane, the lord chancellor, and J. A. Spender, editor of the *Westminster Gazette*. David Lloyd George, the silver-locked chancellor of the exchequer, soon joined the group. They smoked without speaking.

By nine o'clock they had heard nothing from Berlin. Ten o'clock came. Only an hour remained until the ultimatum to Germany would expire. Still nothing from Berlin. The clock on the mantel showed 10:55 PM. Everyone at the table was watching that clock. The room, dimly lit, was silent. Each person sat encased in the most private of thoughts.

Then, from down Whitehall and across Parliament Square and high in the tower beside the Houses of Parliament, resounded the bells of the most famous clock in the world, the deep sonorities of Big Ben. The time was 11:00 PM.

In the cabinet room, Lloyd George later wrote, every face was "suddenly contracted in a painful intensity. 'Doom!' 'Doom!' 'Doom!' down to the last stroke."

CHAPTER 2

The Shining City upon the Hill

1

At exactly eleven o'clock on the morning of June 22, 1897, the huge gate in front of Buckingham Palace swung open and out trotted four white horses pulling a gilded, open carriage. As the equipage started out along the Mall, huge crowds of Britons who had gathered on both sides of the thoroughfare erupted in cheers—for seated alone in the rear of the carriage was their monarch and empress, Queen Victoria, riding forth in celebration of her Diamond Jubilee.

Other carriages followed, forming the procession of processions. Throngs without precedent lined every inch of the route: Charing Cross, the Strand, Fleet Street. The last, reported the *Westminster Gazette*, "looked strangely picturesque with its gay houses and irregular skyline rising above a . . . forest of brilliant masts and flowing creepers. . . . The grenadiers of either side made a glowing line of red along the curved road, dancing pennants and plumes and battle-stained colours, veterans . . . with medals, young men browned by foreign suns."

At last the queen's carriage reached the open square just beyond the end of Fleet Street. Victoria, Queen of England, Defender of the Faith, Empress of India, and Ruler of the British Dominions beyond the Seas, had arrived at the steps of St. Paul's Cathedral.

29

Awaiting her were the living symbols of the British Empire at its apogee: bishops with their miters; generals and admirals gleaming with their brass and braid; scholars robed in the variegated colors of the colleges of Oxford and Cambridge, those twin propagators of the imperial ideology; and a mass chorus swathed in red, white, and purple singing a "Te Deum" that, as someone said, for once was not tedious. Farther up the steps and standing in rows behind all those splashes of color were the emissaries of empire: Hong Kong Chinese in silken gowns; Turkish policemen from Cyprus in fezzes; turbaned officers of the India Imperial Service Corps; cavalrymen in slouch hats from New South Wales; frock-coated prime ministers of the self-governing dominions; and a host of governors of distant possessions. From the windows and rooftops all around St. Paul's a million handheld Union Jacks waved and Cockney voices yelled, "Three cheers for India!" and "Go it, old girl!"

Seated in the carriage at the center of all the attention, as the *Daily Mail* described the scene, "was a little, plain flushed old lady . . . so very quiet, so very grave, so unmistakably and every inch a lady and a queen. [She was] all in black, a silver streak under the black bonnet . . . with the corners of her mouth drawn tight down, as if she were trying not to cry."

The occasion was Queen Victoria's sixtieth year on the throne, but its theme was the grandeur of the empire. As the people of London that day waved their little flags, they had little doubt that Britannia would rule the waves forever.

Only a few weeks later, however, the poet laureate Rudyard Kipling published in the *Times* of London what is probably his best-remembered poem. It was a warning, titled "Recessional":

God of our fathers, known of old,
  Lord of our far-flung battle-line,
Beneath whose awful Hand we hold
  Dominion over palm and pine—
Lord God of Hosts, be with us yet,
Lest we forget—lest we forget!

The tumult and the shouting dies;
   The Captains and the Kings depart;
Still stands Thine ancient sacrifice,
   An humble and a contrite heart.
Lord God of Hosts, be with us yet,
Lest we forget—lest we forget.

Far-called, our navies melt away;
   On dune and headland sinks the fire:
Lo, all our pomp of yesterday
   Is one with Nineveh and Tyre!
Judge of the Nations, spare us yet,
Lest we forget—lest we forget!

If, drunk with sight of power, we loose
   Wild tongues that have not Thee in awe,
Such boastings as the Gentiles use,
   Or lesser breeds without the Law—
Lord God of Hosts, be with us yet,
Lest we forget—lest we forget!

For heathen heart that puts her trust
   In reeking tube and iron shard,
All valiant dust that builds on dust,
   And guarding, calls not Thee to guard.
For frantic boast and foolish word—
Thy mercy on Thy people, Lord!

Kipling knew whereof he wrote. Despite the pomp and circum-
stance of the Diamond Jubilee, Great Britain's economy, the very
engine of empire, had been slipping. The turn had come in the
1870s. Although their capital had still been growing, the British had
chosen, without any real debate, to spend that capital on luxuries.
The managerial class had grown indolent. "Tired of the routine of
trade and flushed with the bucolic aspirations of the country gentleman," an economic historian has commented, "the children of
affluence had worked at play and played at work."

The result had been inevitable. By 1897, more than 20 percent of British steel still came from Bessemer converters, which Germany had all but abandoned. British productivity lagged far behind that of Germany and the United States. Then, starting only two years after the Diamond Jubilee, Great Britain fought an imperial war it almost lost.

Early in October 1899, a small locomotive with a tall smokestack puffed its way over the dun-colored South African veld; the train ran southward from Pretoria in the Transvaal to Bloemfontein in the Orange Free State. In the carriage at the rear of the train sat an untidy-looking old man with hunched shoulders, a long white beard, and a floppy black hat. He was Paul Kruger, the president of the Transvaal, on his way to meet with Sir Alfred Milner, the high commissioner for the British Cape Colony.

The two men were on a collision course. A fervent imperialist, Milner was determined to bring all southern Africa under British dominion. A staunch Boer nationalist, Kruger was equally determined to save his people, the Dutch-descended citizens of the Transvaal and the Orange Free State, from the onslaught of the British Empire.

Great Britain's quarrel with the Boer republics dated back many years. When the British during the Napoleonic wars had taken over Cape Town and its environs, the Dutch farmers there had trekked inland. In doing so, they had situated themselves over great lodes of gold and diamonds. So enter, in time, the archintriguer Cecil Rhodes. The object of Rhodes's scheming was the removal of the Boers so that he could get his hands on the most valuable mineral deposits in the world. Wealthy already, he induced the British government to provoke a war with the Boers, a fight he was certain the Boers would lose.

With British forces concentrated on the borders of the Boer republics, President Kruger met with Commissioner Milner only briefly; there was nothing to say. So on October 8, 1899, Kruger issued an ultimatum, demanding a British withdrawal. No retreat ensuing, the Boer War began on October 11, 1899.

Three years later, the British won the war, barely. Only by burning Boer farmhouses, forcing Boer women and children into concentration camps, and bringing most of the firepower of the empire to bear against a handful of grunting Dutch farmers did Great Britain manage to prevail.

Even in victory, the British government concealed from its people a telling statistic. To pay for the war, London had had to borrow a fifth of the cost from American banks.

Once proud of its splendid isolation, Great Britain after the Boer War began to seek friends abroad. A 1902 alliance with Japan acknowledged the might of the land of the rising sun. A 1904 entente cordiale, a cordial understanding, ended the ancient Anglo-French rivalry. A 1907 treaty with Russia granted the czar a sphere of influence in northern Persia; Great Britain thereby declared its Victorian-era cold war with Russia a thing of the past.

Most important, the Boer War brought home to the masters of the British Empire that their authority abroad rested on support from the United States of America. Given the rise of imperial Germany, the holy grail of British diplomacy became the pursuit of the fidelity of the United States. But since its very inception as a republic, the United States had had little reason to be faithful to its former Britannic masters.

2

The air lay hot and heavy, that May of 1787, as Philadelphia awaited the delegates. The warmest spring since 1750, older city-dwellers remembered, as they gasped in their brick row houses. Such sticky weather for starting a convention! The air was steamy in the Pennsylvania State House, too, as the delegates on the twenty-fifth day of May began to assemble. Perspiring freely, they entered the east room of the steepled brick building, selecting their tables. Most were soon fanning themselves with handkerchiefs or pieces of parchment, although the physical heat was the least of their problems. Their country and their fortunes alike were threatened, or so they feared, and they had journeyed to Philadelphia to see what they could do to save both.

The Constitutional Convention had grown out of a list of post–Revolutionary War woes; almost all these problems had their roots in the continued presence of the British in and around North America. Settlers beyond the Appalachian Mountains lacked protection from the Indians, often armed by the British in Fort Pitt. Trappers who hoped to ship their furs to the markets of Europe found that the Spanish, who then controlled New Orleans, had closed the port to American trade; Spain was allied with Great Britain. Artisans in New England suffered from the competition of English goods. British forces were bivouacked in Ontario and Quebec, and the Royal Navy patrolled the Atlantic Ocean, shutting off American trade with the British West Indies. Without commerce, many Americans feared, their experiment in liberty would be short-lived.

In response to such threats, Maryland late in 1786 urged the states to send delegates the following summer to Philadelphia, there to render the national government, such as it was, "adequate to the exigencies of the Union." All the states save Rhode Island complied.

"The state of Georgia, by the Grace of God, free, sovereign, and independent...": on the morning of Friday, May 25, 1787, the voice of Major William Jackson, a South Carolinian and secretary to the convention, was announcing the credentials of the state delegations. Georgia was the last on his list, but he kept droning on. The delegates had assembled, he stated, to "take into consideration the State of the Union . . . as to trade and other important objects [and] to render the . . . government entirely adequate to the actual situation."

The chamber where the delegates met was about forty feet by forty, with a white plaster ceiling; square-paned windows; and, in the rear, two marble-faced fireplaces. Placed on a small podium between those fireplaces was a chair with heavy mahogany arms and a high, curved back. George Washington, president of the convention, sat in that chair.

It was well that he did so. As presiding officer, he played a quiet but important part in determining the convention's outcome. Throughout the convention, Washington sat in near-silence. He was courteous, firm, and he followed the proceedings with care. He also kept his own counsel. In his stillness lay his strength, a strength that served as an example to the others. They needed all the strength they could muster.

The delegates to the Constitutional Convention were embarking on no mere revision of the older Articles of Confederation, that Revolutionary War–era treaty among the states that had created the flimsiest possible national government. Rather, they were determined to create a dramatically new form of government, one with vastly expanded central powers.

"The Congress," said the eventual Constitution of the United States, in Article I, Section 8, "shall have Power To lay and collect Taxes . . . and provide for the common Defence." During the Revolutionary War, Congress had had no such authority, a shortcoming that had nearly crippled General Washington's efforts against the British. Congress, the framers went on, was to have the power to "regulate commerce with foreign nations, and among the several states." With this, the commerce clause, the national government was able to keep out British economic competition and build a unified national market. And Congress received the right to govern territory outside state control—the lands beyond the Appalachians still in the grip of the British Empire.

In the Federalist Papers, thus, James Madison held that the Constitution not only protected liberties at home but also enabled Congress to defend the United States against the British Empire abroad. Madison envisioned an American people free to expand their own empire all the way across the North American continent.

3

[W]e proceeded down the channel with an Indian dressed in a sailor's jacket for our pilot, and on reaching the main channel were visited by some Indians who have a temporary residency on a marshy island in the middle of the river, where there is a great abundance of water fowl. Here the mountainous country . . . approached the river on the left, and a higher mountain is distinguished towards the southwest. At a distance of twenty miles from our camp we halted at a village . . . consisting of seven ill-looking houses . . . and situated at the foot of the high hills on the right, behind two marshy islands. We merely stopped to purchase some food and two beaver skins, and then proceeded. Opposite to these islands the hills on the left retire, and the river widens into a kind of bay crowded with low islands, subject to be overflowed occasionally by the tide.

We had not gone far from this village when the fog cleared off, and we enjoyed the delightful prospect of the ocean, that ocean, the object of all our labours, the reward of all our anxieties. This cheering view exhilarated the spirits of all the party, who were still more delighted on hearing the distant roar of the breakers.

The river was the Columbia; the ocean was the Pacific; the date was November 7, 1805; and the words, penned in the journal of the expedition, were those of Meriwether Lewis and William Clark. At the request of President Thomas Jefferson, who two years before had effected the Louisiana Purchase, Lewis and Clark had left Fort Mandan, in what is now North Dakota, crossed the Rocky Mountains, and descended along the Columbia River to the Pacific coast.

They returned to the East as national heroes, for their journey had inspired the vision of American dominion "from sea to shining sea." In that sense, Lewis and Clark, and the president who had sent them forth, were the originators of American "imperialism," the vision of dominion over the whole of the continent. And then America would become, in the words of Thomas Paine, that old radical who was forever at Jefferson's side, an "empire of liberty," one that someday would vanquish the European empires of tyranny.

First, though, the Americans had to fight another war. We call it the War of 1812. They called it the Second War of Independence.

America in truth was so far from being an empire that Great Britain, embroiled in the Napoleonic Wars, regarded the United States with contempt. Ships of the Royal Navy impressed American sailors and seized American vessels. British trade restrictions caused crop prices in the American South to plummet. British units in the West encouraged Indians to attack American pioneers. The British seemed on the verge of obliterating large parts of the American economy.

So, bowing to political pressures from the South and the West, Congress on June 18, 1812, declared war on Great Britain. Yet the declaration hardly meant a thing. Opposed to the war—to bankers and shippers in Boston and Manhattan, the loss of an occasional sailor or vessel was just a cost of the business of smuggling goods to the European continent—New Yorkers and New Englanders made even more money by supplying the British forces in Canada. Hoping to invade Canada, the Americans found themselves having to settle for a stalemate. British ships, furthermore, blockaded the Atlantic coast and sailed up the Chesapeake Bay with impunity. Reaching the District of Columbia, they even burned the Capitol and the White House.

America's very existence as a nation, let alone an empire, was in peril. The country was divided, its treasury was empty, its economy was shattered, and its navy was confined to its ports. And then . . .

In the middle of the night, September 13–14, 1814, a heavy rain fell on the Baltimore harbor. Throughout much of the day, British men-of-war had been bombarding Fort McHenry there, and its doom had seemed assured. Not even the rain deterred the gunfire from the ships, the flash of shells flaring through the water-swept sky. Braving the elements, Baltimoreans watching the scene from their rooftops wondered how Fort McHenry could possibly survive. If the fort fell, so would Baltimore and, possibly, the rest of the American republic.

Also watching the action from a sloop about eight miles up the Patapsco River was an officer named Francis Scott Key. Five-fifty was supposed to be sunrise, but the clouds still hung low, and even by looking through a telescope he could make out nothing in the harbor beyond.

Then, however, a breeze sprang up from the west, clearing the air. He raised his glass again and this time he saw it: against the gray of the clouds the red, white, and blue of the American flag still flew from the top of Fort McHenry. The garrison had held out, and we know the rest: "Oh, say can you see by the dawn's early light . . ."

4

On the evening of Saturday, February 19, 1848, an American diplo-mat named James Freanor reached Washington. Two weeks earlier, having completed negotiations with the Mexican government, he had left Mexico City on horseback and headed through mountain passes to the port of Veracruz. From there he had arrived by ship at Mobile and taken a stagecoach north.

Once in Washington he immediately sought out the residence of the secretary of state, James Buchanan. In Buchanan's study, Freanor delivered the Treaty of Guadalupe Hidalgo, the prized instrument of the Mexican surrender, the fruit of President James K. Polk's war.

Americans had sailed along the California coast for decades. Richard Henry Dana's best-selling novel *Two Years before the Mast* had romanticized the Pacific shore, and Polk, president in the mid-1840s, had seen commercial advantages in the possession of the ports at San Diego and San Francisco. There had been only one problem: California had belonged to Mexico.

In the years since the War of 1812, America had gained a new sense of security. The British threat had receded, and Americans had begun to hurtle pell-mell into the West. Justifying their takeover of Native American lands as gifts from God—Manifest Destiny—they had clamored along the Tennessee and the Ohio rivers and beyond. Traveling by steamboat down the Mississippi in 1831, two young French aristocrats, Gustave de Beaumont and Alexis de Tocqueville (the latter of *Democracy in America* fame), had encountered one of those Americans on the move and on the make. He had been a big, rough-hewn, gun-toting former governor of Tennessee who was off to get himself a new country, by hook or by crook. His name was Sam Houston.

The eventual demands of Texans for independence from Mex-ico had given President Polk the opportunity to expand the United States all the way to the West Coast. Late in 1845 he had sent John Slidell, a member of the House of Representatives from New Orleans, to offer Mexico $25 million for California. Incensed, the

Mexican government had refused even to see Slidell; the British ambassador in Mexico City had advised the authorities there to make no deals with those upstart Yankees. Polk thereupon had ordered General Zachary Taylor, in command of a large troop, to encamp on the bank of the Rio Grande; the encampment lay right in the midst of land that the Mexicans claimed as theirs, and the Texans as theirs. A Mexican army thereupon had attacked Taylor's position, and Polk had provoked what he had hoped for all along, a pretext for war. His war message, sent to Congress on May 6, 1846, had stated: "The cup of forbearance had been exhausted. . . . But now . . . Mexico has invaded our territory and shed American blood upon American soil."

Quickly subduing the Mexican resistance, the United States not only negated British influence in Mexico but also acquired that good half of Mexico that stretched from the Rio Grande to northern California. Ratifying the American gains, the Treaty of Guadalupe Hidalgo gave the United States the possibility of having an empire on the Pacific.

5

"What a potato hole of a place, this!" Seeing the U.S. Supreme Court's first-floor room in the Capitol in 1859, a western lawyer thought the justices should be "got up above ground" for some fresh air and sunlight. Two years later, as the Civil War was beginning, the Court indeed moved upstairs to the old Senate chamber. There, seated behind a polished wooden balustrade and facing the attorneys' table, the Supreme Court eight years later heard the *Alabama* case.

Although the Civil War was over, the government of the United States had a score to settle with Great Britain. During the conflict, hoping to smash the northern naval blockade, the Confederacy had commissioned the construction, in Liverpool, of several sea raiders. The most notorious of those vessels had been the *Alabama*, a fast, heavily armed warship that had inflicted heavy damage on the Union blockaders.

Seeking payment of damages from Great Britain, Secretary of State William Seward in 1869 filed suit in the U.S. Supreme Court. Not surprisingly, he won. London refused to pay.

In the next two years, 1870–1871, however, Otto von Bismarck, Prussia's "Iron Chancellor," effected a revolution in European international relations. Defeating France and proclaiming the existence of the German Empire, he presented London with the unassailable fact of a Teutonic colossus bestriding the Continent. From even before the Napoleonic Wars, Great Britain had sought a balance of power, based on the assumption that British security rested on preventing the rise of a Continental superpower. So it had been in the six and a half decades since the defeat of Napoleon. Bismarck, however, overturned the British-led European order.

The Britannic rulers then realized that their world had changed and that they needed a friend abroad. By the Treaty of Washington, ratified in 1871, London agreed to submit the *Alabama* affair to an arbitration tribunal. In 1872 the tribunal awarded the United States $15.5 million for its *Alabama* claims. This time the British paid.

Emboldened, the United States forced Great Britain to submit to arbitration again. This time America chipped away at a corner of the British Empire itself.

6

The year was 1896. The British general election of the year before had ended the era of William Gladstone and the Liberal ascendancy in politics, bringing to the fore the Conservatives (or Unionists, as they often called themselves, in deference to those who opposed independence for Ireland). But the election had done more than substitute one political party for another; it also had ushered in the beginning of the end of England's era of splendid isolation—the empire overseas, the balance of power across the Channel, and no nonsense about having allies. Now Great Britain was saying good-bye to all that.

Presiding over the change was the new prime minister, one who by his very birthright loathed change, the patrician of patricians,

Robert Cecil, Lord Salisbury. Some twenty miles north of London, Hatfield House was the ancestral home of the Cecils: E-shaped and built of brick, it was one of the largest and finest Jacobean mansions in all of England. Queen Elizabeth I had spent her childhood there, and in a house swap, James I had traded it to his prime minister, Robert Cecil, the first earl of Salisbury. With its Long Gallery, which boasted a gold-leaf ceiling and carved paneled walls, the King James Drawing Room, hung with full-length family portraits, and niches that contained letters written by Mary, Queen of Scots, the cradle of the beheaded Charles I, a bust of George III, and flags captured from Napoleon at the Battle of Waterloo, Hatfield was the very essence of the aristocratic life.

Elected prime minister in 1895, Robert Cecil, the ninth earl of Salisbury, was the embodiment of that essence. Tall, in his mid-sixties, massive of build with a heavy bald head and a full, curly gray beard, he once had been a brilliant student at Oxford when he had chosen to exert himself. Regarding himself superior to most other mortals, he bowed to no conventions. When he spoke in public, which was not often, his tone was usually one of sarcasm or mockery. Those whom he mocked the most bitterly were the Americans and their presumptuous Monroe Doctrine. They had had the nerve to assert their primacy in their own hemisphere.

The Americans had been troublesome ever since the end of their Civil War, squabbling with the British over the control of several Pacific islands, including especially Hawaii. They also had been casting covetous eyes on Canada: in 1886, Theodore Roosevelt, a rising star in the American political firmament, had told a Fourth of July audience that he looked forward to the "day when not a foot of North American soil will be held by any European power"; five years later, Secretary of State James G. Blaine had stated that Canada would "ultimately seek . . . admission to the Union." Throughout Central America, but especially in Nicaragua, American fruit companies had been replacing the British.

The Anglo-American crisis, however, arose over disputed territory lying between Venezuela and British Guiana. Most of the region was jungle but, officials in Washington knew, contained massive deposits of oil, petroleum that John D. Rockefeller wanted to tap. Standard Oil's access would be easier if the area were in Venezuela's hands.

So in 1895, President Grover Cleveland demanded that Great Britain submit the dispute to international arbitration. Imperious as always, Lord Salisbury ignored the demand.

Big, bluff, and good-hearted, Cleveland for once became furious, so much so that he ordered his secretary of state, Richard Olney, to present Lord Salisbury with a threat. The Olney Note of July 20, 1896, informed Salisbury that the United States was prepared to invoke the Monroe Doctrine, which had forbidden European colonization in the Western Hemisphere, and to enforce it with the U.S. Navy.

In no way could the American fleet have taken on the British. Preoccupied with the rise of German naval power, however, Lord Salisbury at last paid attention. Although he rejected the Monroe Doctrine as unilateral, which it was, he recognized the need for American friendship. Thus he acceded to Cleveland's demand for arbitration. In 1896 an international panel ruled in favor of Venezuela, and Salisbury accepted the judgment.

In the Caribbean basin, John Bull was making way for Uncle Sam. So it was two years later with the Spanish-American War.

7

Sidney and Beatrice Webb visited the United States in the spring of 1898, hoping to write a report critical of the American system of government. Physically they were an unlikely twosome. Sidney, as the novelist H. G. Wells described him, was "a short sturdy figure with a rounded protruding abdomen and a curious, broad, flattened, clean-shaven face that seemed nearly all forehead. He peered up with reddish-swollen-looking eyes over gilt-edged glasses. . . . [H]e was artlessly rude and egoistic in an undignified way." Nearly a full head taller than her husband, Beatrice had a pale, emphatic face, dark hair, aquiline features, and the bright, brown eyes of a hawk. They were devoted to each other and to their political causes: Fabian socialism (they were among the founders of the London School of Economics); the British Empire (they hoped to make it gentler, kinder); and anti-Americanism (an attitude shared by many of their fellow Britons). Friends of Wells and George Bernard Shaw, they considered themselves among Great Britain's leading intellectuals.

As such, once in Washington, they expected mere American politicians to be deeply deferential. Few, however, bothered to give them the time of day. Summoned from the floor of the Senate for an interview with the English inquisitors, the Boston Brahmin, Henry Cabot Lodge, could scarcely stifle his yawns; at the first break in the conversation, he fled back to his desk to take part in debate.

Lacking anyone to cross-examine on American shortcomings, the Webbs ended up in the gallery of the House of Representatives. The date was April 11, 1898. Shortly after noon, Beatrice Webb wrote in her diary, "a seedy looking old gentleman appears in one of the gangways with a large folio of paper under his arm." Given over to a clerk who read it aloud in a dull monotone, the document turned out to be a "long-winded epistle" from President William McKinley. It was an official request that Congress declare war on Spain.

John Hay, then U.S. ambassador to the Court of St. James's, called it a "splendid little war." Much of the rest of the world did not agree. To Continental Europe especially, the Spanish-American War was a case of David and Goliath, with Goliath the victor. However hypocritically, the French, the Belgians, and the Germans saw America's expulsion of Spain from Puerto Rico, Cuba, Guam, and the Philippines as naked imperialism.

Not so the British. Despite his disdain for the Yankee upstarts, Lord Salisbury saw his opportunity and took it: needing the United States on Britain's side, he feigned support for the American cause. Indeed, he orchestrated a press campaign to welcome the United States as a partner in Great Britain's own imperial enterprise.

Americans, at least those not of Irish descent, returned the sentiment. During the Boer War, the United States was the only major country to take the British side. Nevertheless, Theodore Roosevelt, once president, lost little time applying the big stick to the British Empire.

8

By the morning of September 23, 1901, the furnace that was the Washington summer had begun to cool, and residents were starting to loll about on the benches of Lafayette Square. Seated in the shade of the magnolias and beech trees, people could observe the time-honored rituals of a capital weekday morning: the congressmen in their buggies heading toward Capitol Hill; female secretaries in their choke collars and long dresses strolling to government offices; the naval officers in their crisp white uniforms entering the doors of the State, Army, and Navy Building, just west of the White House. The president's home was nearly a century old.

All around the square were reminders of the past. Off to the east was the buff-colored Cosmos Club; Dolley Madison had lived there. Right across Sixteenth Street were twin, side-by-side red brick mansions: in one lived Secretary of State John Hay, who had begun his career as private secretary to Abraham Lincoln; in the other dwelt Henry Adams, grandson and great-grandson of presidents. And on Pennsylvania Avenue, facing the executive mansion, was Blair House: four-storied with gables and square-paned windows, it had been built in 1824.

Lafayette Square and its immediate surroundings were stately, serene, and sedate. On the morning of September 23, 1901, Theodore Roosevelt burst upon that scene like John Philip Sousa's marching band.

Having succeeded the slain President McKinley, TR strove to consolidate his predecessor's imperial gains, sending forces to put down insurrections in Cuba and the Philippines. He also took aim at the British Empire.

The 1896 discovery of gold in the Klondike inflamed a dispute between the United States and Canada over the border of the Alaskan panhandle. Warning British friends that "I'm going to be ugly," Roosevelt sent army units to Alaska. Agreeing to submit the argument to "six impartial jurists," he selected three Americans who were anything but impartial or, for that matter, jurists. Sir Wilfred

Laurier, the Canadian prime minister, denounced TR's appointments as outrageous. He himself appointed two Canadian judges. And according to the arbitration agreement, London selected one more—who voted with the Americans and gave Roosevelt exactly the land Americans had wanted to take from Canada. Ottawa charged a double cross, which it was. Britain was quite willing to sacrifice Canadian interests to those of the United States.

The same was true in Central America. Back in 1850, Great Britain and the United States had signed the Clayton-Bulwer Treaty, by which the two countries had agreed not to build or fortify a canal across Central America, save in cooperation with each other. During the Spanish-American War, however, the battleship *Oregon*, stationed in San Francisco Bay, had received orders to proceed to the Caribbean. Because of the length of the voyage around South America, the ship had reached its destination only after the hostilities were over. The late arrival had given rise in the United States to a clamor for a transisthmian canal. The Clayton-Bulwer Treaty stood in the way.

Once in office, Roosevelt resolved the issue. He demanded and got from Great Britain the Hay-Pauncefote Treaty, ratified in November 1901; it gave the United States the right alone to dig the Panama Canal. Once again, the British had appeased the Americans.

Later came the Roosevelt Corollary to the Monroe Doctrine, enunciated in December 1905: "Chronic wrongdoing, or an impotence which results in a general loosening of the ties of civilized society, may in [Latin] America as elsewhere, ultimately require intervention by some civilized nation, and in the western hemisphere the adherence of the United States to the Monroe Doctrine may force the United States, however reluctantly, in flagrant cases of such wrongdoing, or impotence, to the exercise of an international police power."

Faced like their Conservative predecessors by what they saw as the menace of Germany, the ministers of Britain's Liberal government, after their victory in the election of 1905, welcomed America as the policeman of the Caribbean. Nine years later, desperate for American support in what they were certain would be a war with Germany, that same government went further: as the request of

President Woodrow Wilson, London reversed its diplomatic recognition of revolutionary Mexico.

9

As viewed from the Gulf of Mexico, Veracruz would have been an artist's delight. At the entrance of the harbor, the ancient fortress of San Juan de Ulva, with its massive white-walled sides, stood guard over the city. Inside the seawall, gulls and pelicans rode the waves or dropped in vertical dives for their prey. Behind the waterfront, the city nestled in low, sandy hills that were green throughout the year; the houses—blue, green, or red, as well as muted pastels—took their colors from nature. Some of the wealthier residences were built of white coral. In the distance loomed the perpetual snow of the Pico de Oriza, at eighteen thousand feet Mexico's highest mountain.

Veracruz also was the port where President Woodrow Wilson, on April 17, 1914, staged his most significant military action until the American entry into World War I. Four years before, Francisco Madero, a liberal landowner from just south of El Paso, had overthrown Porfirio Díaz, Mexico's long-reigning dictator. Early in 1913, however, Victoriano Huerta, an Aztec-looking crony of Díaz, had mounted a countercoup and had had Madero murdered. Assuming power in Mexico City, Huerta had quickly received diplomatic recognition from most of the great powers, including Britain.

But not from the United States under its new president, Woodrow Wilson. Huerta's bloody measures had exemplified exactly the "wrongdoing" of which Theodore Roosevelt warned in the corollary. Much in the spirit of TR, Wilson resolved to bring about in Mexico what we now call a "regime change."

Conservative by instinct—he had been born in Virginia and grown up in the South—Wilson also reflected the imperial attitudes that had taken root in the United States. Given Wilson's career as an academic, a professor at Bryn Mawr, Wesleyan, and Princeton, and the president of Princeton from 1902 to 1912, Wilson's espousal of American imperialism may seem strange. Intensely ambitious, however, he had never been a cloistered scholar. In both his teaching and his writing he had mastered the art of saying what his audience wanted to hear. Thus he had adopted the language of the most important political movement of his day, progressivism: good government, sound reform, and the expansion of democracy at home and abroad. And he had linked such ideas with those of freedom of trade and investment. Despite his dour appearance, Wilson was a master politician. He had learned how to link diverse interests under his personal leadership.

A southerner who lived in the North, he was a conservative progressive who, a Presbyterian minister's son to the core, could infuse whatever he said with a messianic fervor. Woodrow Wilson espoused both realism and idealism, and he applied both to America's role in the world.

He told a delegation of businessmen who had come to the White House,

> Lift your eyes to the horizons of business. Let your thoughts and your imaginations run abroad throughout the whole world, and with the inspiration of the thought that you are Americans and are meant to carry liberty and justice and the principles of humanity wherever you go, go out and sell goods that will make the world more comfortable and more happy, and convert them to the principles of America.

Horrified by the violence of the Mexican revolution, Wilson would make that land safe for democracy as well as for American investment. Wilson's was the American version of the "white man's burden": south of the border, nonrecognition was to secure American interests and ideals alike.

Unfortunately, for Wilson, his policy of nonrecognition had just the opposite effect: opposed by the gringos to the north, Huerta had gained steadily in popularity among the Mexican people. Using as a pretext the arrest of two American seamen who had gone ashore in Mexico, Wilson turned to war.

On the morning of April 17, 1914, William W. Canada, the U.S. consul-general in Veracruz, climbed to the roof of his building.

Apprised of the impending attack, he wanted to witness the event. Just below the rooftop lay the inevitable plaza, fringed with palms; beyond the open space was the harbor. Beyond the harbor, American troopships stood at anchor. Shortly after eleven in the morning, Canada could make out a launch full of marines passing by the breakwater. Soon the harbor was alive with boats, all loaded with troops. Two hours later, Veracruz was in American hands.

The Mexican press reacted with outrage, but Wilson had his way. Frightened by the American invasion, Huerta on July 15, 1914, relinquished his claim on the presidency of Mexico and sailed off into exile.

Wilson had his way in another regard as well. At the Foreign Office in London, Sir Edward Grey had considered Wilson's policy of nonrecognition to be absurdly moralistic. Nonetheless, on the eve of World War I, Grey did exactly what Wilson wanted: in the climax of Great Britain's prewar effort to secure a rapprochement with America, he withdrew recognition of the Huerta regime.

10

At exactly eleven o'clock in the evening of August 4, 1914, the moment when Great Britain was at war with imperial Germany, a ship called the *Telconia* slipped out of the harbor at Portsmouth and steamed up the English Channel to the German coastline. The *Telconia* was a strange-looking vessel. With a huge crane at its prow, it looked top-heavy, even likely to tip over forward, for the *Telconia* was a cable layer. But the vessel was actually quite stable, and the crane was now fitted with pincers. And upon reaching a certain spot in the sea just above the German-Dutch border, the pincers dropped into the water. There they cut, at the point of origin, the five German transatlantic cables.

In an age before the widespread use of radio, Germany would be unable to relay its side of the war to the United States. Only Great Britain could do so. To the British government, an American intervention was to be brought about no matter what the cost, even in human life.

CHAPTER 3

The *Lusitania*

1

The Old Head of Kinsale was a rocky, steep peninsula that stuck out into the Atlantic from the southwestern coast of Ireland. Atop its crest were a coast guard station and a lighthouse, both on a clear day visible from many miles at sea. Behind the cliff lay the fishing town of Kinsale and, a dozen miles to the northeast, twin promontories that formed the opening of a harbor leading to the British naval base at Queenstown.

If any ship, under threat of an attack by a submarine, could pass through that aperture, it would have reached safety. Such was the hope of Captain William Thomas Turner as, on the morning of May 7, 1915, he resolved to leave the Atlantic and steer toward Queenstown. At the moment of his decision, he had only twenty miles to go. His ship was the *Lusitania*.

2

A week before the outbreak of the war, Churchill had sent the bulk of the Royal Navy to Scapa Flow; from the naval base there, high over Scotland, the ships had a straight shot at the German coastline and, with the declaration of war, they took that shot.

Their mission was to institute a blockade, intended in time to starve Germany into submission. The German High Seas Fleet was strong enough to keep the blockade at a distance. But in sea duels that ranged from the North Sea to the Pacific Ocean, British forces soon swept German vessels from the waters of the world. Germany's far-flung trade became almost nonexistent. With the British Isles lying athwart the western face of the European continent, further-more, the Royal Navy had little difficulty squeezing off German commerce with Holland, Denmark, Norway, and Sweden, the nearby neutrals. The British blockade held Germany in a grip of iron.

In response, Germany resorted to submarine warfare. The submarine, or U-boat (the anglicized version of the German word *Unterseeboot*), was a shocking new weapon. Undetected in the depths of the North Sea, the English Channel, and the Atlantic Ocean, a single German submarine could create havoc with shipping and bring sudden death to hundreds of people. So while the British blockade, conducted with conventional surface ships, brought about an encirclement of Ger-many, the German retaliation, carried out with unconventional sub-marines, effected a counterencirclement of Great Britain.

Britain faced other troubles, too. Counting on a short war, its political leaders thought they had enough money to finance the fighting. They were wrong. Having entered the war as the world's leading creditor, Great Britain soon found itself plunging into debt to the major banks of the United States. Britain also started to run out of just about everything: butter, cheese, cloth for uniforms and leather for boots, guncotton, shells, and gasoline. These the British had to purchase largely in the United States, leaving themselves even more deeply in debt.

With the outbreak of hostilities, furthermore, the generals believed that they could have their troops home before the leaves fell. They, too, were wrong. From the sunny days of August 1914 to the overcast chill of December, the armies in northeastern France grappled, bled, died, and bogged down in stalemate. As 1914 ended, thousands of men on both sides were spinning coils of barbed wire along the 350-mile front from Switzerland to the sea. No one could advance and no end was in sight.

It is little wonder that on Christmas Eve 1914, Churchill asked, "Are there not other alternatives than sending our armies to chew barbed wire in Flanders?" Thus, for the British, was born the disaster at Gallipoli.

3

On the day after the war began, the *Sicilia*, an Italian steamer, was making its way up the Aegean Sea, bound for Constantinople; the route lay through the Dardanelles, the strait that led to the Sea of Marmara. Aboard the vessel was the Wertheim family: the parents, two older sisters, and the toddler Barbara. (As an adult she would gain fame as the historian Barbara W. Tuchman.) They were on their way to visit Mrs. Wertheim's father, Henry Morgenthau, the New York developer who by dint of his contributions to the Wilson campaign in 1912 had become the ambassador to Turkey. While still at sea, the family witnessed an event that became a legend to them. "I've told it many times," Mrs. Tuchman would say, "but I don't remember it personally." Nonetheless, in her most renowned book, *The Guns of August*, she described their bringing to her grandfather "an exciting tale of the boom of guns, puffs of white smoke, and the twisting and maneuvering of faraway ships."

On the night of the British declaration of war, Churchill, from his post in the Admiralty, ordered ships still in the Mediterranean to chase down two German warships, the cruiser *Breslau* and the battleship *Göben*. Steaming in tandem, they had come out of their berths in a Croatian port (part of the Austro-Hungarian Empire) and had been making their way toward the southern coast of France. Coming under British fire, they had escaped.

The Wertheim family witnessed the flight. Then, as Ambassador Morgenthau watched from his hilltop embassy, the German warships anchored in the sanctuary of the waters off Constantinople. The waterway was safe because Turkey on August 3 had signed a treaty of alliance with Germany.

With Turkey on the side of the Central Powers, Great Britain could not ship supplies to Russia through the Black Sea. Turkey, however, was weak from the rot of centuries. Its minister of war, Enver Pasha, was a notorious drunkard. Most of its soldiers were illiterate and its defenses were spread thin. Turkey seemed ripe for defeat. Besides, Churchill wanted to avenge the humiliation of having lost the *Breslau* and the *Göben*.

> Cease your preaching! Load your guns!
> Their road our mission tells.
> The day is come for Britain's sons
> To seize the Dardanelles!
> —London music hall song

The idea of an attack on the Dardanelles was hardly Churchill's alone. It appealed to nearly every Briton, especially to those empire loyalists who longed romantically for a blow that would overcome the ignominy of the Boer War as well as strike the Central Powers at their soft Mediterranean underbelly. The vision attracted even that supposedly most rational of human beings, Prime Minister Asquith. With the man on top approving a naval attack on Turkey, Churchill was only the executor, albeit one who threw himself wholeheartedly into the role.

The promised rewards of Churchill's alternative were immense: outflanking the Central Powers from the rear; reestablishing a supply line to Russia; eliminating Turkey from the war; even bringing about the collapse of the Austro-Hungarian Empire. For the British the possession of the Dardanelles would have been the richest prize in the world; it might even have decided the war against imperial Germany.

In the middle of March 1915, the attack on the Dardanelles got under way. Six British and four French battleships entered the strait, opened fire on Turkish forts that stood on both sides, and bombarded them for more than two hours. At the end of the barrage, the batteries in the forts were silent.

Almost immediately, though, the Allied forces ran into trouble. Several of the ships struck mines, and two sank. A month later, the soldiers, mostly Australians and New Zealanders, went ashore. They landed at the bottom of the Gallipoli Peninsula, which formed the European side to the strait. They soon were able to establish a row of beachheads. Then everything seemed to go wrong. In their briefings, the men had been told that beyond the beach they would find level ground that would be easily crossed. Instead, a cliff loomed up right before them and, as they hauled themselves upward, clutching at roots and boulders, kicking footholds into the rocks, heavy fire came down on them from above. Shouting and crying out, the men kept losing their grips and tumbling down into gullies. Those who did manage to scale the cliffside went charging off toward well-dug Turkish trenches, there to expose themselves to machine-gun fire. Those who followed had no idea where to go, and struck off on paths of their own. Officers lost touch with their men; units became hopelessly mixed; signals failed altogether.

The Gallipoli campaign would drag on for months, but the first month, up to mid-April, determined the outcome. Trained by German advisers, Turkish gunners commanded the heights and kept the beachheads under constant fire. Thus the flanking operation through Turkey, intended in London to bypass the stalemate on the Western Front, itself bogged down in immobility. By May 1915 Gallipoli had become an open, seeping wound. And since the Admiralty had presided over the attack, Churchill became the scapegoat for the disaster.

The debacle at the Dardanelles showed that, alone, the Allies could not win the war, at least not until the naval blockade took a sufficient toll. The British government could see only one way out: American intervention in the war as soon as possible. And Churchill had a personal reason to hope for such an intervention. He was desperate for a success that would salvage his reputation. But what to do?

In his memoirs of World War I, Churchill proffered an answer to that question: "At the summit true politics and strategy are one," he wrote. "The maneuver which brings an ally into the field is as serviceable as that which wins a great battle. The maneuver which gains an important strategic point may be less valuable than that which placates or overawes a dangerous neutral."

Of what maneuver was Churchill writing? It had to do with the *Lusitania*.

4

A month and a half after the outbreak of the war, Churchill, in his capacity as first lord of the Admiralty, visited Loch Ewe, a deepwater fjord near the northern tip of Scotland. Warships for which Scapa Flow had no room were at anchor there, and Churchill was on an inspection tour. The main object of his attention, however, turned out to be not the fleet but rather a clifftop house he had spotted from the wardroom of the battleship *Iron Duke*. Mounted atop the house was a searchlight, and Churchill, having imbibed a quantity of the admiral's brandy, convinced himself that the houseowner must be using the device to send signals to German submarines. So, commandeering pistols and bullets from the ship's armory and rounding up a posse of officers, Churchill led a nocturnal raid on the house.

The mission was a fiasco. The searchlight did not work, and the owner proved to be a seventy-five-year-old former member of Parliament. The adventure nonetheless showed Churchill, Asquith put it, with "all his war paint on." Brilliant but undisciplined, his imagination abounded with thoughts of conspiracies and counterconspiracies.

Churchill had long been the bad boy of British politics, overtly ambitious when members of the aristocracy into which he had been born were supposed to be merely covertly so. Rebellious as a student, he had entered the army, only to find life in the barracks of India confining and remote from the centers of power. Turning to journalism, he found an outlet perfect for his gift of self-promotion.

While covering the Boer War, he was taken prisoner by the enemy, then managed to slip away. In an account of his flight, wired on December 21, 1899, from Lourenço Marques (now Maputo), in the Portuguese colony of Mozambique, to the London papers, he brought himself to the attention of a fascinated British public. His account, in part, went thus:

On the afternoon of the 12th, the Transvaal government's secretary for war informed me that there was little chance of my release. I therefore resolved to escape the same night, and left the State Schools Prison at Pretoria by climbing the wall when the sentries' backs were turned momentarily. I walked through the streets of the town without any disguise, meeting many burghers, but I was not challenged in the crowd. I got through the pickets of the Town Guard, and struck the Delagoa Bay Railroad. I walked along it, evading the watchers at the bridges and culverts. I waited for a train beyond the first station. The 11:10 goods train from Pretoria arrived, and before it had reached full speed I boarded with great difficulty, and hid myself under coal sacks. I jumped from the train before dawn, and sheltered during the day in a small wood, in company with a huge vulture, who displayed a lively interest in me. I walked on at dusk. There were no more trains that night. The danger of meeting guards of the railway line continued; but I was obliged to follow it, as I had no compass or map. I had to make wide detours to avoid the bridges, stations, and huts. My progress was very slow, and chocolate is not a very satisfying food. The outlook was gloomy, but I persevered, with God's help, for five days. The food I had to have was very precarious. I was lying up at daylight, and walking on at night-time, and, meanwhile, my escape had been discovered and my description telegraphed everywhere. All the trains were searched. . . . But on the sixth day I managed to board a train beyond Middleburg, whence there is a direct service to Delagoa.

Inside Mozambique, Delagoa was just across the border from the Transvaal. Churchill was free.

How much of this account is true is impossible to say. Churchill's melodramatic tale of his escapade, nonetheless, appealed to the newspaper-reading public back home, so much so that it earned him a seat in the House of Commons in the general election of 1900.

Churchill sat as a Conservative. But in a party dominated by the landed aristocracy—Churchill's father, Lord Randolph Churchill, had been born the second son of the duke of Marlborough and hence had not inherited the ancestral estate at Blenheim—Churchill saw little future for himself. Only four years after entering the House, and just in time for the victory of the opposition in the election of 1905, Churchill crossed the floor to join with the Liberals.

The Conservatives for years thereafter regarded Churchill as a traitor, and the Liberals saw him as an opportunist. Probably both had a point. Certainly in the Liberal Party, which despite a smattering of its own landed aristocrats, such as Sir Edward Grey, had its roots in the Non-Conformist middle class, Churchill was an exotic; isolated, he represented no constituency. Still, he was not to be ignored. In the popular press, he was always good copy. Lacking the social polish of one who had glided through Cambridge or Oxford, he appealed to the British public as a man of action. He stood for empire, and the working classes loved him for it.

Elected prime minister at the head of the Liberal Party in 1905, therefore, Sir Henry Campbell-Bannerman took Churchill into the cabinet, assigning him to the Board of Trade. To Churchill with his soaring imagination, however, import and export and balance of payments statistics were a colossal bore. All the same, his tremendous ability to concentrate on the work of his department made him a formidable member of the ministry. So when Campbell-Bannerman died in 1908, H. H. Asquith, his successor, elevated Churchill to the Admiralty.

At the Admiralty, with an office that overlooked St. James's Park and the Mall, Churchill could expand his realm of activity. As always, he could find vivid words to portray that action as vital to the future of the British Empire.

After Churchill had returned from his spy-hunting misadventure to the wardroom of the *Iron Duke*, anchored in Loch Ewe, he had a conversation with Commodore Roger Keyes, one of the officers who had accompanied him ashore. Keyes was an angry man. Some of the cruisers on patrol off Germany, he informed Churchill, were unfortified along the waterline; they were prime targets for submarines with their torpedoes. The men of the navy, Keyes went on, had nicknamed the ships the "Livebait Squadron."

Four days later, Churchill was in Liverpool, scheduled to address an audience of naval recruits. Before giving his speech, he visited the Merseyside docks. There, lashed with many ropes to its berth, stood the tallest ship he had ever seen. It was the *Lusitania*. Quizzing a naval architect who was one of the first lord's hosts, Churchill learned that like the cruisers off Germany, the *Lusitania* lacked waterline armament. He expressed astonishment.

Reassuring Churchill, the architect mentioned the *Lusitania*'s great speed and added, "The navy hasn't anything like her."

Reporters nearby noted Churchill's reply. "We have," he said. "To me she is just another 45,000 tons of livebait."

5

Launched at Clydebank, the shipyard at Glasgow, on June 7, 1906, the *Lusitania* was the largest and fastest ship in the world. Reporting the event, the shipping correspondent for the *Times* of London was so overcome by the magnificence of the vessel that he mixed his metaphors mercilessly: "She is a veritable greyhound of the seas . . . a worthy tribute to her illustrious lineage . . . a credit to the august and noble stable which conceived her."

Whether dog or horse racing was the better figure of speech for describing the *Lusitania*, the ship was majestic indeed: all who saw the vessel at first marveled at its height. If somehow placed beside the Admiralty, which had subsidized the construction of the Cunard-owned ship, the *Lusitania* would have dwarfed the buildings of Whitehall; it was higher and longer than the Capitol and the Senate and House office buildings in Washington all taken together. After the *Lusitania* was put into commission, regularly plying the great circle route in the North Atlantic between Liverpool and New York and back, the jumbling of metaphors continued. To some, it was the "Greyhound of the Seas"; to others "a skyscraper afloat." Newspaper advertisements, placed in Great Britain and the United States by the Cunard Company, described the *Lusitania* as the most luxurious hotel in the world.

It may well have been so. The first-class cabins and suites, placed amidships, where the motion of the vessel would bother the passengers the least, were outfitted with the finest giltwork and marble basins. The dining room was double-tiered, with white fluted columns, gilded railings, and crisp white linen tablecloths and napkins. The cuisine and the wines were France's finest. After their many-course dinners, the first-class passengers could retire to the smoking room, its walls all gilt and white, and its ceiling a stained glass dome; the walls of the Robert Adam–style library and writing room were of a delicate gray and cream silk brocade. Even the second- and third-class quarters, fore and aft, bore the trappings of luxury.

The prestige of sailing aboard the *Lusitania* was like that of taking the Concorde many years later. The ship, moreover, was renowned for its record of safety. Unlike the *Titanic*, of course, but many other ocean liners as well, it had made the North Atlantic run for year after year without incident. Safe, luxurious, and fast, and apparently devoted wholly to commercial purposes, the *Lusitania* appeared to be the ultimate nonbelligerent ship.

Except that it was not. On May 12, 1913, the *Lusitania* went into dry dock at Liverpool. The Cunard firm stated that the ship needed to be outfitted with the latest-model turbines. The *New York Tribune* on June 19, 1913, however, carried a different story: "The reason why the crack liner *Lusitania* is so long delayed at Liverpool has been announced to be because her turbine engines are being completely replaced, but Cunard officials acknowledged to the *Tribune* correspondent today that the greyhound is being equipped with high-power naval rifles in conformity with England's new policy of arming passenger boats."

Two and a half months later, the *Lusitania* resumed its transatlantic voyages. And on March 16, 1914, Churchill told the House of Commons that "some forty British merchant ships have been defensively armed." He did not define *defensively*.

Under the strictures of international law, unarmed merchant ships were regarded as nonbelligerent, immune from attack as enemy

ships of war. To be sure, one can (as did all the great powers once
World War I got under way) regard the treaties that made up international law as mere scraps of paper, nothing but propaganda to be
used by one side against the other. Nonetheless, in arming the *Lusitania*, which carried American passengers, Churchill was taking a
step almost guaranteed to make the Germans regard it as a belligerent. And if Germany so regarded it, and killed Americans, then
Berlin was bound to become embroiled with the United States.

There was yet another problem with the *Lusitania*. Although
the ship had not been designed to carry cargo, during its refitting
in Liverpool, the walls of the hold had been shifted to allow for
the storage of freight. German intelligence learned about the transformation and feared that Great Britain would use the *Lusitania* to
ship food and munitions to the home islands. If that were the case,
then in German eyes the ship would be doubly a belligerent vessel.

Despite such considerations, the *Lusitania* on April 17, 1915,
again left Liverpool for New York. It arrived on April 24.

New York at the time seethed with international intrigue. Commanded by Sir Courtenay Bennett, Great Britain's consul-general
in the city, British agents were constantly placing orders with America's farms and factories, receiving the purchased goods at the rail
yards, supervising their transportation across the city, and oversee-
ing their emplacement in the holds of ships bound for Britain.
Under the neutrality laws of the United States, such activities were
illegal, but they were good for American business—the United
States was in a recession—and with the tacit approval of the Wilson
administration in Washington, they went on anyway. For the Allies
(the French and to an extent the Russians also participated in obtaining supplies from the United States), the Atlantic Ocean was a veritable pipeline of the instruments of war.

The Germans knew it, too. With its large and sympathetic Irish
American and German American communities, New York provided
a haven for German spies. Their chieftain was Captain Franz von
Rintelen, a tall, lean German naval officer who reached New York
aboard a Norwegian ship. His mission was twofold.

First, by placing his own purchasing orders, he hoped to keep American goods out of Allied hands. Here he failed; so stupendous was America's agricultural and industrial output that, he lamented, "if I bought up the market on Tuesday, there would still have been an enormous fresh supply on Wednesday."

Second, by infiltrating German agents (and Irish ones, too, for they were dedicated to the downfall of the British Empire) onto the docks of New York Harbor, he wished to determine just what was going aboard what ships. Here von Rintelen succeeded: in his reports he indicated having seen "numerous English, French, and Russian transports waiting to take munitions onboard." He also observed a "large number of German sailors, mates, and captains . . . hanging about the harbor with nothing to do" and Irish dockhands "who were far from friendly to England or those allied to her." From those various sources, he came to the conclusion that the *Lusitania*, scheduled to sail from New York on May 1, was being loaded with huge quantities of munitions, especially explosives.

The list of what illegally was going aboard the *Lusitania* was truly impressive. It included cloth; furs; sundries; bacon; 300 tubs of butter; some 80 cases of lard; 500 boxes of candy; 125 boxes of cheese; stacks of knit goods; at least 200 cases of oysters; 4 full storage rooms belowdecks packed with quarters of beef; at least 150 cartons of brass rods; 200 reels of wire; 1,700 ingot bars of copper; 191 barrels of brass; 1,248 cases of shrapnel; and 4,927 boxes of cartridges. Right below the waterline and close to the first boiler room the *Lusitania* also stored 75 barrels of oil. The total weight of the explosives taken aboard was slightly more than 10½ tons.

Whether von Rintelen was able to send this information to Berlin is unclear. What was plain, however, was that by dint of its cargo, the *Lusitania* was the ultimate vessel of war.

Others, too, were thinking about the *Lusitania*. George Viereck, a German American poet who headed the German propaganda office in New York, commented, "Sooner or later some big passenger boat with Americans aboard will be sunk by a submarine and there will be hell to pay." Convinced that such an action would lead the United States into the war against Germany, Viereck placed a black-rimmed warning in several American newspapers. It read:

NOTICE!

Travelers intending to embark on the Atlantic voyage are reminded that a state of war exists between Germany and her allies and Great Britain and her allies; that the zone of war includes the waters adjacent to the British Isles; that, in accordance with formal notice given by the Imperial German government, vessels flying the flag of Great Britain, or of any of her allies, are liable to destruction in those waters and that travelers sailing in the war zone on ships of Great Britain or her allies do so at their own risk.

Imperial German Embassy
Washington, D.C., April 22, 1915

Neither the Cunard Company nor the British government wished to cancel the trip of the *Lusitania*. London needed the cargo desperately. All the Admiralty could do was keep on the lookout for any submarine that might be waiting for the ship.

British intelligence had broken the German naval code: divers had extracted a codebook from a sunken German ship, and so the Admiralty could track the paths of the U-boats with exceptional accuracy. The system worked like this. Listening stations along the coastlines of England and Ireland picked up radio messages from the U-boats, and relayed them immediately to Room 40, an innocuously designated chamber in the basement of the Admiralty in London. There decoders and translators deciphered the contents, presenting them to Captain William R. Hall. Nicknamed "Blinker" because of a twitch in an eyelid, Hall must have blinked considerably when he read the following intercept dated April 25, 1915, and sent out of Wilhelmshaven, the German submarine command post on the North Sea shore:

U-30 puts to sea from Ems to the west coast. *U-9* after completion of repairs goes from Wilhelmshaven to Heligoland. . . . [T]he naval staff . . . decided that three stations be occupied as quickly as possible for interception of troop transport ships in front of Dartmouth, Bristol Channel, and Liverpool. *U-30* pursuant to the following radiotelegraphic message is ordered to Dartmouth [on the southern Devon shore, just south of Torbay]: "Await large English troop transports coming out from west and south coasts of England. Head via the most rapid route around Scotland for the English Channel. Take position in front of Dartmouth. Attack transports [and] merchant vessels [and] warships. Keep position for as long as supplies allow. *U-20* and *U-27* to Irish Sea and Bristol Channel."

On its way to Liverpool, the *Lusitania* would sail right past the Bristol Channel and into the Irish Sea. The British Admiralty was fully aware of the route. To protect the *Lusitania*, therefore, orders went out to the *Juno*, a cruiser based at Queenstown, on the southern Irish coast, to rendezvous with the *Lusitania* forty miles off the Fastnet lighthouse, at the far southwestern tip of Ireland.

Fastnet Rock stood at the point where the North Atlantic steamer routes to Britain converged. It was an obvious place for a submarine to await the arrival of the *Lusitania*.

At eight on the morning of May 1, 1915, the *Lusitania* was ready to receive its passengers. In the customary manner, several of the ship's officers lined up at the head of the main gangway to extend their official welcomes. To their surprise, however, down on the pier the reporters seemed to outnumber the passengers; a movie newsreel team was even setting up its cameras. Coming up the gangway, one correspondent showed John Lewis, the senior third officer, what was going on. In his hand the journalist was holding up a copy of that morning's *New York Tribune*, folded open to the warning placed by the German embassy. Lewis dismissed the notice as unimportant, a practical joke, perhaps even a hoax.

He recited what would become a litany. The fastest ship in the world, the *Lusitania* could outrun any submarine.

At last the first of some twenty-five hundred passengers started to come aboard. The first-class list included some of the richest and most famous people of the day: Oliver Bernard, an English-born theatrical designer who was hoping to enlist in the British army; Charles Frohman, the best-known impresario of the day and the producer of more than five hundred plays on both sides of the Atlantic; Elbert Hubbard, a best-selling author; Alfred Gwynne Vanderbilt, a tall, lean, handsome playboy who had inherited the largest part of his ancestors' fortune; and David Thomas, a Welsh coal magnate, and his daughter, Lady Margaret Mackworth, both hoping to contribute to the British war effort.

Like them, most of the Britons who reached the top of the gang-way that morning considered it their patriotic duty to sail home specifically aboard the *Lusitania;* they had read the German warning as a challenge to their honor. Besides, as Captain William Thomas Turner, a short, stocky, broad-faced taciturn old sea dog promised them, "There is always a danger but the best guarantees of your safety are the *Lusitania* herself, the fastest ship in the world, and the fact that wherever there is danger your safety is in the hands of the Royal Navy."

Shortly after noon on that May 1, with the Union Jack and the Cunard Company's own flags fluttering from the tops of the masts, the *Lusitania* was eased out and away from its pier. Then, under its own power, it steamed down the Hudson River, passed through the Narrows, and under a cloudless sky nosed into the springtime blue of the Atlantic Ocean. The *Lusitania* was on its way to Liverpool.

6

On that same morning, Captain Hall, the intelligence chief in the British Admiralty, received information from the coastal stations that three submarines of the German flotilla described in the April 25 intercept were moving toward the Irish Sea. He duly passed the report along to Churchill, first lord of the Admiralty, and to Admiral Sir John Fisher, formerly and now again first sea lord (because of his German surname and despite his relationship to the royal family, public opinion had forced Prince Louis Battenberg to step down from the post). One detail in the intercept was particularly worrisome: the submarine designated *U-20* had already made its progress up through the North Sea and was nearing the tip of Scotland. Soon it would be making its turn toward the south.

Having received orders to put out from Queenstown, Vice Admiral Sir Horace Hood, aboard the cruiser *Juno* on the evening of May 4, was steaming toward Fastnet. He was about to enter the zone where he would make contact with the *Lusitania*, and escort the liner to Liverpool.

That same night, Kapitän Leutnant Walter Schwieger, the commander of the *U-20*, was coming around Scotland off Loch Ewe, where Churchill had had his nocturnal misadventure. According to his official photograph, Schwieger was a rather round-faced, blue-eyed young man with closely cropped light brown hair. German submarine commanders were youthful, often barely out of their teens, and adventurous. Schwieger was of just that sort: he was out for kills. Moving along the surface of the sea and down past the Scottish western coastline, he soon made a notation in his log. From out in the night, he had spotted the lights of Belfast.

On May 4, as the *Lusitania* sliced through the waves of the North Atlantic and, rounding Iceland, started down toward Ireland, all was peaceful and serene. The sun was bright and the water was calm. The passengers played deck tennis on the promenade and in the evening enjoyed an uneventful repast.

7

Scheduled to take the noon boat-train to Paris, where he was to participate in Anglo-Italian naval negotiations (having entered the war on the side of the Allies, Italy was most desirous of what we now call military aid, and what was traditionally known as bribery), Churchill on the morning of Wednesday, May 5, was up unusually early. Before he left London, he had to join Admiral Fisher in the map room at the Admiralty.

The Admiralty's wall map of the North Sea and the North Atlantic was divided up by horizontal and vertical lines that formed a grid; each square of the grid designated an area of thirty-two square miles. Inside those areas, pins of variegated sizes and colors represented the locations of all known vessels; red pins stood for U-boats. Serving as briefing officer, Vice Admiral Henry Oliver used a pointer to bring the *U-20*'s position to Churchill's attention. As its red pin showed, the *U-20* had passed Dublin and, traversing St. George's Channel, was approaching the Old Head of Kinsale.

At this point the Admiralty war diary, usually kept meticulously, was silent; the relevant pages have long been torn out. No one can say why. Nonetheless, shortly after noon on May 5, with Churchill now on his way to Paris, the *Juno* received a new order: it was to return to Queenstown. Who authorized the order we shall most probably never know, but the responsibility lay with Churchill.

Furthermore, no one informed Captain Turner, aboard the *Lusitania*, that the *Juno* was steaming back to port. At the time he was off Galway Bay, where he might have found protection. What was happening? In a book entitled *The Freedom of the Seas*, published in 1929, Commander Joseph M. Kenworthy, who had been present at the May 5 briefing in the Admiralty map room, wrote: "The *Lusitania* was sent at considerable reduced speed into an area where a U-boat was known to be waiting and with her escort withdrawn."

While Churchill was on the train to Dover, Captain Turner was on the bridge of the *Lusitania*, thinking ahead. Off Ireland the sky was still cloudless, but he had noticed several patches of mist. If a fog became thick, he realized, he would have to reduce his speed; otherwise he might collide with the *Juno*.

Knowing that on the night of May 6–7 he would have to be on the bridge all the time, alert for danger, he went down to his cabin. He took a long afternoon nap.

Aboard the *U-20*, Kapitän Leutnant Schwieger was wide awake. Having reached the area around the Old Head of Kinsale, he submerged and sank a sailing schooner, the *Earl of Latham*. About twelve miles east of Kinsale, he fired a torpedo at a steamer and missed.

Vice Admiral Sir Henry Coke, the commanding officer at Queenstown, soon learned of the two assaults and reported them promptly to the Admiralty. In Churchill's absence, the Admiralty did nothing.

Shortly after nine in the evening, Churchill arrived at the Ritz in Paris. For whatever the reason, he registered under the name of "Mr. Spencer."

8

At dawn on May 6, the southern Irish coastline was thick with fog, with visibility almost everywhere reduced to no more than a few feet. Through the periscope in the *U-20*, however, Schwieger, in the course of the day, was able to make out two steamers, the *Candidate* and the *Centurion*, and to sink them both. At seven in the evening, a worried Admiral Coke on his own initiative sent out a warning to the *Lusitania*, now about to round Fastnet Rock.

Captain Turner received the message with considerable alarm. He was unable to make radio contact with the *Juno*.

In the first-class smoking room aboard the *Lusitania* on the evening of May 6, Captain Turner, decked out in his naval blues, spoke to the assembled passengers. They needed reassurance. Earlier in the day, they had noticed that crewmen had been swinging out all forty-eight wooden lifeboats, putting them in position to be lowered to the water. Now, after the fall of darkness, Turner had ordered a blackout of cabin portholes. No one, furthermore, was to go out onto the decks and light the customary after-dinner cigar.

What was going on? passengers asked. Had there been something to that German warning, after all?

All such precautions, Turner told his listeners, were purely routine. In any case, he asserted—perhaps wondering about the truth of his own words—by morning they would be around Fastnet and in the company of the *Juno*, with its protecting heavy artillery.

9

At dawn on May 7, the fog was so thick that from the bridge Captain Turner could hardly see a thing. Hoping still to make contact with the *Juno*, he sounded his foghorn. He heard no reply.

Roughly a hundred miles to the east, the *Juno* was steaming slowly around the Old Head of Kinsale, heading for the two promontories that formed the mouth of Queenstown Harbor. There, at about noon, the cruiser dropped anchor.

Twenty miles still farther to the east, the *U-20* was on the surface, recharging its batteries. The submarine's fuel was running low and Kapitän Leutnant Schwieger saw that he would have to return to the base at Wilhelmshaven. Before he left the Irish coast, however, he decided to submerge once again. The fog had cleared, and the visibility through his periscope was about twenty miles.

At Queenstown, Admiral Coke saw the return of the *Juno* and sensed that, back in the Admiralty, which was supposed to provide the *Lusitania*'s protection, something had gone wrong. Frightened, he sent another warning to Captain Turner.

Underwater at 11:00 AM, Schwieger had felt the throb of propellers overhead. Raising his periscope, he made out the form of a British cruiser moving away from him toward Queenstown. It was the *Juno*. It was out of torpedo range. Schwieger would wait about another hour, perhaps a bit more, and then start out northward around Scotland for home. Through his periscope, nonetheless, he kept watch on the western horizon.

Shortly after noon, having received the warning from Queenstown, Captain Turner swung the *Lusitania* violently to the north; at the same time he threw the ship into its highest speed. Passengers at their luncheon tables were aghast: wineglasses and dishes flew about, and some of the diners were thrown from their chairs.

Ahead of him, in the now clear air, Turner saw a lighthouse atop a cliff: it was, he calculated, the Old Head of Kinsale. If he could get the *Lusitania* past that bluff and into the mouth of the harbor at Queenstown, the vessel would be safe.

Manning the *Lusitania*'s guns, seamen peered intently over the sparkling surface of the water. For quite a while they detected nothing to worry about. Then, at 2:10 PM, May 7, 1915, they saw it: just below the surface a length of white foam was streaking toward the *Lusitania*, coursing directly toward the forward part of the ship, the part that housed the first boiler room and the seventy-five barrels of oil. They did not have time to fire.

Written in dry naval prose, Kapitän Leutnant Walter Schwieger's logbook told the rest:

> 2:35 PM [Greenwich time, 1:35].
>   The steamer turns starboard, takes a course to Queenstown and thus makes possible a drawing near for the firing. Up to 3 PM [2 PM] ran at high speed in order to get a position up-front.
>   3:10 PM [2 PM].
>   Pure bowshot at 700 meters range. Angle of intersection 90 degrees, estimated speed 22 knots. Shot strikes right behind the bridge.

10

The next morning, the *New York Times* carried a side-view photograph of the *Lusitania*. The banner headline ran: "LUSITANIA SUNK BY A SUBMARINE, PROBABLY 1,000 DEAD; TORPEDOED OFF IRISH COAST,

SINKS IN 15 MINUTES; AMERICANS ABOARD INCLUDED VANDERBILT AND FROHMAN; WASHINGTON BELIEVES THAT A GRAVE CRISIS IS AT HAND."

In the sinking, nearly 1,200 people died, including 128 Americans. American hatred toward Germany grew white-hot.

Churchill had spoken of the *Lusitania* as "livebait." Whether or not he had conspired to allow the ship to be sunk, the British government now could reel in the biggest catch of all: American intervention in World War I.

When President Woodrow Wilson learned the news, his immediate response was to summon Joseph P. Tumulty, his red-haired, usually cheerful chief of staff. When Tumulty heard what Wilson wanted, though, he was no longer cheerful. Shipping correspondents in various newspapers, Wilson said, were speculating whether the speed of the sinking was due to an explosion of illegal cargo. At Wilson's request, Tumulty got in touch with Robert Lansing, legal counsel to the State Department, who in turn asked an official in the Treasury Department to investigate. Was the speculation, the White House wanted to know, correct? Over the weekend, the report from Treasury came back to Wilson: "practically all [the *Lusitania*'s] cargo was contraband of some kind."

So Wilson realized what had been aboard the *Lusitania*. Yet he chose to condemn Germany exclusively for the atrocity. Unbeknown to most of the American public, and for reasons of his own, he had already abandoned neutrality.

CHAPTER 4

The Fourteen Points

1

On the evening of April 2, 1917, horse-drawn carriages from all around Washington clip-clopped through rain-moistened streets to the Capitol of the United States. Up on the Hill, most of those in the gathering crowd carried little American flags and shouted anti-German slogans, drowning out the chants that emanated from little groups of protesting pacifists. In the Capitol itself, the House galleries were packed with spectators; below them were seated the representatives and the senators, the justices of the Supreme Court, the diplomatic corps, and the members of the cabinet, the last seated in the front row. All had come to hear President Woodrow Wilson ask for a declaration of war against Germany.

Among those seated in the gallery was a tall young woman named Eleanor Roosevelt. And having pushed in among the members of the cabinet, where all could see him, was her husband, the assistant secretary of the navy, Franklin D. Roosevelt.

Any understanding of Franklin Roosevelt has to begin with Springwood, the Hyde Park, New York, house in which he grew up, a mansion situated on a bluff overlooking the Hudson River. Surrounded by woods and orchards and filled with dark paneling and heavy Victorian furniture, the home conveyed a sense of security. It also bespoke the family history: the lobby was filled with huge Chinese vases. Operating out of Hong Kong, Franklin's grandfather, Warren

Delano, had made a fortune from the sale of opium. The British Empire had led the way into the Chinese drug market, and Delano had followed where the British had led. His grandson would reverse the pattern.

Born into the apex of the American aristocracy, Franklin grew up a treasured boy. His father, James Roosevelt, was an elderly lawyer who clipped coupons, rode to the hounds, and doted on his son. Sara Delano Roosevelt, inheritress of her father's wealth, was much younger than her husband; she practically smothered the boy with her love. And although he had a considerably older half brother, James Roosevelt Roosevelt, Franklin was in effect an only child. His was the sense of being at the center of the world.

Yet he was no brat. While Franklin was still a small boy, his father was diagnosed with heart disease and became bedridden; Sara made clear to Franklin that any rowdy behavior could precipitate his father's death. Franklin early on thus learned to be a good boy, sunny and cheerful always, keeping his feelings to himself. Throughout his life he would wear the mask of shallow affability. Alice Roosevelt, his distant cousin and elder daughter of Theodore, thought him a mere feather duster.

Such was the opinion, too, of most of those who knew Franklin at Groton Academy and Harvard College. In Cambridge he contented himself with the "gentleman's C," and he flitted from ballroom to ballroom in Boston's fashionable Back Bay. The only collegiate activity he took seriously was his work on the college's newspaper the *Crimson*, of which he became an editor. After his graduation in 1904, he stayed on an extra year to run the paper. His interests were hardly profound, confined to the fate of the football team and the like. At the *Crimson*, nonetheless, he learned to think like a newspaperman, an invaluable gift for an aspiring politician.

For all his frivolousness, Franklin had a resolve of iron—this may have been what Eleanor saw in him—and a sure instinct for power. He was determined to capitalize on his name, imitating his distant cousin Theodore Roosevelt at every possible turn, and thus go into politics. Theodore said "dee-lightful"; Franklin at college kept saying "dee-lightful." Theodore wore the pince-nez; Franklin affected the same. Theodore had gone to Harvard; so did Franklin. Theodore had attended Columbia Law School; Franklin followed suit. And Theodore had won a seat in the New York Assembly.

Here Franklin had to break the mold: Theodore was a Republican, and his several sons were expected to hold office as Republicans. No more Republican Roosevelts needed to apply. Franklin became a Democrat, and as such ran for a seat in the New York Senate.

Receiving the Democratic nomination in the district around Hyde Park—the district was heavily Republican and no other Democrat was willing to hazard a race—Roosevelt in early October 1910 said, "We are going to have a very strenuous month." "Strenuous" was one of Theodore's favorite words.

Tall, thin, and nervous, Roosevelt was a poor public speaker. "He spoke slowly," Eleanor would remember, "and every now and then there would be a long pause, and I would be worried for fear he would never go on."

But he did go on, running as if he were the reincarnation of Theodore. He denounced the party bosses, as Theodore had done. Addressing the voters, he would tell a story: "A little shaver said to me the other day that he knew I wasn't Teddy—I asked him 'why' and he replied: 'Because you don't show your teeth.'" Throughout the campaign Franklin sounded the themes long popularized by Theodore Roosevelt: honesty and economy in government.

On Election Day, November 8, 1910, Roosevelt carried his district by only a narrow plurality. But he won, and he was now a public official.

Early the next year, a story went, Big Tim Sullivan and another Tammany boss were lounging in the lobby of an Albany hotel. A tall young man wearing a frock coat and a gold-rimmed pince-nez strode in. It was Franklin Roosevelt. "You know those Roosevelts," Big Tim muttered. "This one is young. Wouldn't it be safer to drown him before he grows up?"

Roosevelt, however, had no intention of staying in Albany. Hardly had he been elected than he went to Trenton, New Jersey, there to proclaim fealty to the new governor and rising star in the Democratic Party, Woodrow Wilson. Roosevelt thereby established his bona fides as an early Wilson supporter. And in March 1913, after Wilson had been sworn in as president, Secretary of the Navy Josephus Daniels offered Franklin the post of assistant secretary, exactly the position Theodore had once held.

But Elihu Root, a wealthy Manhattan attorney, secretary of state under the earlier Roosevelt, and now a New York senator, warned Daniels, echoing Big Tim Sullivan: "Whenever a Roosevelt rides, he wishes to ride in front."

2

"Sometimes a man's rootage means more than his leafage," Woodrow Wilson once said. He, too, wished to ride in front, and he, too, was best explicable in terms of his background.

Situated on a hilltop in Staunton, Virginia, not far from Charlottesville, the house in which Thomas Woodrow Wilson was born in 1856, the first son in his family, was a Presbyterian manse. His parents were of Scottish background; his mother, née Jessie Woodrow, was a direct immigrant, and his father, the Reverend Dr. Joseph Ruggles Wilson, was the brilliant offspring of a family that had settled in Ohio. Despite his northern origins, Dr. Wilson had taken his first pastorate in the South, fully identifying himself with the region. He also won fame as a preacher, so much so that a year after Tommy's birth, he received a call to a much more prestigious parish in Augusta, right in the heart of the Deep South.

"My earliest recollection is of standing at my father's gateway in Augusta, Georgia, when I was four years old, and hearing someone pass and say that Mr. Lincoln was elected and there was to be war," Woodrow Wilson would tell an audience many years later. "Catching the intense tones of his excited voice, I remember running to ask my father what it meant."

Across the street from his father's large church, built of sandstone with a crenellated rooftop, the boy would have been standing at the edge of what was then a wide, unpaved street. Running up the stoop into the three-story brick manse, he would have passed along a hall-way floor covered with an early version of linoleum, yellow and brown, laid to protect the rest of the house from mud and horse dung, and entered his father's book-lined, tobacco-smoke-filled study.

The study was Dr. Wilson's sanctuary as well as Tommy's first classroom. As Woodrow Wilson (he dropped the "Tommy" while in college) was the first to acknowledge, his father's influence on him was profound. He drilled his son constantly in the correct use of the English language, and while he may have been something of a mar-tinet, his son absorbed the lessons willingly.

The father also taught by example. On Sunday mornings, Mrs. Wilson, her two daughters, and Tommy habitually sat in the fourth row of pews, close enough to the pulpit that the boy could look almost straight up into his father's face. Dr. Wilson prepared his sermons carefully and eloquently, and his sonorous voice carried without difficulty to congregants in the very back of the church. "I wish that I could believe," Woodrow Wilson would write as an adult, "that I had inherited that rarest gift of making great truths attractive in the telling and of inspiring with great purposes by sheer force of eloquence or by gentle stress of persuasion." As the future would show, he manifestly inherited that "rarest gift."

After Augusta, the Wilson family moved on to churches in Columbia, South Carolina, then Wilmington, North Carolina. In Wilmington, the time came for Tommy to go off to college. So in September 1875 tall, thin, angular, and carrying an old black bag that had belonged to his father, Tommy Wilson stepped down from a train carriage onto the platform of the little station at the foot of the hill by the College of New Jersey, now Princeton University.

3

A drawing of the college sketched in the 1870s shows twenty or so buildings, a good half of them private houses, straggling along Nas-sau Street. The rest of the picture is taken up with the farms and orchards of the rolling New Jersey countryside. Rural and at the time isolated from the temptations of the cities, Princeton was ideal for the education of young men who expected to follow their fathers into the ministry.

Young Wilson, however, had set another goal for himself. "And now we come," he wrote in his diary during his sophomore year, "to the chief and best means of training the orator—the imitation of classic models. The greatest and truest model for all orators is Demosthenes. One who has not studied deeply and constantly all the great speeches of the great Athenian is not prepared to speak in public. . . . Only as the constant companions of Demosthenes, Cicero, Burke, [Charles] Fox, [George] Canning, and Webster, can we hope to become orators."

Wilson was laying out what he wanted from Princeton: not grades, not academic prizes, and not a mastery of a curriculum imposed on him by others; but rather a self-directed discipline intended to prepare himself for some great purpose.

For he had resolved to go into the world of politics. In September 1879, therefore, having graduated with his class that spring, Wilson set off from his parents' home in Wilmington to the law school at the University of Virginia.

"The profession I chose was politics; the profession I entered was the law," he would write. "I chose the one because I thought it would lead to the other."

The law took Wilson nowhere. As at Princeton, he spent much of his time in Charlottesville studying the art of oratory. At the end of May 1882, to be sure, he passed the Georgia bar and set out his shingle. But he had just one client: his mother.

After about a year of living off money sent by his parents, Wilson's life changed. On his mother's behalf, he went by train to Rome, Georgia, to confer with a relative over the settlement of an estate. The journey through the green hills of northwestern Georgia must have been pleasant; so must have been the carriage ride through Rome, with its broad market street and stately mansions surrounded by magnolias, dogwoods, and azaleas, all in full bloom.

While staying with his relatives, Wilson attended the Sunday service at the local Presbyterian church. Once seated, he noticed a young woman in a nearby pew. "I remember thinking," he wrote to her later, "what a bright, pretty face; what splendid mischievous, laughing eyes! I'll lay a wager that this demure little lady has lots of life and fun in her!"

The young woman, Wilson learned after the service was over, was Ellen Louise Axson. Four years younger than he, she was the widely read, artistically talented daughter of the Reverend Samuel Edward Axson, the minister of the church and an old friend of Wilson's father. Half a year later, Woodrow and Ellen were engaged to be married.

Woodrow in the meantime had decided to abandon the law and to pursue a career as a professor of history and politics; such a choice, he knew, would make almost impossible the fulfillment of his dream of becoming a renowned statesman. Nevertheless, in the autumn of 1883 he enrolled in the new graduate school at Johns Hopkins University in Baltimore.

Woodrow wrote to Ellen in October,

> My room [on Charles Street in Baltimore] is not large, but it is a cheery front room with good-looking, shapely furniture in it and lighted by a broad, generous window which looks out upon a handsome square and plats of grass and ornamental shrubs which are grateful to the eye in the midst of a great city; and across the brave architecture of the noble Peabody Institute, as well as upon the graceful shaft of the beautiful Washington Monument.

Yet Wilson was almost immediately dissatisfied. Less than six weeks after his arrival at Johns Hopkins, he complained to Ellen:

> Style is not much studied here; ideas are supposed to be everything —their vehicle comparatively nothing. But you and I know that there can be no greater mistake; that, both in its amount and in

its length of life, an author's influence depends upon the power and the beauty of his style; upon the flawless perfection of the mirror he holds up to nature; upon his facility in catching and holding, because he pleases, the attention; and style shall be, as under my father's guidance, it has been, one of my chief studies. A writer must be artful as well as strong.

At Johns Hopkins Wilson distinguished himself academically as he had never done before. He also worked hard at his literary technique. He sought to compose well every time he put pen to paper, whether in letters, reports, to his graduate seminar, or even notes taken during lectures. "My chief study," he wrote to Ellen, "is the art of writing."

Woodrow Wilson still clung to his hope, however seemingly unreachable, of exerting political influence. Even in graduate school he was seeking to make himself what in time he became: the great communicator of his day.

After finishing his coursework (the completion of the doctorate would come later), Woodrow Wilson in the summer of 1885 married Ellen Axson. In the autumn he took his first teaching position, at Bryn Mawr, then a new Quaker college for women just outside Philadelphia.

The Wilsons (two baby girls came in rapid order) stayed there only three years. Woodrow's record of publication landed him a better-paying job at Wesleyan University in Middletown, Connecticut.

Wilson thrived at Wesleyan; he was a superb teacher. One of his students wrote in 1924, the year of Wilson's death,

Every man in his class felt inspired to do his best, not because of any exhortation or threat, but from the very atmosphere of his personality; not a feeling of fear of consequences was present, but a feeling that you were ashamed if you were not at your best. I can see him now, with his hands forward, the tips of his fingers just touching the table, his face earnest and animated; many times illuminating an otherwise dry and tedious subject by his beautiful language and his apt way of putting things.

The students at Wesleyan had no idea how hard Wilson worked to put things in an "apt way." Night after night, the light in his study in his house on High Street would shine into the darkness. Determined to get every lecture just right, Woodrow Wilson was striving for mastery. He was educating himself, in the classroom, to capture the interest and fire the imagination of an audience.

But his time at Wesleyan lasted only two years. In the spring of 1890, Wilson received the call from Princeton, for him the holy grail.

When Woodrow and Ellen Wilson, with their three little girls—Margaret, four; Jessie, three; and Eleanor (born in Middletown), just over one—moved to New Jersey in September, Princeton was still the village it once had been. The college, however, was now full of young faculty members who wanted to throw off the shackles of parochial Presbyterian control and turn the campus into a secular, national university. And Woodrow Wilson represented the kind of change that his new colleagues craved. When he had first stepped off the shuttle at the base of the hill, he had been a shy freshman, unknown and knowing no one. Now, accompanied by his family, he was greeted by a coterie of cheering undergraduates who had heard of his stellar reputation in the collegiate world.

In the years he taught at Princeton, Wilson's enrollments almost exactly doubled. His main course was in public law, not necessarily a popular topic, but the subject did not matter. Year after year, the student grapevine—a college's true advisory system—buzzed with two words: "Take Wilson!"

Lecturing in the chapel, Princeton's largest classroom, Wilson would look out on his students and, when the bell rang, say, "Good morning, gentlemen"; and from that moment through the rest of the period they would be under his spell. After making a few abstract points, he illustrated them with stories from the news or with pictures-in-words from the past. Throughout all his lectures ran the central drama of the age-old struggle for democracy.

Wilson knew that he had found his voice. "I seem myself to have become in so many ways another fellow," he wrote to Ellen during a time away, "more confident, steady, serene . . . enjoying in a certain degree a sense of power."

Wilson made his mark as the idol of the undergraduates, the college's most noteworthy speaker, and the most ardent faculty fan of the athletic teams. At Princeton football games, Wilson would march alongside the band, then once in the stands thump a cane in encouragement, and afterward, win or lose, visit the players in the locker room. He also became the leader of younger faculty discontented with what they saw as the college's inertia. With a sure grasp of politics, Wilson had made himself the embodiment of what Princeton might be.

Halfway through his time as a teacher, Wilson had cried out to Stockton Axson, his brother-in-law, that "I am tired of a merely talking profession! I want to do something!" During the week of commencement in 1902, the board of trustees offered him the presidency of Princeton. Now his chance to "do something" had arrived.

4

Saturday, October 25, 1902, the date set for Woodrow Wilson's inauguration as the president of Princeton, was a beautiful, cloudless day, and the air was crisp and clear. Beneath the azure morning sky, the leaves on the trees throughout the village were brilliant in tones of red and yellow. Banners of black and orange, the colors of the Princeton football team, hung from turrets and towers around the campus. The crowds that lined the walkways were dense and, according to the local newspaper, "extra carriages had to be imported from Trenton."

At about eleven o'clock, various dignitaries—famous professors, best-selling authors, notable public officials, and captains of industry, all of whom had arrived to take part in the inaugural procession —assembled under the medieval arches of the library. Garbed in academic cap and gown as the group started forward were Frank Murphy, the governor of New Jersey, and the bulky figure of former president of the United States Grover Cleveland, who had chosen to live in Princeton and who served on the board of trustees. Just behind them, striding in tandem, were Francis L. Patton, the outgoing president, and slim, erect, and keen-faced, Woodrow Wilson, the president-elect.

Wilson gave his inaugural address in the auditorium of Nassau Hall, Princeton's most venerable building. Wearing a plain black mortarboard cap and gown, adorned with an orange and black honorary doctoral hood conferred on him earlier by the university, Wilson spoke to the topic "Princeton for the National Service."

The title presaged Wilson's university presidency. Once a college largely for the sons of Presbyterian clergy, Princeton had become a country club for sons of the rich. Wilson espoused a third purpose: Princeton, he believed, should educate the young for the service of the nation. As the new president of Princeton, he was putting himself forward as one who would educate "efficient and enlightened" youths. Although not yet embarked on a political career, he was presenting himself as one who would provide a benefit to the country at large.

In his first four years at the helm of the university, Wilson concentrated on modernizing the curriculum, hiring new professors, and introducing British-style tutorials. Then he went much farther. First he launched an attack on the "eating clubs"—Princeton's version of fraternities grown wealthy and housed in spacious mansions—as undemocratic and inimical to serious learning. Later he proposed locating a new graduate school, not on the edge of the campus, as its dean, Andrew West, wanted, but rather at the very center, so that graduate and undergraduate students could mix freely. Such steps, Wilson contended, accorded with the American democratic tradition.

The Princeton board of trustees rejected Wilson on both issues: board members had received voluminous correspondence from alumni who definitely wished to preserve the eating clubs; and in his pursuit of a segregated graduate school, Dean West had secured a huge financial gift from William C. Procter, a Princeton alumnus and cofounder of the soap company Procter & Gamble. Wilson had lost decisively twice, and in May 1910 the majority of the board concluded that he had outlived his usefulness as the president of Princeton.

During the week of commencement in 1910, Wilson in public kept his feelings to himself. He gave a graceful speech to the class of 1910, the new graduates cheering him so long and so loudly that tears streamed down his face.

The young men cared nothing about the graduate school controversy. They just knew that Wilson had been an inspiration to them all, and they lauded him by singing new words to an old Princeton song:

> Here's to Wilson, king of men,
> He rules this place with 1910.
> We have no fear he'll leave this town
> To try for anybody's crown!

But, of course, Wilson was going to leave that town. Colonel George Harvey was showing the way.

Editor of *Harper's Weekly*, a magazine underwritten by the financier J. P. Morgan, Harvey, round-faced with owlish glasses, fancied himself a kingmaker and had long thought Wilson to be of presidential timber. Looking ahead to the election of 1912, Harvey reasoned that William Howard Taft, the incumbent president, could be defeated with ease. The most prominent of the old-line Democrats, furthermore, was William Jennings Bryan, now balding and portly, and the loser in three previous presidential races. Wilson, a Democrat, could give the party a fresh face. There did exist a widespread belief that a southerner could not be elected president, and Wilson was a southerner. In Harvey's view, however, Wilson had lived in Princeton long enough to qualify as a northerner, and his struggles at the college aligned him with the nation's dominant political movement, progressivism. Besides, Wilson had proven himself the most renowned orator of his time. So in January 1910 Harvey arranged a luncheon at Delmonico's in Manhattan with a former senator, James Smith.

Tall, handsome, brawny, and florid of face, Smith was the undisputed boss of the New Jersey Democratic Party. His specialty was lobbying. With huge corporate bribes, he spread the wealth among his largely Irish American followers, making sure that the party picked loyal Democrats to sit in the statehouse in Trenton and enact laws dear to the hearts of Smith's clients. If he wished, he could even make someone governor, and that was why Colonel Harvey invited him to lunch: if Wilson were to run for president, he had to hold public office first, and with its proximity to the New York newspapers, the governorship of New Jersey seemed ideal.

Smith understood the game, but he was uneasy. If made governor, what would the reform-minded Wilson do to the "boys," Smith's political hacks on state patronage jobs?

The best Harvey could give by way of an answer was to arrange a meeting of Smith and Wilson. The encounter took place on the evening of June 26, 1910, in Harvey's beach house at Deal, New Jersey. What Wilson promised, if anything, is not recorded. Smith nonetheless left satisfied. Wilson soon thereafter became the Democratic nominee for governor and on November 10 won the election.

Surrounded by gilt-edged oil portraits of governors from New Jersey's past and backed by a huge bookcase lined with legal texts, Wilson in his office in the statehouse sat behind an uncluttered mahogany desk. Across an oriental carpet stood a cluster of brass-studded leather armchairs for visitors, and hovering nearby usually was Joe Tumulty, Wilson's stocky, red-haired private secretary. Tumulty was ready and willing always to go outside the office and to fight, trade, and cajole on Wilson's behalf.

Wilson had committed himself to the passage of a four-point reform program: a bill that would strike down patronage in the state's governmental hiring; a measure for the regulation of the utilities companies; an anticorruption act; and a workers' compensation law. All were intended to reduce the power of Boss Smith's machine. Few thought he could succeed. By the late spring of 1911, nevertheless, Wilson had driven all his measures through the legislature.

James Smith and other regular Democrats, including those of Tammany Hall in New York, regarded Wilson as a traitor. Because of the success of his progressive, antiboss program, however, Wilson was now in a position to seek the Democratic nomination for president.

Late in June 1912, William Jennings Bryan arrived by train at Baltimore's Union Station. Cheers from crowds followed him all the way to his hotel, and he waved back in acknowledgment. As he entered his room, he knew he could not win a fourth nomination. Yet he hoped to influence the convention's outcome.

Democratic delegates were taking possession of Baltimore. The first to arrive were the Champ Clark men from Missouri and its neighboring states; Clark was the Speaker of the House. One hundred fifty strong, they had traveled in a train called the Hound-dog Special. Delegates for Judson Harmon, the governor of Ohio, pulled in from Columbus. Supporters of Representative Oscar Underwood came from Alabama. Tammany Hall forces dominated the New York delegation. Wilson people from Georgia and the Carolinas, along with New Jersey, held high banners of black and orange, the Princeton colors. As was the custom, Wilson kept away, staying with his family at the governor's cottage at Sea Girt, on the Jersey shore.

When the Democratic convention officially opened on the afternoon of June 25, 1912, the Baltimore Armory, site of the gathering, was hung inside and out with American flags and bunting of red, white, and blue. James Cardinal Gibbons of Baltimore opened the convocation with a prayer. Robed in red with a scarlet skullcap on his white hair, he intoned: "Let the light of Thy divine wisdom direct the deliberations of this convention."

In the heat of the Baltimore summer, the convention droned on and on. The nominating speeches seemed endless and, although Champ Clark started with a substantial lead, the voting went on to the fourteenth ballot. At that point, Bryan announced his support for Governor Wilson. With hard bargaining taking place in smoke-filled rooms, the momentum shifted to Wilson. Finally, on the afternoon of July 2, 1912, amid a tumult of shouting and cheers, the convention acclaimed Woodrow Wilson its nominee for president.

Hand in hand, Governor and Mrs. Wilson came out onto the porch of the cottage at Sea Girt. His eyes moist, Wilson said to reporters that "at this moment I feel the tremendous responsibility [the nomination] involves even more than I feel the honor." In her mellifluous Georgia accent, Mrs. Wilson added, "Now I'm going to quit worrying."

All was quiet until Labor Day. Then the presidential campaign of 1912 got under way. Although the majority of Americans were Republicans, Theodore Roosevelt, running again as head of the new Progressive Party, had broken the GOP in two. But could Wilson, the nominee of the party that since the Civil War had won the White House only twice, succeed? It was anybody's guess. Correspondents thought it would be quite a race.

Poor Taft! He may have wanted to be reelected, and his wife, Helen, certainly wanted to stay in the White House, but he just did not want to work for it. When fellow Republicans insisted that he go out onto the hustings and start an energetic campaign, he exclaimed: "I couldn't if I would and I wouldn't if I could!"

Theodore Roosevelt conducted his own campaign with all his renowned energy, and he displayed all his magnetism of old. When his special train reached Providence, journalists estimated that ten thousand people had crowded into the railway station. In the rail yard at Springfield, Missouri, he spotted some Taft campaign buttons and called out, "They are the appropriate color of yellow!" In Duluth, the throng of people was so dense that security guards had to surround Roosevelt all the way to a hotel. Roosevelt pushed on to Washington and Oregon, then down the coast to Los Angeles. There he faced a welcoming multitude of some two hundred thousand people.

It was not enough. Although Roosevelt came in second to Taft's distant third, Wilson—carrying the South and enjoying the support of New York backers such as Henry Morgenthau—won a plurality of the popular votes. He carried the electoral college with a substantial majority.

March 4, 1913, Inauguration Day, in Washington dawned cloudy, but the sky soon cleared and the snow that had fallen in the night glittered in the sunshine. In the chilly brightness, the crowds assembled at noontime on the plaza east of the Capitol strained for a view of the inaugural stand. All was quiet. Suddenly, though, a thousand voices or more roared out their greeting. Woodrow Wilson had appeared at the top of the platform.

Standing beside the ponderous outgoing president, Taft, Wilson in his morning coat and striped trousers looked lean and alert. Side by side, Wilson and Taft started down the red-carpeted steps. As they descended, they passed by the justices of the United States, seated in their black robes; the leaders of both houses of Congress; and the members of the diplomatic corps, resplendent in sashes, colorful cummerbunds, and ornate medals. Occupying chairs at the bottom of the stairs, just behind the white-painted railing, were Mrs. Wilson and her three daughters. As her husband reached the rostrum, Mrs. Wilson rose, making certain that she missed not a word.

With his wife by his side and his left hand on the Bible of his late father, to whom he owed so much, Woodrow Wilson repeated after Chief Justice Edward D. White, "I, Woodrow Wilson, do solemnly swear."

5

Once the Wilsons had settled into the White House and become accustomed to the place, the Oval Office took on the appearance of the president's study back in Princeton. Books from Wilson's personal library filled the white-painted shelves, and some of his old armchairs lined the edges of the room. Wilson himself enjoyed a leather swivel desk chair with padded arms. On the desk were a calendar; a brass lamp with a half-globe green shade; and on one corner every day was a tall glass vase with freshly cut flowers. The white desk blotter was almost wholly devoid of clutter. The overall impression was one of neatness and order.

Off by one wall, however, was a large globe, the kind that portrayed all the realms of the British Empire in red. A reporter with access to the president would remember Wilson "standing there, turning the globe with one finger, tracing out the relationships of America with Europe, with Mexico, with Japan and the Philippine Islands. It was a symbol of preoccupations that were unexpected when he came into office, of duties for which he had never deliberately prepared."

Shortly before going to Washington, Wilson himself had said to a former colleague at Princeton: "It would be an irony of fate if my administration had to deal chiefly with foreign affairs." Wilson had devoted his career to politics at home. Yet from the moment he took the White House he discovered that he had to deal with politics abroad.

To this point, Wilson's life had taken place during an era in which Americans were beginning to lay claim to Great Britain's title as the world's greatest power and, at the same time, to expect a stable world. Now, however, the globe was bursting into violence in Mexico, Central America, the Caribbean, and East Asia. But the most dangerous of the crises overseas was the explosion of war in Europe.

Soon after the outbreak of World War I, Wilson asked the American people to be "neutral in fact as well as in name," "impartial in thought as well as in action." Few Americans, however, could maintain such disinterest. Irish Americans and German Americans loathed the British Empire; recent Jewish immigrants regarded Russia with similar hatred. Yet British propagandists swamped America with stories of German atrocities, and white Protestant Americans clearly favored the Allied cause.

Wilson's closest aides also were divided. William Jennings Bryan, whom the president as a political payoff had made secretary of state, was resolutely neutral. But Colonel Edward M. House, Wilson's frail and shadowy éminence grise, favored the Allies. And Robert Lansing, the handsome, square-jawed legal adviser to the State Department, was keenly pro-British.

Lansing, in fact, was neutral in neither thought nor action. When to enforce their blockade of Germany the British began to board American ships, Lansing acquired the task of drafting protest notes. But he also, in his own words, turned them into "long and detailed" messages intended to prolong controversies with London: he hoped thereby that in time "the American people [would] perceive that German absolutism was a menace to their liberties."

Lansing's stratagem worked: most of the American public saw the sinking of the *Lusitania* as an outrage perpetrated solely by Germany; Wilson directed his protests to Berlin only. And when Bryan insisted that Wilson also denounce the British, the president refused to do so. Bryan resigned, and Wilson replaced him with Lansing.

After the *Lusitania* went down, Germany foreswore unrestricted submarine warfare. Wilson's tilt toward the Allies nonetheless became ever more pronounced. In September 1915 he allowed them to float huge loans on Wall Street. He also made sure that Germany had no access to such funds; thereby, a historian has noted, he "had become a partner, and not always a silent partner, in the Allied economic campaign to strangle Germany."

Given that partnership, Germany early in 1917 resumed total submarine warfare, and Wilson in March ordered armaments placed aboard American merchant ships. On March 18, German submarines sank three American ships. And on April 2, with the young Roosevelts in attendance, President Wilson asked Congress for the declaration of war.

During luncheon at the White House four days later, a messenger approached the table where President and Mrs. Wilson were dining. (This was the second Mrs. Wilson, the former Edith Bolling Galt; Ellen Axson Wilson had died two years before, of kidney disease.) Vice President Thomas R. Marshall had just signed the war resolution, passed by both houses of Congress, Wilson was told, and it had reached the White House. The Wilsons arose at once and, accompanied by the president's cousin, Helen Bones, walked directly to the office of the White House usher, just inside the North Portico. There Rudolph Forster, the executive secretary, was waiting with the parchment document in his hand. Wilson sat at a desk, took up a pen, and affixed his own signature. The United States was now in a state of war with imperial Germany.

6

But why?

That was a question raised not only by anti-Allied ethnic communities but also by leaders of business. Only the year before, British, French, Russian, and Italian representatives had met secretly (so they thought, but the news had leaked) in Paris, agreeing jointly to use government subsidies, higher tariffs, and controlled markets to fight off American competition in the postwar world. Furious, Wilson had stated that "our businessmen ought to organize their wits in such a way as to take possession of foreign markets"; he much favored, he had added, the "righteous conquest of foreign markets."

Wilson had done more than talk. He had sponsored the Webb-Pomerene Act, a measure that freed American corporations from antitrust laws, allowing them to combine for the "conquest of foreign markets." In the autumn of 1916, moreover, he had sent to Congress a huge naval appropriations bill. To help defeat Germany? To be sure. But also to beat down British economic and maritime power. "Let us build a navy bigger than [Great Britain's]," he had said to Colonel House, "and do what we please."

Why, then, did America intervene in World War I? The sinking of the *Lusitania* had created in the nation an undeniable clamor for war, but Wilson wanted to earn the right to demand that the British open their empire to American business. And *that*, as much as hostility toward Germany, was the theme of Woodrow Wilson's famous Fourteen Points.

Just before noon on January 8, 1918, a mounted honor guard escorted Wilson to the Capitol. Believing that he needed to clarify his war aims, Wilson had arranged to speak to a joint session of Congress.

The impression he made was excellent. Speaker Champ Clark afterward wrote to Wilson: "Your speech was clear as crystal. Anybody that can't understand it, whether he agree with it or not, is an incorrigible fool." The *New York Tribune* the next day termed the address "one of the great documents in American history." It was the speech for which Woodrow Wilson had been preparing all his life—and it shocked the British to the core.

The Fourteen Points included:

One. "Open covenants of peace, openly arrived at, after which there shall be no private international understandings of any kind." Wilson was rebuking not the Germans but rather the Allies for their earlier anti-American collusion.

Two. "Absolute freedom of navigation upon the seas . . . alike in peace and in war." Here was a slap not only at Germany's submarine warfare but also at Great Britain's naval embargo and its boarding of American ships.

Three. "The removal, so far as possible, of all economic barriers and the establishment of an equality of trade conditions among all the nations." Wilson was calling for a worldwide open door, which meant above all the elimination of British imperial trade barriers.

Four. "Adequate guarantees given and taken that national armaments will be reduced to the lowest point consistent with domestic safety." With the German High Seas Fleet virtually useless, Wilson was implying the need for the reduction of the size of the British Royal Navy.

Five. The "adjustment of all colonial claims," with the colonized enjoying "equal weight" with their colonizers in deciding their futures. Since the British, French, and Japanese had shorn Germany of its colonies, this was a clear shot at the British Empire.

Fourteen. "A general association of nations must be formed under specific covenants for the purpose of affording mutual guarantees of political independence and territorial integrity to great and small nations alike." This, Wilson's call for a League of Nations, had deep roots in the American faith in freedom. In its proclaiming "political independence and territorial integrity," it was asserting America's right to re-create the world in its own image. The hope of such a re-creation underlay everything Wilson sought during the peace talks in Paris in 1919.

CHAPTER 5

The Peace of Paris

1

On August 8, 1917, a special train left the depot at Zurich, steaming northward into Germany. The German government had arranged for its journey and had ordered that it be sealed. During transit, no one was to leave and no one was to come aboard. For on the train were some thirty passengers, all of them Bolsheviks, the most extreme of the Russian revolutionaries, who had been in exile in Switzerland. The leaders of the group were a rather short, chunky woman named Nadezhda Konstantinovna Krupskaya and her husband, Vladimir Ilyich Ulyanov, the stocky, paunchy, balding, red-goateed theorist and orator who had taken the code name of Lenin.

Lenin and Krupskaya had been staying in a greasy, ill-lit single room in the rear of a cobbler's house; their only view had been that of a wall of a Zurich sausage factory, and the stench had been so foul that they had spent most of their time in the city's library. Lenin had been disconsolate, fearing that they might have to live like that forever. On a night in the middle of March 1917, however, as they were getting up from the boardinghouse table, a Polish comrade burst in, exclaiming, "Haven't you heard the news? There's been a revolution in Russia!"

Czar Nicholas II had abdicated and had been replaced by a provisional government headed by Alexander Kerensky. But the new government had maintained the Russian military effort, such as it was, against Germany. Hoping for a regime that would pull

Russia out of the war altogether, Berlin had quickly decided to send Lenin home.

As he and his wife looked out the train windows at the passing railroad stations, farm fields, and city streets of Germany, they noticed the absence of men: only women and children were outside, dutifully carrying out the chores of daily life. There were no signs that Germany was on the verge of a revolution; all was eerily passive. When they got to Stockholm, they were gratified to see that Swedish socialists had hung a red flag in the waiting room. Once inside, they partook of a smorgasbord, the first substantial meal they had eaten in months. One of the attending Swedes took Lenin to a downtown shop and bought him a new pair of shoes: the future leader, the Swede explained, needed a firm understanding.

From Sweden Lenin and Krupskaya crossed by sleigh into Finland. There, Krupskaya wrote, "everything was already familiar and dear to us: the wretched third-class cars, the Russian soldiers. It was terribly good."

At Helsinki, they mounted a train for St. Petersburg, now renamed Petrograd. It arrived late on the evening of April 16, 1917, at the Finland Station.

The depot was little more than a stucco shack, oily gray and smoky pink. The waiting room reeked of smoke, and its wooden benches were grimy from the filth of innumerable bundles of peasants who sat and awaited their trains. On this night, though, no one was sitting. As the train hissed to a stop, hundreds of fellow Bolsheviks, released from prison, rushed forth in greeting.

During the journey from Switzerland, Lenin had feared that he might be riding into arrest. When he looked down upon the throng of comrades gathering along the platform, though, he exulted. Leaping down from the carriage, he was so excited that he neglected to button his coat. But a neatly uniformed naval officer stepped forward and snapped a salute. Lenin returned the honor. The officer shouted an order and, suddenly visible, a squadron of sailors from the Kronstadt naval base stood at attention. Searchlights of the fortress of Peter and Paul came on, bathing the platform with light.

A military band struck up the "Marseillaise." The crowd erupted with a roar.

Unbelieving, Lenin stepped back toward the train and asked someone nearby, "What is this?"

The answer came back from the crowd, rhythmically chanting one word: "Lenin!"

Then he was up on shoulders, being carried to an armored car parked outside the station. With Lenin inside, the automobile moved forward, passing through a multitude of soldiers, sailors, and textile- and metalworkers. The searchlights illuminated red banners with gold letters hung along the roadside. At last the car reached the Kshesin-skaya Palace, taken over by the Bolsheviks for their party headquarters.

Inside were mirrors, crystal, frescoes, and a wide staircase, but Lenin displayed no interest in the luxury. Bounding up the steps, he raced to a balcony and looked down at all the people assembled below. Beginning to speak, he denounced "robber capitalists . . . the destruction of the peoples of Europe for the profits of a gang of exploiters . . . the defense of capitalists against everybody else." Excoriating the provisional government, he cried out, "We don't need any parliamentary republic! We don't need any bourgeois democracy! We don't need any government except the Soviet of workers, soldiers, and peasants!"

Lenin's speech, which marked the beginning of the Bolshevik Revolution in Russia, coincided with the utter collapse of the country's war effort. At the front, troops were deserting by the hundreds of thousands. In their rush to return home, hordes of soldiers clinging even to freight trains, as Count Leo Tolstoy described them, "were killed under the wheels and smashed their heads against the cross-girders of bridges." But still the human tide continued to flow.

As the soldiers streamed onward, Russia descended into anarchy. "All the dark instincts of the crowd, irritated by the disintegration of life and by the lies and filth of politics, will flare up and fume, poisoning us with anger, hate, and revenge," wrote Russia's famed proletarian author Maxim Gorky. "People kill one another, unable to suppress their own animal stupidity."

Lenin and his associate Leon Trotsky, who had returned from exile in Vienna, found the course of events to exceed their fondest hopes. As Bolsheviks won majorities in the soviets of Petrograd, Moscow, and Kiev early in September, Lenin declared that "all the objective conditions exist for a successful insurrection."

To ensure that success, Lenin on the night of October 10 secretly convened other prominent Bolsheviks in an obscure flat on the edge of Petrograd's proletarian quarter; he pledged them to the support of an armed uprising against the Kerensky regime. Two weeks later, on October 26, the uprising took place. Driving Kerensky from office, Lenin's forces seized control of the city and set up Russia's first "people's government."

The October Revolution was such a triumph that even Lenin was stunned. "To pass so quickly from persecution and living in hiding to power," he exclaimed, "*es schwindelt* [it vanishes]—it makes one's head spin!"

Lenin's victory over all Russia, however, was far from certain. The old empire was falling apart, its many nationalities asserting their independence from Petrograd. Faced with the prospect of a civil war, Lenin saw no choice but to withdraw altogether from the European conflict. On March 3, 1918, he signed the Treaty of Brest-Litovsk, allowing Germany to send new divisions to the Western Front and to grab off Finland, Poland, and the little Baltic states, severing them from the old Russian Empire.

Lenin had only exchanged one war for another. In April 1918 a Japanese army marched into Siberia, and only three months later President Wilson sent several American battalions into Russia through ports on the Arctic Ocean. Working in cooperation with the British, Wilson justified the intervention as necessary to prevent a German takeover of the ports and their environs. The Anglo-American units, though, soon found themselves entangled not with Germans but rather with Bolshevik Russians.

Almost inadvertently, Wilson had joined with Great Britain in its reversion to the Victorian era's "great game": the containment of the Russian "menace." And although the intervention foundered on distance, cost, and the wish of the American public to get the boys home, that "menace" hung over the Paris peace conference even a year later. As Ray Stannard Baker, a reporter and Wilson's first major biographer, put the problem, there had arisen a "black cloud of the east, threatening to overwhelm amd swallow up the world. . . . Russia played a more vital part at Paris than [Germany]. For the Prussian idea had been utterly defeated, while the Russian idea was still rising in power." As David Lloyd George, the British prime minister, confessed, he found it nearly impossible to discuss Germany without also mentioning Russia.

Throughout much of the nineteenth century, British statesmen had seen Russia as a gigantic and hideous serpent, flicking its tongue in every direction, probing always for a weak spot in the armor of the British Empire. Bismarckean and Wilhelmine Germany had emerged as the new colossus to the east. With Germany defeated, however, the old specter of Russia the aggressor had arisen again: Lenin, after all, was calling for a worldwide, Soviet-led revolution.

Wilson accepted that British view without reservation. Indeed, at Paris he took the lead in devising a defense against the hordes from the heartland of Asia. Kneeling on a carpet in his Paris hotel with a map spread out before him, he sketched out a column of new nations—a cordon sanitaire, or a "sanitary barrier," from Finland through the Baltic republics of Estonia, Latvia, and Lithuania; the newly independent Poland; the unified Czechoslovakia; and, skipping over Austria, Hungary, and Romania, the combination of Balkan ethnic groups called Yugoslavia.

In time, of course, that pillar of states crumbled under assaults from Nazi Germany and the Soviet Union. In 1919, though, Woodrow Wilson was taking upon the United States the imperial British task of the containment of Russia.

But Ray Stannard Baker did exaggerate: just as important as the containment of Russia, for Wilson, was the establishment of a general peace. In going to Paris, he intended nothing less than to make of the United States the redeemer of the world—even if the world was not ready to be redeemed.

2

Wilson's most formidable opponent at the Paris peace talks was the French premier, Georges Clemenceau. A member of the American delegation would liken Clemenceau "in face and figure [to] a Chinese mandarin of the old empire. . . . He had the sallow complexion, the prominent high cheekbones, the massive forehead with protuberant brows, the slant of the dark eyes, the long down-curving gray moustache, the short neck, the broad, rounded shoulders." The French had another way of describing Clemenceau. They called him, simply, the Tiger.

Born in 1841 in the Vendée, a region near the Atlantic with hedgerows, stone cottages, and stony farmland, Clemenceau had descended from a line of country doctors. As a young man he had gone to Paris to learn medicine. His studies had not lasted long. Falling in with radical circles, he had become a political agitator and in 1862 spent two months in jail. Released, he had received an allowance from his father to spend time in the United States. Living in Greenwich Village, he had picked up an American wife. The marriage had not endured, but the couple had returned to Paris in time to witness the German invasion of France in 1870, the siege of Paris and the starvation of its inhabitants, and the humiliation of France's surrender, signed on January 18, 1871, in the Hall of Mirrors at Versailles.

In and out of political office over the next five decades, Clemenceau had never forgotten his country's debasement. And now, with the Great War over, he sought his revenge. He was determined to do all he could during the peace talks to tear Germany asunder, no matter what Woodrow Wilson wished to propose.

Clemenceau's desire for vengeance led him to do all he could to thwart Wilson; but his British counterpart, Lloyd George, did all he could to court Wilson. Before World War I as after, Britain's leaders recognized their dependence on American goodwill.

John Maynard Keynes, the Cambridge economist who was part of the British delegation to Paris, described Lloyd George as this goat-footed bard, this half-human visitor to our age from the hag-ridden magic and enchanted woods of Celtic antiquity[.] One catches in his company that flavour of final purposelessness, inner irresponsibility, existence outside or away from our Saxon good and evil mixed with cunning, remorselessness, love of power, that lend fascination, enthrallment, and terror to the . . . magicians of the northern European folklore. . . . Lloyd George is rooted in nothing . . . he lives and feeds on his immediate surroundings; he is an instrument and a player at the same time which plays on the company and is played on them too; he is a prism . . . which collects light and distorts it and is most brilliant if that light comes from many quarters at once; a vampire and a medium at once.

Some of this was nonsense, the sneering of a Cantabridgean at the humble region of Welsh miners and farmers from which Lloyd George had sprung. But much of it was accurate. Short and stocky, with a large head and a mane of flowing white hair, Lloyd George was the perfect politician. Like quicksilver, he was impossible to pin down. Sharp in debate, he could shift in a flash from a swoon of romantic oratory to a riposte so swift that he left an opponent impaled. He was the master of inconsistency: an imperialist who had railed against the Boer War, and a social reformer who wanted to balance the budget. One of his Conservative opponents, Stanley Baldwin, destined to be prime minister in the 1930s, said of Lloyd George that "he spent his whole life plastering together the true and the false, and therefrom manufacturing the plausible."

Above all, Lloyd George was a realist. Late in 1916, with Great Britain's war effort going nowhere, he had sensed Asquith's political vulnerability and, entering into a coalition with the Conservatives, had seized the premiership. Two years later, with Germany defeated and knowing where the power lay, he set out to beguile Woodrow Wilson: in the part played by so many British prime ministers ever since, Lloyd George took on a poodlelike obeisance.

On December 4, 1918, fully prepared to dictate the terms of the peace, Woodrow Wilson sailed to France aboard the battleship *George Washington*. As tugboats eased the great ship into the mainstream of the Hudson River, crowds along the waterfront waved handkerchiefs and hats; dirigibles floated overhead, bidding the president a fond farewell. Once past the Statue of Liberty, the ship was surrounded by a phalanx of destroyers and other battleships, charged with escorting Wilson and his party safely to France.

Foremost among those accompanying Wilson was the first lady. Rather plump and wide of mouth, the second Mrs. Wilson had sparkling eyes and the easy manner of a gentlewoman from Virginia; Wilson adored her, perhaps in part because she was a fellow southerner. Widowed herself, she responded to Wilson's affection with a ferocious loyalty. So much did they treasure each other's company that during the Atlantic crossing they seemed aloof, usually dining alone in their stateroom or strolling hand-in-hand around the decks, hardly speaking to anyone else.

The "anyone else" included Secretary of State Robert Lansing, whom Wilson barely consulted; Henry White, a diplomat with whom Mrs. Wilson would discuss matters of etiquette; and no Republicans. "I'll tell you what," the stand-up humorist Will Rogers pictured Wilson saying to the Senate Republicans, "we will split fifty–fifty—I will go and you fellows can stay." Wilson's refusal to take along even Senator Henry Cabot Lodge, chairman of the Committee on Foreign Relations, was to prove costly: it would undercut Wilson's ability to sell to America his vision of a new world order.

But what, concretely, did that vision entail? William Bullitt, a young man in the delegation from Philadelphia's rich and influential Main Line, summoned up his courage and approached Wilson during one of the presidential strolls. Speaking for the other staff members aboard—the White House had scoured the government and universities for Americans most knowledgeable about European affairs— Bullitt protested that while they had brought along crates upon crates of books, they did not know what they were looking for. What did Wilson want of them? What advice did he expect? What were his goals?

In many ways Woodrow Wilson was still the professor. "I am going to teach the South American republics to elect good men," he had said at one point in his first term. In the same spirit he explained to Bullitt that he was going to teach the Europeans to accept his idea of a League of Nations.

When the *George Washington* on December 13, 1918, reached Brest, at the northwestern tip of France, Charles Seymour, another of Wilson's aides, counted up to eighty warships, British, French, and American, all in two straight lines. As Wilson's vessel passed between them, a band aboard each ship played "The Star-Spangled Banner." Various boats came up to the battleship, one of them bearing the American victor, General John J. Pershing. Seymour described him as "very tall, enormous in breadth . . . walks with a bit of a swagger." Once the *George Washington* was at anchor inside the harbor, President and Mrs. Wilson, along with General Pershing, descended to a launch, heading for the shore.

All along the quay before them stood Breton fishermen in wooden shoes and velvet coats; the women were adorned with their best peasant bodices and headdresses. The cheering was unceasing and, as the American party climbed the gangplank, Wilson tipped his silk top hat over and over. After ceremonies beside the quay, the Americans set off in the evening by train for Paris.

All along the roadbed, even in the middle of the night, people stood shoulder-to-shoulder as they shouted their greetings of welcome. In the capital itself, under a crisp, clear morning sky, all France seemed to be present. From the Bois de Boulogne to the Arc de Triomphe, the streets were completely packed and spectators were looking down from every window and rooftop. Dozens of military bands were lined up in attendance, the musicians with their instruments tested and their scores in place. Aside from the clomping of the hoofs of the cavalry, all was quiet in expectation, a crowded, motionless tableau.

Then, at ten o'clock, from the distant guns of the fort at Mont Valérien outside the city, came the signaling booms of artillery. Wilson's train had reached its station at Paris.

Those waiting along the Champs Élysées may have thought they were hearing the roll of approaching thunder. For as Wilson, seated beside Raymond Poincaré, the president of France, and preceded by mounted members of the Garde Républicaine, started forth, the sound of cheering rolled on in deafening waves all the way to the Arc de Triomphe.

As the carriage began its course down the Champs Élysées, a huge banner, lettered in English, stretched across the boulevard: "HONOR TO WILSON THE JUST!" The air was dark with caps and hats, then jackets and coats, all thrown aloft; flowers rained down on the presidential carriage. Trotting alongside, the Secret Service men were terrified, for any crowd control was impossible. As the carriage made its way to the Place de la Concorde, hands stretched forth, trying to touch Wilson or even the wheels of the carriage. The screaming seemed about to go on forever: "*Vive* Wilson!" "*Vive* Wilson!" "*Vive* Wilson!"

"No one ever had such cheers," an American journalist wrote. "I, who heard them in the streets of Paris, can never forget them. . . . I saw [Marshal Ferdinand] Foch pass, Clemenceau pass, Lloyd George, generals, returning troops, banners, but Wilson heard from his carriage something different, inhuman—or superhuman."

At a luncheon in the Élysée Palace, the American and French presidents exchanged toasts. Wilson spoke from behind a dais covered with roses: "All that I have said or tried to do has been said and done only in the attempt to faithfully express the thoughts of the American people. From the very beginning of this war the thoughts of the people of America turned toward something higher than the mere spoils of war. Their thought was directed toward the establishment of the eternal principles of right and justice."

Despite the excitement of the day, Wilson's French listeners were disappointed. The very purpose of the reception for Wilson had been to win his support in securing the spoils of war. Indeed, after Wilson had sat down again, the applause in the palace was distinctly muted.

Wilson, however, was unperturbed. The day after Christmas—the Boxing Day holiday in Great Britain and its empire—he and the first lady left for a visit to England.

Across the English Channel, Wilson's welcome was as tumultuous as it had been in France. The lord mayor of Dover greeted him in wig and robe; guns in the Tower of London announced his arrival in the metropolis. The Grenadier band and a detachment of Scots Guards were present in Waterloo Station and so was King George V, bearded and trim in a khaki field marshal's uniform. Following a red carpet laid along the platform, the Wilsons mounted red-and-gold carriages that carried them over the Waterloo Bridge, through Trafalgar Square in front of the National Gallery, and down the Mall. As in Paris, crowds lined every inch of the route; the London newspapers estimated the presence of two million persons. The nearby churches rang their bells, and flags with the emblems of the British Empire decorated the lampposts. At Buckingham Palace the Royal Horse Guards band struck up the American national anthem. Once inside, the American president and first lady joined the English king and queen on a balcony. Below they could see nothing but people from Green Park to Piccadilly on the left, St. James's Park to the Foreign Office and the Treasury on the right, and back along the Mall to the Admiralty straight ahead. Hundreds of thousands of voices were chanting in unison: "WE WANT WILSON!"

That night, the Britannic majesties hosted their first state dinner since the beginning of the war. On the long polished table under the chandeliers, everything—knives, forks, spoons, dishes, and the candelabra—was gold. The dinner took place in the ballroom, where Beefeaters from the Tower of London stood motionless in their red uniforms, their backs stationed at even intervals along the ivory-colored walls. Liveried servants exchanged the plates and served the courses in silent formality. Everything was exquisite, intended to impress the president of the United States.

Wilson nevertheless made clear that he was pursuing his own, American, purpose. The British should have been forewarned. During the war, the president had consistently referred to the "Allies," meaning the British, the French, the Italians, and the Russians (until Lenin pulled out of it all), and the "Associates," primarily a United States that would fight, but do so for its own reasons. Even before going from Paris to London, then, Wilson had stated to a colleague of Clemenceau: "If England insists on maintaining naval dominance after the war, the United States can and will show her how to build a navy!" At Buckingham Palace, finally, during a gala reception before the banquet, Wilson told a British official (who, of course, passed the remark along) curtly: "You must not speak of us who come over here as cousins, still less as brothers; we are neither." Although the two countries shared a common language, Wilson went on, the United States was far more diverse ethnically than the so-called mother country. "No," he concluded, "there are only two things which can establish and maintain closer relations between your country and mine: they are community of ideals and interests."

Wilson may have been alluding to the dictum expressed in the middle of the nineteenth century by Lord Palmerston, then Great Britain's foreign secretary: "Great powers have no permanent friends and no permanent enemies. They only have permanent interests." If the British wished a special relationship with the United States, Wilson implied, then they would subordinate their interests to those of the United States.

During the dinner at Buckingham Palace, Wilson took the British aback even farther. After the king read out a toast, Wilson replied, without notes, addressing his host not as "Your Majesty" but simply as "sir." "There was no glow of friendship," Lloyd George noted, "or of gladness at meeting men who had been partners in a common enterprise and had so narrowly escaped a common danger."

After an excursion to Carlisle, a town near the Scottish border, where Wilson's maternal grandfather had been a minister, the presidential couple headed off for a brief tour of Italy. Then they returned to Paris for the beginning of the peace conference. There, on January 12, 1919, the delegations of twenty-seven Allied and Associated countries started their deliberations.

3

Paris still had the look of a city at war: the streets were littered where toward the end of the conflict German bombs had fallen. Most of the once-famed chestnut trees were merely stumps, cut down for firewood. Coal, flour, and milk were in short supply. Men without legs begged on street corners; about half of the women wore the black of mourning.

Into this gloomy scene came delegations from countries as far away as China and Japan and as close by as the fragments of the war-shattered and defunct Austro-Hungarian Empire. Australians, New Zealanders, Canadians, and South Africans also were present. The British themselves stayed at the Hôtel Majestic, an establishment near the Arc de Triomphe. John Maynard Keynes described the atmosphere among the Britons there as one of "feverish, persistent, and boring gossip [which] developed in full measure the peculiar flavour of smallness, cynicism, and self-importance." The members of the British delegation may have realized that their heyday was passing and that the dominant delegation in Paris was the American.

The Americans certainly were housed in the greatest splendor of all: the magnificence of the Hôtel Crillon. On the western side of what became the Place de la Concorde, King Louis XV had commanded his architects to construct pavilions and balustrades, and two splendid buildings on the northern side of the square. The eastern one became the Crown Storehouse; the other, on the rue Royale, in time became the Hôtel Crillon. The hotel had a venerable history: on February 6, 1778, it had been the site of the signing of the Treaty of Friendship between France and the thirteen American states; most prominent among the American signatories had been Benjamin Franklin. Now, more than a century later, a new American delegation could enjoy views of the Seine River to the south; the Champs Élysées to the west; and, across the square, the Louvre and the gardens of the Tuileries. The rooms were elegant, with high ceilings, wide fireplaces, and white-paneled walls. Despite the food shortages in France, the breakfasts, Charles Seymour wrote, "turned out to be about the best in our experience—bread very nearly white and with the finest crust, the most perfectly fried sole I ever tasted, plenty of delicious butter and all the sugar one wanted." Not by accident, the French had put the American delegation up in the most prestigious hotel in Paris.

Keeping apart from their fellow Americans, the Wilsons stayed at the Palais Murat near the Parc Monceau, about half a mile north of the Champs Élysées. Dating back to the eighteenth century, the palace was three stories high and eleven windows wide, surrounded by trees and set back from the street. Its rooms, James T. Shotwell, librarian to the American delegation, wrote, "have costly paintings and the ceiling is filled with original frescoes, but the most distinctive note of decoration is that afforded by the electroliers which give an indirect lighting through a mass of crystal and twisted bronze. These lights are multiplied by huge wall mirrors, so that one can hardly tell how many rooms are real and how many are only reflections."

Wilson and Clemenceau met for the first time in the Palais Murat, sitting together in a small library on the second floor. Clemenceau let Wilson do most of the talking, for he wanted to find out what the American president really wanted. The answer was almost unbelievable: neither territory nor colonies nor even reparations for the American lives lost in the war. Wilson, quite simply, wanted the League of Nations.

Later Clemenceau described Wilson as a man of noble *candeur*. The French word *candeur* has a double meaning: frankness and naïveté.

On the morning of January 18, 1919, a small ceremony took place by the Seine along the Quai d'Orsay. While a company of soldiers stood at attention, a brass band announced the arrival of a huge automobile from which Woodrow Wilson emerged. While cameramen photographed the moment, he tipped his top hat and entered the Ministry of Foreign Affairs. The first plenary session of the Paris peace conference was about to get under way.

Protected by a tall iron fence, the edifice had a formal, riverside entryway that opened into a foyer and a grand staircase. Past the stairs, a corridor led to reception rooms and diplomatic offices, all with tall windows, high ceilings, and sparkling chandeliers. Heavy tables and chairs with gilded legs stood on oriental carpets; most of the rooms seemed to be colored red, gold, and ebony. The inner sanctum, the office of the foreign minister, revealed dark wood paneling covered with faded, ancient tapestries. Double doors led out to a walled rose garden.

When Wilson entered the room, Clemenceau and Lloyd George, along with Baron Sidney Sonnino, the Italian foreign minister, were already present. As host, Clemenceau presided from a massive armchair placed alongside the hearth, its logs aflame to ward off the January cold. The others took their seats in armchairs beside which were little tables for their papers; aides and advisers perched behind them on tiny gilt chairs. As the only head of state, Wilson was ushered to a chair with the highest back in the room. Without secretaries, he sat alone. Then the peace talks began.

Since Clemenceau's English was fluent, if heavily accented, and Sonnino's command of the language was passable, the discussions took place in English. For centuries of European history, most diplomatic discourse had taken place in French. The switch to English was the Big Four's acknowledgment of the Anglo-American dominance in international relations.

The first issue confronting the statesmen as they talked in the Quai d'Orsay was the disposition of Germany's former colonies. In a treaty signed in London in 1915, an understanding supposedly secret but well known in Washington, the Allies had agreed to divide those spoils among themselves. Now, however, Wilson would have none of it. Like most of his fellow Americans, he abhorred the idea of renewed colonialism, and he had espoused the principle of national self-determination throughout all the colonized areas of the world. But what was he to do? America could hardly attack the Allies. So he discovered quickly that he had to compromise: the victors would take over Germany's colonies, especially in Africa, under the guise of League of Nations "mandates."

Having already written the Covenant of the League of Nations, Wilson begrudgingly accepted the arrangement. Then, on February 14, 1919, he left Paris for a month back in Washington.

On Capitol Hill, Wilson's enemies were waiting to do combat. In the election of 1918, the Republicans had gained control of both houses of Congress, putting Henry Cabot Lodge of Massachusetts in charge of the Foreign Relations Committee. A close friend of Theodore Roosevelt and like Roosevelt an American aristocrat, Lodge was a slender, neatly bearded man so snobbish that at concerts, it was said, he applauded only with the tips of his gloved fingers. Lodge regarded Woodrow Wilson as southern riffraff and, a scholar himself, sneered at the president's academic achievements. His suspicion, dislike, and even hatred of Wilson were bottomless; he resented Wilson's not having taken him to Paris. Most important, he was convinced that Wilson had succumbed to "vaulting ambition," having been the president of Princeton, being now the president of the United States, and aspiring next to being the president of the world.

Led by Lodge, ranking members of the Senate, which under the Constitution of the United States had the authority to grant or withhold its consent to treaties, confronted Wilson personally in the White House. They could support a peace treaty, they informed the president, but not the League covenant as it stood. In its Article Ten, it pledged the United States to abide by the will of the majority of the League members. That would not do, they said: they would not tolerate having America committed to go to the aid of British and French imperialism.

Wilson shot back, stating that he would bind the peace treaty and the covenant so tightly together that the Senate would have to take or leave both. Wilson believed that he had won a political victory.

Then, however, on March 4, 1919, Lodge dropped his bombshell. He had circulated, he announced, a round-robin that declared the League of Nations, "as now proposed," to be unacceptable. Thirty-nine senators, well more than the two-thirds required to reject a treaty, had signed the document.

Believing that he could still bring the Senate around, Wilson returned to France. What he needed was international support for the League. Then, treaty in hand, he would come back to the United States and, taking his case to the American people, savor his culminating triumph.

He landed at Brest again on March 13. This time he ran into a new challenge, the naked demands of the victors for their spoils.

In Paris, too, Wilson's opponents were poised, like cats in an ambush. Clemenceau struck first, demanding that Germany be held guilty for all the war's destruction, that Germany be forced to pay billions in reparations, and that the iron and coal region of southwestern Germany be placed under French control. Both Wilson and Lloyd George were horrified: they had no wish to see Germany beaten back into the Middle Ages. With Lloyd George following Wilson's lead, however, they gave "the Tiger" much of what he wanted: a fifteen-year French occupation of the Rhineland and an international commission that would require unspecified but huge reparations from Germany.

Then Vittorio Orlando, the Italian prime minister, emerged from his lair. Italy, he informed the others, wanted Fiume, a northern Adriatic port where the population was partly Italian and partly Slavic. Despite protests from the southern Slav delegations, Wilson gave way.

Finally, the Japanese showed their claws. Early in World War I, Tokyo had declared war on Germany, seizing the Shandong Peninsula, a German colony on the northern coast of China. Japan wanted to retain its power there, and Wilson caved in.

Wilson yielded in the face of all these demands because France, Italy, and Japan alike had threatened, implicitly or explicitly, otherwise to refuse to join the League. But in subordinating his principle of self-determination to the League, Wilson lost the support of many Americans and earned the contempt of many Europeans.

Yet he did win agreement on the League, and the signing of the treaty took place in the Hall of Mirrors at Versailles on June 28, 1919, five years to the day after the Sarajevo murders. Wilson then sailed home once more.

4

On July 10, 1919, President Wilson went before the Senate formally to present his treaty and the covenant. When he entered the chamber, two of the senators refused to stand.

Looking down from the gallery, Henry L. Stoddard, a journalist, was dismayed. Although pallid and worn, Wilson seemed suffused with arrogance. He struck Stoddard as the "coldest man I ever saw." Wilson's tone implied that he had remade the world and it was the Senate's duty simply to approve his work. The Senate, as Alice Roosevelt Longworth, also watching from the balcony, put it, was to be "merely a pawn in Mr. Wilson's campaign for the presidency of the Federation of the World." Her father's daughter always, she wished a plague on Woodrow Wilson.

Such was also the general opinion down on the floor of the Senate. There two factions banded together to deny Wilson his treaty. The first, made up of progressive Republicans such as William Borah of Idaho and Hiram Johnson of California, feared that by joining the League of Nations the United States would be drawn into the defense of colonialism. Headed by Lodge, the second group, the so-called reservationists, condemned Wilson for having abandoned his advocacy of national self-determination. In fact, when the Committee on Foreign Relations sat down to look at Wilson's work, Lodge scratched out "Japan," wherever the president had inserted it, and penned in "China," thereby asserting China's right to its own territory.

Furious at having to face such treatment, Wilson got out of Washington. Accompanied by Dr. Cary T. Grayson, the White House physician, and the ever faithful Joe Tumulty, President and Mrs. Wilson left Union Station on the evening of September 3, 1919. Wilson intended to speak in the Midwest and in almost every state west of the Mississippi.

At first the trip went well. On Broad Street in Columbus, Ohio, hundreds of schoolchildren, dismissed from their classes, broke away from their teachers and rushed to the presidential limousine; airplanes from the landing field at Ohio State University dropped roses on the parade. Speaking without notes to a crowd, Wilson said, "This is what the League of Nations is for: it is to prove to the nations of the world that the nations will combine against any nation that would emulate Germany's example." At Richmond, Indiana, Wilson spoke from the rear platform of his train and asked, "Shall we or shall we not sustain the first great act of international justice?" Under the hot September sun, Wilson declared in St. Louis that "if we keep out of this arrangement war will come soon. If we go into it war will never come." "I have come to fight for a cause," he said in Kansas City, "and that cause is greater than the U.S. Senate!"

Wilson's voice was growing hoarse. Then came Des Moines and Omaha, and he developed a headache, located in the rear of his skull. Sioux Falls, St. Paul, Bismarck. The message was the same, and the headache continued. Then on westward to Helena; Coeur d'Alene, Senator Borah's hometown; and on to Spokane. Wilson was having trouble breathing. Seattle, Portland, and San Francisco. Wilson could not sleep, and the headache was moving to the front of his head. Los Angeles. The Mormon Tabernacle at Salt Lake City. Cheyenne and Denver. At Pueblo, Colorado, Wilson did something he had never done before: he stumbled over a sentence. His words were becoming slurred.

Just beyond Pueblo, Dr. Grayson suggested a walk in the fresh air of the evening. After the train had stopped, he, the president, and the first lady stepped down for a stroll in the countryside. After they had returned to their cabins, the train resumed its progress toward Wichita.

Woodrow Wilson did not give his speech in Wichita. On the evening of September 26, 1919, aboard the presidential train, he suffered a paralytic stroke. He never functioned properly again. And the Senate of the United States, as a coup de grâce, rejected American membership in the League of Nations.

5

But while Woodrow Wilson for the rest of his term in office lay personally defeated, shrouded in the darkness of his White House bedroom, Wilsonianism—the idea that America should and could remake the world in its own image—lived on.

Consider Wilson's opponents. Borah, Johnson, and Lodge did not dispute the proposition that the United States had a large role to play in the world; what they rejected was the thought that America should be beholden to discredited European imperialists. And that, in the Fourteen Points, had been Wilson's theme exactly.

America's duty and opportunity was to free the world not only from European aggression but also from European imperialism.

In Wilson's vision, the League of Nations was to be the means of containing the evils of the world. Wilson had called for "the establishment of an organization of peace which shall make it certain that the combined power of free nations will check every invasion. . . . There must now be, not a balance of power, not one powerful group of nations set off against another, but a single overwhelming, powerful group of nations who shall be the trustee of the peace of the world."

What "group of nations" did Wilson have in mind? Russia had dropped out of the war, and Japan had entered the war for reasons that were purely opportunistic. Italy's contribution to the fighting had been minimal. France and Great Britain were exhausted, bankrupt. Allied membership in the League would be useful. But the only country that could provide "overwhelming" power was the United States of America.

Toward the end of World War II, American military and diplomatic planners explicitly developed the doctrine of preponderant power: the descending *Pax Britannica* would be replaced by the ascending *Pax Americana*. The idea, however, was not new. It originated with Woodrow Wilson. His failure, if failure it was, lay in the fact that he was ahead of his time. He stands out as the prophet of the American empire. Ironically, his very enemies on the American political scene began to turn his prophecy into reality.

Part II
The Interwar Years

CHAPTER 6

The Washington Conference

1

At precisely eleven o'clock on the morning of March 4, 1921, Woodrow Wilson for the last time reached the Capitol of the United States. Helped from the official limousine, he got out at the freight entrance; then, refusing to use a wheelchair, he braced himself on the arm of an attendant and walked slowly to the elevator. Riding up to the President's Room, he signed a few remaining bills, carrying out the last rituals of office. Just as he finished, Senator Lodge entered the chamber. Wilson glared at him, then departed.

Too frail to attend the inaugural ceremony, he made his way, unobserved and alone, to a side door of the Capitol. From there he could hear the cheers, but they were no longer for him. Another automobile took him back down Pennsylvania Avenue, passing in front of the White House, and turned off Massachusetts Avenue into S Street, stopping at 2340, his new brick-and-limestone residence set back by a shallow driveway from the deserted street. Helped by his wife, the former president ascended the stone steps and disappeared through the front door.

"Today," a Democratic senator wrote in his diary, Wilson is "bereft of popularity." Indeed, as he retreated into his private home, Woodrow Wilson entered into what seemed the certainty of oblivion and the disgrace of defeat. His body was broken and his hopes for the League of Nations lay shattered. Just as bad, the Democratic Party, the vehicle by which his dream might have been reborn, had been crushed by his Republican opponents in the presidential election of 1920.

Without question, 1920 was a Republican year. The popular reaction against Wilson had been profound, for, "at the bottom," as Charles Hand, an official in the Ohio Republican Party put it, "the people desire a return to common sense. They are tired of viewing rainbows and soap bubbles."

The Democrats in the meantime chose a remarkably ineffective presidential candidate. When they convened in San Francisco in the summer of 1920 for their nominating convention, the leading contender was William Gibbs McAdoo, secretary of the treasury and a son-in-law of Woodrow Wilson. Originally a lawyer from Tennessee, McAdoo had gone to New York, organized the construction of the Lincoln Tunnel, then emerged as a major Wilson backer at the 1912 convention in Baltimore. Tall, hawk-nosed, and commanding of manner, he had been a captain of industry and a master of politics. He had overseen the financing of America's participation in World War I, and he was a progressive who could appeal across the South and the West. In that era of Prohibition, however, he also was a dry, which left him unpopular with the machine bosses in the Northeast and the Midwest.

Hoping to take advantage of McAdoo's vulnerability was the attorney general, A. Mitchell Palmer. Originally a Pennsylvania Quaker, then a senator from that state, and finally another backer of Wilson in 1912, Palmer had gained fame, or infamy, as the propagator of the 1919 "Red Scare." His Washington house had been bombed, true, but his subsequent crackdown (carried out by the young J. Edgar Hoover) had led to the arrests of hundreds of thousands of socialists, anarchists, and even ordinary immigrants, most of whom were innocent of any crime. Palmer's detainees were overwhelmingly of central and eastern European background, which made him popular in white Protestant circles. By the same token, he had little support in the big cities.

When the San Francisco convention deadlocked between McAdoo and Palmer, the Democrats turned to the governor of Ohio, James M. Cox. The owner of several newspapers, Cox was a small man with a pinched, bespectacled face. He seemed cocky: even his friends thought his manner Napoleonic. Unknown to the public at the time of his nomination, he ran a disastrous campaign. The only bright spot on the Democratic ticket in 1920 was the vice presidential nominee, Franklin D. Roosevelt.

Roosevelt had thrust himself ahead with immense skill. He had been unable, to be sure, to translate his assistant secretaryship of the navy into military heroism, as Theodore Roosevelt had done in Cuba in 1898. Like TR (who had died in 1919), however, he had used his position in Washington to his political advantage, letting out contracts to naval yards from Puget Sound to the Boston harbor and thus acquiring supporters far from his native New York. Known in New York itself as an opponent of corruption in government, he also had refused to fight the bosses on liquor; he had even signaled quietly his opposition to Prohibition. As a New Yorker he had given the Ohioan Cox a chance to balance the ticket.

"I don't like Roosevelt," Charles F. Murphy, head of Tammany Hall, had said to Edmund H. Moore, Cox's campaign manager, who had sought out his opinion about Roosevelt as a vice presidential candidate. "He is not well known in the country, but, Ed, this is the first time a Democratic nominee for the presidency has shown me courtesy. That's why I would vote for the devil himself if Cox wanted me to. Tell him we will nominate Roosevelt on the first ballot as soon as we assemble." Murphy was true to his word.

Once nominated, Roosevelt met with Cox and discussed the campaign's strategy. Hovering around, many Democratic politicos urged them to forsake Woodrow Wilson and everything about the League of Nations. At Roosevelt's urging, Cox went just the other way. Traveling to the White House, they paid homage to Woodrow Wilson. Out on the South Portico, Wilson sat gray and gaunt, a shawl covering his paralyzed left arm. "Mr. President," Cox declared, "we are going to be a million percent with you and your administration, and that means the League of Nations."

Wilson stirred in his chair, managing to say, "I am very grateful." The Democratic nominees left Washington, presenting themselves to the nation as Wilson's successors.

Once out on the hustings, starting at Chicago on August 10, Roosevelt stole the show. Traveling in a private railroad car, the Westboro, which was attached to a series of regular passenger trains, he set out on a wide swing out into the Northwest, back into New York and New England, out again as far as Colorado, and finally back home to Hyde Park for the end of the campaign. All in all, he gave at least a thousand speeches.

He did not campaign alone, for Louis Howe, the wizened, ash-strewn former Albany reporter who had been at Roosevelt's side through all the years in Washington, dispensing political advice, settled in aboard the Westboro. Also present was Marvin McIntyre, a reporter from Kentucky who had handled Roosevelt's public relations at the Navy Department and whose task on the campaign trail was to keep local reporters wined and dined. And traveling ahead of Roosevelt, functioning as an advance man, was Stephen Early, still another reporter who had covered the Navy Department before the war and then edited the army newspaper *Stars and Stripes*.

Early's job was to wire back to McIntyre and thus to Roosevelt observations on the lay of the political land: what journalists and politicians should be flattered, what town traditions the candidate should mention, what issues he must avoid. One such telegram was typical: "Washington state is DRY. Interest centers on reclamation of lands and destruction of Non-Partisan League [a farmers' organization with socialist overtones, crushed by the federal government during the war]. The Boss will be asked to express himself on Non-Partisan League and their kind of radicals. This section of country vitally interested. . . . Advise strongly that you do not hit the NPL directly. Lumber is the big industry. Wheat is the big crop. Agricultural development is the aim of all."

But not the League of Nations. Just about everywhere, Early informed the candidate, attitudes toward Wilson's League of Nations ranged between apathy and hostility. "New Hampshire is hopeless," one wire from Early stated; "the Irish are rampant." In Minneapolis, the citizenry was thinking of its "breadbaskets and not of war allies. . . . The bitterness toward Wilson evident everywhere."

Roosevelt nonetheless stuck to his promise to Wilson, praising the League and doing so always with his suave manner and electrifying smile. Roosevelt "gets the last ounce of appeal-power out of each sentence," a reporter wrote. "The physical impression leaves nothing to be asked—the figure of an idealized college football player, almost the poster type in public life . . . making clean, direct, and few gestures; always with a smile ready to share. . . . He speaks in a strong clear voice, with a tenor note in which it rings—sings, one is tempted to say—in key with . . . [an] intangible, utterly charming and surely vote-winning quality."

Roosevelt's name also cast its spell. Shaking hands with him, people would say things like, "I voted for your father," meaning Theodore Roosevelt. Franklin did little to correct the misimpression.

Yet he sustained, as he put it, "nary an illusion." When the election was over, the Democrats were the minority party, by wide margins, in both houses of Congress, and they lost the White House in one of the most sweeping landslides in American presidential history.

The results left Woodrow Wilson even more disheartened than before. "We had a chance to gain the leadership of the world," he said. "We have lost it, and soon we shall be witnessing the tragedy of it all." The last thing Wilson could imagine was that his successor, Warren Gamaliel Harding, would follow in the very path he himself had laid out.

2

"He's not a bad man," Alice Roosevelt Longworth was supposed to have said of Harding. "He's just a slob."

Warren G. Harding's rise to the presidency and the denigration to which he was thereafter subjected had a common source: he seemed an anachronism. In a nation so long dominated by progressives he was a conservative, and in a White House so long occupied by men from the cities—Roosevelt from New York; Taft from Cincinnati; and Wilson from Princeton, close to Manhattan and Philadelphia—Harding had been a country boy, a newspaperman from the small town of Marion, Ohio. In a nation of great cities with vast immigrant populations, Harding was a hick.

Yet Harding won the presidential election of 1920 by 277 electoral votes and more than 7 million popular votes. He did so in part because he was not Wilson and in part because he represented something that great numbers of voters took to their hearts: Americanness.

As far back as the 1830s, Alexis de Tocqueville, the young French aristocrat whose nine-month journey through the United States culminated in that incomparable work *Democracy in America*, commented that Americans saw themselves as a new people. Wherever he traveled—Newport, Albany, Philadelphia, Baltimore, and beyond—Americans told him that they had rejected the evil, corrupt, and tyrannical ways of the Old World and were starting a New World free from the clutches of a hereditary nobility. Americans—white Americans, at least—were not enslaved as peasants. They considered themselves a people of the middle class, free, prosperous, and democratic.

Tocqueville also noted the powerful current of religion that everywhere ran through American culture. In his journal he recounted a visit to Boston's Faneuil Hall and hearing the Reverend Lyman Beecher, father of Harriet Beecher Stowe, ask the members of his congregation to bestow upon the Polish people, then in rebellion against their Russian oppressors, the gift of two American flags.

Although Tocqueville did not use the word, all this was Americanness: the desire of a free, democratic people to inspire the rest of the world to be like them. As surely as did Woodrow Wilson, Warren Harding embodied that American tradition.

Such was how Harding, born in Ohio right after the Civil War, described his childhood years. He wrote in his campaign autobiography,

> I grew up in a village of six hundred [Caledonia, Ohio], and I know something of the democracy, of the simplicity, of the confidence in—aye, better yet, of the reverence for government and the fidelity to law and its enforcement, as it exists in the small community. I do not believe that anywhere in the world there is so perfect a democracy as in the village.... About everybody starts equal. And in the village where I was born the blacksmith's son and the cobbler's son and the minister's son and the storekeeper's son all had just the same chance in the opportunities of this America of ours.

Harding exaggerated somewhat. When he was seventeen his father, a homeopathic doctor, searching for more patients, moved the family about seven miles southwest to Marion, the seat of Marion County. About forty miles north of Columbus and lying in the flatlands of north-central Ohio, Marion at the time had a population of about four thousand, so it was a bit more than a village. For young Harding, nonetheless, it was indeed a place of opportunity. At age nineteen he went to work on the *Marion Star*. Even with little capital he made the nearly lifeless newspaper thrive. Two years later, he bought it outright, and the *Star* became the basis of his eventual wealth.

Since Harding made the paper a voice for the Republican Party in a predominantly Republican state, the *Star* also became the basis of his rise in politics. A handsome man with dark eyes and black hair, and the backslapping ways of the small-town booster so derided in the novels of Sinclair Lewis, Harding was a natural joiner. The local Kiwanis, Elks, Rotary, Masons, and Shriners, the fraternities of businessmen across the heartland of America, all listed Harding on their membership lists. The *Literary Digest*, a New York journal, eventually would write of Harding: "Like the town, he is kindly of manner, good to look at—and conservative. There are no jangling notes of liberalism in the Harding philosophy, nor any traffic cops in Marion. Seeing Marion . . . one can understand a little better [his] standpatism. . . . Harding is Marion."

Marion was the door to Harding's entry into politics: a Republican delegate from Marion to the state convention; local party orator; county auditor; election to the Ohio Senate, the local party's reward for faithful service; and two terms in that body. There Harding "took orders," an Ohio Democrat noted, "and desired to be known as a man who carried them out without question. He had things to protect; he wanted to rise; he hoped with the turn of the wheel to find himself . . . at Washington."

Friendly to all, Harding did favors and worked out deals. "There may be abler men in the [Ohio] Senate than Harding," the governor told a reporter, "but when I want things done I go to him." Harding delivered the goods for the Ohio Republican machine.

His reward was the Republican gubernatorial nomination in 1910. That year was a Democratic one, and Harding lost narrowly to James M. Cox, the eventual Democratic nominee for the presidency. In 1912, however, Harding, always the party regular, supported William Howard Taft over Theodore Roosevelt; in the 1914 race for the U.S. Senate, Taft in turn gave his endorsement to Harding. That year, the first in which Americans voted directly for their senators, Harding won. Six years later, he secured the Republican nomination for the presidency.

Why Harding? His six years in the U.S. Senate were undistinguished: he spoke rarely; he introduced no legislation of national importance; and two times out of five he failed to show up for roll-call votes. When the Republicans met in the summer of 1920 to choose their presidential nominee, he was at best a dark horse.

Yet one by one, Harding's rivals for the nomination fell out of the race. The front-runner was General Leonard Wood, the one-time actual commander of Theodore Roosevelt's Rough Riders; the Old Guard Republicans feared him as another TR. Next in line was Herbert Hoover, a man of proven ability but autocratic and inarticulate; Republican bosses thought he would offend the electorate. Senator Hiram Johnson of California was popular in the western states but too progressive for the power brokers. Governor Frank O. Lowden of Illinois was popular with the Old Guard but had done poorly in the primaries.

With the prospects of other candidates fading, Harding believed that he could count on the friends he had cultivated in every state delegation. For although he had presented himself as a reluctant candidate, he had followed a simple rule: be a pal to all. As he later explained, "Other fellows, just as competent as I, or more so, had made enemies, and it looked to me that there was no one in sight that the convention could unite on except myself." Warren Harding became the Republican candidate for president because he had become the available man.

He was also the underestimated man, shrewd enough to turn his limits into strengths. Being in no way as articulate as Wilson, Harding clouded every issue with words so vague that no one could tell where he stood on issues, left or right, north or south, up or down. Even H. L. Mencken, the Baltimore editor famed for his attacks on the American "booboisie," had to admit that what he sneered at as "Gamalielese" was "so bad that a certain grandeur creeps into it."

Presenting himself as just an ordinary American, Harding popularized the term *normalcy*. America had to return to hearth, home, and country—normalcy.

Making the most of his background, he ran almost exclusively (following the example of William McKinley in 1896 and 1900) from his front porch. By doing so, as Mark Sullivan, a particularly perceptive reporter, noticed, he appeared to stand for "an orderly world, a neat world, a world of carefully graveled paths, and nicely clipped hedges—above all, a world that stays the same from day to day . . . a world that stays put. Harding winces at all the mess the war has made in the world, and he wants to get it all cleaned up and get back to 'normalcy.'"

Close beside his home in Marion, Harding constructed a three-room bungalow exclusively for the convenience of reporters: he was deft at using the press to convey the image he wanted to the American people. Once or twice each day he would stroll in, greet the correspondents by name, swap stories, pitch horseshoes out in the yard, and answer questions. Knowing how newspapers operated, he routinely handed out beforehand copies of speeches he made from his porch, making sure that the reporters could meet their editors' deadlines. Since he went out of his way to make their jobs easier, the journalists went out of their own way to present Harding as the sure and certain winner. Harding's good relations with the press were not equaled until the presidential campaign of Franklin D. Roosevelt.

From his sickbed in the White House and through the medium of his wife, Woodrow Wilson had stated that the 1920 election would be a "solemn referendum" on the League of Nations. This was not to be so. The election was a contest of personalities. Seeing Cox as a stand-in for the unpopular Wilson, the American electorate voted heavily for the popular Harding.

Yet the election had little effect on America's foreign policy, a policy so clearly defined by Woodrow Wilson. Wilson and Harding both abhorred the chaos of the world beyond the water's edge. Both believed in America's superiority to the nations of Europe and in the New World's responsibility to redeem the sins of the Old World. And both reflected the culture of the American democracy, that desire portrayed by Tocqueville to remake the world in the American image. So it is not surprising that once in the White House, President Warren G. Harding perpetuated the ideas of Woodrow Wilson.

3

But was not the Republican era of the 1920s a time of isolationism, an era of American withdrawal from world leadership? The answer is a resounding "No!" Rather than following a policy of isolationism, the Harding, Coolidge, and Hoover administrations pursued what at least one historian has termed an "American structure of world order": keeping American hands as free as possible to build a world order in which Americans could prosper, a world no longer run by Great Britain.

Harding himself never articulated such a vision, but for his cabinet he chose three prominent figures who did so. Some of Harding's cabinet choices were undistinguished at best and disastrous at worst. Nonetheless, his three sterling appointments were Andrew W. Mellon as secretary of the treasury, Herbert Hoover as secretary of commerce, and Charles Evans Hughes as secretary of state. Together the trio translated the American search for order at home into one for order abroad, an international system reconstructed by the United States of America.

To Harding, a worshiper of big business, Andrew Mellon was the "ubiquitous financier of the universe." At the time of his government appointment, he was sixty-six years old but looked as if he were going on eighty-six. Of medium height and quite slim, he wore the homburg hats, chesterfield coats, and three-piece pinstriped suits that gave him an air of dignity and taste. But over his white mustache, his long, bony face and sunken cheeks made him look haggard, even ill. His also had what Lucius Beebe, a prominent writer who knew the Mellons, called a "measureless shyness."

Mellon's frailty and diffidence, however, masked a mind of piercing intensity. By the time he went to Washington, he had transformed the family's Pittsburgh banking business into a network of commercial alliances—including, among others, Alcoa, Gulf Oil, and the enterprises of Henry Clay Frick—that, indeed, reached around the globe. Some calculated that he was the second-richest man in the world. Certainly he practically owned Pittsburgh and, almost single-handedly, he kept the Republican Party financially afloat. His move to Washington delighted his fellow financiers; they knew that he would work to cut taxes on the rich.

He sought to benefit the rich in yet another way. Working behind a massive, orderly desk in the Treasury Department, Mellon gave his full support to the Webb-Pomerene Act. That measure, passed under the leadership of Woodrow Wilson, had removed antitrust restrictions from American corporations engaged in export.

The idea of the law had been to free American business to compete as freely and as massively as possible in the markets of the British Empire. Secretary Mellon's responsibility was to make certain that the Wilson-era law remained in full force in the time of Warren G. Harding.

To head the Commerce Department, Harding, who despite his own intellectual deficiencies was unafraid to select the "best minds," went for Herbert Hoover. The Hoover appointment also was shrewd politics: born in 1874 in West Branch, Iowa, and later a resident of California, Hoover gave western populists and progressives representation in the Harding cabinet. And Hoover was one of the brightest stars in the American firmament.

Enrolling at Stanford, a new university in Palo Alto, California, the almost morbidly shy and virtually tongue-tied Hoover had proven himself a brilliant student of geological engineering. After graduation and marriage he had made a fortune as a director of mining in the American Southwest, China (he and his wife, Lou Henry, had helped organize the foreigners' defense during the Boxer Rebellion of 1900), Latin America, and Russia. Later he had turned to philanthropy; he also had organized famine relief in wartime Europe and in the Soviet Union. A staunch Republican, Hoover had worked for the election of Warren G. Harding.

Once installed at the Commerce Department, Hoover displayed an engineer's understanding of what he wanted to achieve: he wanted to erect an international system designed to resemble America. Insisting that he be included in the shaping of American foreign policy, Hoover believed that as it had built the United States, so could "American individualism" provide the girders for the rest of the world. "I insisted that spiritual and intellectual freedom could not continue to exist without economic freedom," Hoover wrote in his memoirs. "If one died, all would die."

He went farther. "I am thus making a plea for individualism in international economic life," Hoover testified before Congress in 1921, "just as strongly as I would make a plea for individualism in the life of our own people. . . . This system [of individualism] cannot be preserved in domestic life if it must be abandoned in international life." Then Hoover became specific: "Special privileges," he declared, referring to the British and French colonial empires in Asia and the Middle East, were "not to be allowed."

As far as Hoover was concerned, what was good for America was good for the world. Secretary of State Charles Evans Hughes wholeheartedly agreed.

Everything about Charles Evans Hughes—from his Baptist upbringing in New York State, to his years as a crusading progressive attorney in Manhattan, to his two terms as governor of New York, his appointment to the U.S. Supreme Court, his nomination by the Republicans to run against Woodrow Wilson in 1916, and his erect posture and Jove-like beard—bespoke uprightness and integrity. His also was the reputation of having one of the best legal minds in the nation. So it was scarcely surprising that Harding, conscious of his own meager knowledge of world affairs, asked Hughes to serve as secretary of state. Hughes accepted the post without hesitation: he was part of the long chain of prominent lawyers from New York, with that city's internationalist outlook, who became America's top diplomats.

The Hughes appointment elicited widespread approval. "If the nation believed that all the cabinet appointments were to be of a similar caliber," the *New York Times* asserted, "it would thank God and take courage." The *Baltimore Sun* concurred: "Mr. Hughes' name is luminous throughout the country." And the *New York Evening Mail* opined that no "man has set higher standards of public service."

Lost in the acclaim was a special aspect of Hughes's public life. He had come out in favor of the League of Nations.

On the day of the Harding inaugural, Hughes took possession of the office of the secretary of state, a large, rectangular room in the big, shambling State, War, and Navy Building (now the Executive Office Building) just west of the White House. Tall windows afforded a view of the Washington Monument; oil portraits of earlier American statesmen looked down from the walls; and over the stone-faced fireplace hung a gilt mirror crowned by the U.S. coat of arms. From this office, Secretary of State Charles Evans Hughes set out to realize his vision of what America should do in the world.

He left no doubt as to the nature of that vision. The United States, he believed, was to seek to "establish a *Pax Americana* maintained not by arms but by mutual respect and good-will and the tranquilizing processes of reason." The important phrase in this statement was *"Pax Americana"*; Hughes intended it as a replacement of the older *"Pax Britannica."* And to bring that substitution into being, Hughes in late 1921 summoned eight other nations to send representatives to a conference in Washington, where they were to submit to American dictates.

The meeting was titled the Conference on the Limitation of Armament or, simply, the Washington Conference. Presiding over it with his full white beard and penetrating blue eyes was the dignified and ruthlessly intelligent presence of Secretary of State Hughes. But the spirit of the conference was that of the broken man who lived in the big red-brick house on S Street in Washington, Woodrow Wilson.

4

The eleventh hour of the eleventh day of the eleventh month—11:00 AM, November 11, 1921, the first Armistice Day—found the American nation wrapped in an almost religious fervor, a passion for peace. Standing before the flag-draped Tomb of the Unknown Soldier in Arlington National Cemetery, President Harding called for universal disarmament and, alluding to the war just over, asserted solemnly and repeated for emphasis: "It must not be again." He closed his speech with a recitation of the Lord's Prayer.

Catching the mood of the moment, Senator Frank B. Kellogg of Minnesota said later,

> I thought as I looked out over that vast crowd of fifty thousand people that there were others there in spirit, even though we could not see them. I thought that I saw standing there in the

mists the figures of a hundred thousand boys who gave up their lives over yonder that there might be peace and the preservation of free government. I thought I saw those boys standing there at "Present Arms" to do honor to the memory of this soldier, the unknown dead. . . . In high purpose this nation then and there resolved that it must not be again.

That afternoon, two thousand people marched down Pennsylvania Avenue carrying banners that denounced war. One of these proclaimed: "We will not give our children for another war!"

Devoted to peace, the Armistice Day ceremony might well have marked the high point of public fervor. Led by Charles Evans Hughes, however, the Harding administration held in reserve an even more striking event, timed to open the next day: the Washington Conference.

Despite a sharp, wintry wind, as early as eight-thirty on the morning of November 12, the streets and walkways around Continental Memorial Hall (part of the complex of buildings owned by the Daughters of the American Revolution and situated at the corner of Seventeenth and D Streets, just down the hill from the White House) were full of onlookers, hoping to catch glimpses of the delegates. Their hopes were rewarded because, for the next hour or so, limousine after limousine parked before the building and let out the conferees. In their dark overcoats and top hats, the delegates filed between the Grecian columns that lined the front of the building, disappearing inside.

Gathering in the anteroom were Hughes; Elihu Root, a former secretary of state and a member of the American delegation; Arthur Balfour, the tall, white-haired, languid former prime minister and foreign secretary (who during World War I had promulgated the Balfour Declaration, the promise of a Jewish homeland in Palestine) and now head of the British delegation; Aristide Briand, the premier of France; and delegates from Holland, Belgium, Italy, Portugal, China, and Japan. At about ten twenty-five they all entered the central hall and found their places around a rectangular arrangement of tables.

Nearly a thousand persons were present inside. The balcony and one side of the auditorium had been reserved for U.S. senators and representatives; members of the cabinet and the diplomatic corps were seated along the other side. On the main floor sat advisers to the delegations and prominent newsmen.

Up in a booth, Mrs. Harding sat beside the vice president, Calvin Coolidge. Mrs. Hughes was nearby. So were Chief Justice and Mrs. William Howard Taft (appointed by Harding, Taft had taken up the chief justiceship only the month before). Positioned in the front row of the journalists, playing his sometime role of special correspondent, was William Jennings Bryan, wearing a flowing black cape. When the delegates began to come in, the crowd shouted, and mispronounced, the name of the French premier, Briand. Bryan stood up to take a bow, but the people ignored him. He sat back down in a huff.

Backed by the balustrades along one wall of the auditorium, along with two clusters of potted palms and a row of the flags of all the nations represented, the seating arrangement around the grouped tables reflected the new realities of international power. The American delegation, which included Hughes, Root, and Senator Henry Cabot Lodge, was placed exactly at the center of the top of the rectangle. Also at the head table, the British sat on the Americans' left and the French on the right. On the side table next to the British were the Italians and the Belgians. Across from them were the Portuguese, the Dutch, and the Chinese. At the bottom of the table arrangement were the Japanese, led by Prince Tokugawa Iyesato, Tokyo's foreign minister. The Japanese seemed to have been put as far from the others as possible, as if they were diplomatic pariahs.

In front of each delegate was a desk pad, a pen-and-ink set, and small stacks of writing paper. Once all had taken their places, there was a moment of hushed expectation.

Then, amid a burst of applause, President Harding entered from a door at the back of the chamber. Reaching the head table, he stood for a moment, bowing in acknowledgment of his reception, and then sat beside Hughes. The time was 10:30 AM.

At that moment Hughes, as the temporary chairman of the convention, rapped for order. The Reverend W. S. Abernethy offered a prayer. After he said his "Amen," Hughes stood and said simply: "The president of the United States." Harding rose to deliver a speech of welcome.

With his typical vacuousness, Harding described the convocation as "an earnest expression of the awakened consciousness of twentieth-century civilization. It is not a convention of remorse, not a session of sorrow. It is not a conference of victors to define terms of settlement. Nor is it a council of nations seeking to remake humankind." The nine nations had met, Harding stated, to reduce the evils of armament and war. But he added: "I do not mean surrendered rights, or narrowed freedom, or denied aspirations. Our republic would no more ask for these than it would give. No pride need be humbled, no nationality submerged, but I would have a mergence [sic] of minds committing all of us to less preparation for war and more enjoyment of fortunate peace."

When Harding finished, those present rewarded him with polite applause. Nothing in his speech had conveyed the slightest impression of what was to come.

After Harding had left, it was Hughes's turn to speak. Offering his greetings, he disposed of several routine matters. The foreign delegations seemed to think that he would stop with words of welcome. How wrong they were!

"I am happy to say," Hughes declared after he had finished his preamble, "that I am at liberty . . . to submit to you a concrete proposition for an agreement for the limitation of naval armament." As Hughes spelled out the sacrifices America might make, his biographer tells us, the "delegates caught their breaths and moistened hot lips." The "United States," Hughes proclaimed, "is willing to scrap all [its battleships and cruisers]." He then challenged the other powers to do the same.

The Britons were stunned. Scribbling some notes, Lord Balfour did manage not to change his expression. Admiral Sir Ernle Chatfield, however, "turned red and then white, and sat immovable." Lord Lee of Farnham, first lord of the Admiralty, "half rose and whispered to Balfour." Admiral Earl Beatty, first sea lord and the "very embodiment of the idea that Britannia ruled the waves," leaned forward with the belligerent expression of "a waking bulldog that had been poked in the stomach by the impudent foot of an itinerant soap-canvasser."

"With the acceptance of his plan," Hughes concluded nonchalantly, "the burden of meeting the demands of competition in naval armament will be lifted. . . . Preparations for offensive war will stop now."

As Hughes uttered these words, the Americans in the hall erupted with cheers. People hugged each other and waved their hats. William Jennings Bryan fluttered a large silk handkerchief as he wiped huge tears from his cheeks. The occasion, wrote the renowned Kansas editor William Allen White, "furnished the most intensely dramatic moment I had ever witnessed."

By no means did the United States or anyone else scrap all the great ships; Hughes's speech served simply as a bargaining ploy. Nonetheless, dominated by Hughes, the Washington conferees reached four principal agreements. First, in return for the right to keep its Pacific islands (confiscated from Germany during the war), Japan consented to leave China's Shandong Peninsula. Second, Japan promised to abide by the Nine-Power Treaty, a guarantee of nonaggression toward China: signed on February 6, 1922 by the United States, Great Britain, France, the Netherlands, Portugal, Italy, Belgium, China, and Japan, the treaty, in the first paragraph or its first article, read: "The Contracting Powers, other than China, agree . . . to respect the sovereignty, the independence, and the territorial and administrative integrity of China." Third, the United States, Great Britain, and Japan agreed to a five-five-three ratio: for every five American battleships, Great Britain would reduce its number to five and Japan to three. And fourth, Hughes persuaded the delegates to consider the Washington Conference as the foundation of a larger and longer-lasting entity called the "Association of Nations." One journal believed that the United States thereby had entered "into an international partnership in which this nation is certain to attain experience and confidence of a sort that will gradually allay American fears of larger cooperation in safeguarding of peace. . . . The first step is the hardest. At least we have taken it."

Each of these agreements was Wilsonian. Japan's return of Shandong to China accorded with Wilson's principle of national self-determination. The Nine-Power Treaty gave voice to Wilson's advocacy of international nonaggression. The five-five-three battleship ratio was wholly in line with Wilson's challenge to Britain's naval supremacy. And the "Association of Nations" was Secretary Hughes's effort to give new life, under a new name, to the League of Nations.

Few of these agreements, to be sure, endured. Facing sure opposition, Harding in the end did not submit the Association of Nations treaty to the Senate. In its 1931 invasion of Manchuria and in its 1937 attack on China proper, Japan shredded the Shandong and nonaggression accords. If we look back on the Washington Conference from the vantage point of World War II, we can see that the convocation produced little more than a parchment peace.

Only the naval ratio agreement with the British remained in effect. Great Britain could not afford to challenge the United States.

The Washington Conference nonetheless symbolized a profound change in international relations. It did so in two ways.

First, unlike its Ottoman and Habsburg counterparts, the Russian Empire had not collapsed; it had taken on a new name. As Lenin gradually subdued his rivals, Great Britain's ancient concern for the security of India was resurrected. Worse still for Britain, Russia was governed by revolutionaries dedicated to the overthrow of British and French colonialism.

Second, the United States had stayed in the ranks of the great powers. As Sir William Wiseman, a British diplomat in Washington, warned London, there was in America a growing sense of rivalry with Britain. "Which is going to be greater, politically and commercially," Wiseman asked, "Britain or America?" The Washington Conference answered the question: Great Britain had no choice but to accept Hughes's principle of naval parity.

Great Britain stood revealed as a power in decline. Then, just before the Washington Conference adjourned, early in 1922, Lord

Balfour announced another concession: Great Britain would hand back to China its lease to Weihaiwei.

5

Weihaiwei, meaning the "oceanic guard station at Wei," lay near the northern tip of the Shandong Peninsula; Port Arthur, on the southern tip of Manchuria's Liaoning Peninsula, was only eighty miles away. Facing each other across the Gulf of Zhili, therefore, the two harbors formed a gateway to Tianjin and Beijing. To guard that gateway from the Russians, the British late in the nineteenth century had leased the land around Weihaiwei.

The British action had been a sort of climax to the imperial land-grab that had sent Britain, France, Germany, Japan, and Russia pushing in to control the East Asian littoral. They all had snatched off pieces of the territory, the French completing their conquest of Indochina, the Germans colonizing Shandong, the Japanese seizing Korea and Taiwan, and the Russians moving across inner Asia into Manchuria. The Russian drive especially had alarmed the British, already having defined the czar as the main enemy. Ever on the lookout for Russian incursions, the British had set up defenses in and around Weihaiwei.

Britons also found Weihaiwei delightful as a tourist attraction. With its "exquisite climate, russet-colored mountains, blue sea, and lovely bay," wrote the *Times* of London, Weihaiwei as a summer resort could not be surpassed, and every year "hundreds of foreigners journey from the fierce heat of Shanghai and Tianjin. There are boating, fishing, golf, lawn tennis, riding, the best swimming in the world, snipe, hares, and woodcock to shoot in season, and enchanting walks. It is possible to dance, play bridge, and talk scandal every night, or live the life of a hermit with equal ease. And there are no telephones."

The good times ended. Citing the cost of maintaining a garrison at Weihaiwei, Lord Balfour while still in Washington announced that His Majesty's government in less than a decade would withdraw from the port. And so it came to be. After a brief ceremony on September 28, 1930, Reginald Fleming Johnston, the tutor to the last Chinese emperor and later the governor of Weihaiwei, signed an official agreement and boarded a steamship for Britain.

Newspapers around the world played up the departure. In itself, Weihaiwei was insignificant. What mattered, however, was that Great Britain was relinquishing a fragment of its empire, for Johnston's sailing back home symbolized what had been taking place ever since the Washington Conference: the beginning of what Rudyard Kipling had prophesied two decades before, the Britannic recessional.

CHAPTER 7

Imperial Decline

1

Shortly before moving to Washington, the Hoovers bought a colonial-style house at 2300 S Street, almost next door to the Wilson residence. Flanked by oak trees, the yard was about an acre deep, and from the spacious back porch, where they often ate when the weather was warm, they enjoyed the view of the Capitol dome and the Washington Monument. Hoover's ride to his office was easy: back along Massachusetts Avenue to Dupont Circle, then down Nineteenth Street to a corner room in a rented apartment building.

Such was the headquarters of the Commerce Department, or at least what passed for a department. Hardly unified, it consisted of about fifteen bureaus, such as Lighthouses and Fisheries, most of which predated the department and were so independent that some even placed their names alone on their letterheads. They had long run themselves, and Oscar Straus, a former secretary appointed by Theodore Roosevelt, told Hoover that the job would require no more than two hours of work a day. Hoover wrote that putting "the fish to bed at night and turning on the lights around the coast were the major concepts of the office."

Hoover had no intention, however, of sitting around. With his usual energy, he plunged into a range of activities such as centralizing the department; eliminating waste in industry; providing flood relief; meting out water resources; and, above all, beating down foreign trade combinations against the United States. The worst example of such cabals, in Hoover's judgment, was the action of the British government in 1922 of curtailing the empire's production of rubber and thus driving up the commodity's world price. Hoover's response was a virtual declaration of economic war: the last thing he would tolerate was having the American automobile industry held hostage by the Britannic overlords. So by threatening to call in Great Britain's wartime loans and by helping Firestone and other American rubber companies expand the output of their African and Asian plantations, Hoover forced the British to their knees. In just three months in mid-1925, he drove the world price of rubber down from $1.21 a pound to a mere $0.40 a pound.

The loser in the fight over the price of rubber was the British secretary of state for the colonies, Winston S. Churchill. Yet the loss was only one part of Churchill's growing distress.

2

Despite demotion to a minor cabinet post after the Gallipoli disaster and despite the distrust he inspired among all political factions, Churchill proved himself a survivor. It was better to keep him on the inside, Lloyd George reasoned, than to have him loose on the outside. Indeed, by 1922, Churchill was back in power as the colonial secretary.

As if to celebrate his new role, Churchill, who already possessed a town house at Sussex Square, near Hyde Park, and who had inherited several thousand pounds from the death of a cousin, sallied forth in search of a country home; such an establishment would befit his position as an English gentleman who was Tory at heart. The place he settled on, early in 1922, was called Chartwell, a Kentish estate about twenty-five miles and an hour's train ride south of London. Sited on the crest of a hill, the manor looked down and out on some eighty acres of meadows, slopes, and woods. Churchill later said that he had bought Chartwell for that view.

Dating back to the fifteenth century, however, the house itself was rotten to the core and had to undergo a wholesale reconstruction. Originally long and rectangular with chimneys and a sloped roof, the mansion under Churchill's direction acquired high gables and a perpendicular brick wing for the drawing room, the dining room, and Churchill's writing studio. He also dug gardens, planted trees, dammed the stream, and erected brick walls, doing most of the work himself. The renovation went on for two years, costs mounted, and Clementine, Churchill's wife, hated the place, perhaps because he had bought it without consulting her.

At Chartwell, however, from the mid-1920s well into the 1930s, Churchill could play the grand host. Guests came in great numbers and variety—politicians, authors, publishers, artists, scientists, and even actors (the last including Charlie Chaplin, who delighted the Churchill children by breaking into the dance from his 1925 movie *The Gold Rush*)—but they all shared one trait: they served as foils for Churchill's soliloquies. Churchill had become a master of the English language, and he knew it. He dominated dinner conversations, and well into the early hours of the morning his houseguests would hear him pacing the floor of his study, talking aloud in the cadences he had absorbed from his youthful readings of Edward Gibbon's *The Decline and Fall of the Roman Empire*, and dictating to young assistants the histories that were starting to earn real money: a reminiscence of his early days as a subaltern and reporter; an account of the part he played in World War I; and a massive biography of his famous ancestor John Churchill, the duke of Marlborough, who two centuries before had defeated the French at Blenheim and as a reward had received the Oxfordshire palace of the same name.

Throughout all these works, Churchill wrote largely about himself. So, of course, do many politicians. But Churchill's self-idolization had a special quality; it was elegiac, as if he saw himself of an earlier era of English life. He lived in Chartwell, yes, but a reading of Churchill's histories conjures up pictures of Blenheim with the height of its chimneys, the sweep of its columns, and the vistas piled upon vistas as they create a sense of drama, battle, and victory, all of it a dedication to the glory of one Englishman, a direct lineal ancestor of Winston S. Churchill.

Clearly Churchill believed himself the inheritor of that legacy: the faith that he could be the preserver of the British Empire gave meaning to his life. Yet that faith was illusory, and the tragedy of Winston Churchill—tragedy in the classical sense of the fall of a great man who pursues great dreams that, because of his own actions, cannot be realized—was in the background of all his writing. Even in the 1920s, as he was rebuilding Chartwell, it was becoming apparent to so many others in Britain, if not to Churchill himself, that the empire could never be rebuilt.

3

In the middle of the 1920s, the British Empire *seemed* to be a thing for all eternity. Such was the point of the British Empire Exposition, which opened on April 23, 1924, St. George's Day, at Wembley. At the commencement of the exposition, the *Daily Mail* of London reported: "The Lord's Prayer was recited reverently by the multitude. [The composer] Sir Edward Elgar, a lonely figure in black in his lofty pulpit, raised his baton." A massed choir above him sang his "Jerusalem"; the empire was being baptized.

Erected by a public-private consortium at the northern terminus of the London Underground, the show was spectacular. Into its fifteen square miles, exposition managers had packed anything and everything that appeared remotely imperial. A stadium (still in use) signified sportsmanship. A sculptor had used Canadian butter to fashion a statue of the prince of Wales. Someone had erected a miniature version of Niagara Falls, intended to remind ticket purchasers of the grandeur of the imperial wilderness. Someone else had modeled the tomb of King Tutankhamen in an effort apparently to link the most ancient and the most recent Mediterranean empires. A company of Tibetans stood about, moaning into long, drooping horns; they were supposed to look like Indians.

Traveling from site to site, visitors could ride an elevated track of the "Never-Stop Railway." The British Empire was always on the move.

The Wembley exhibition was a sham: even in the English-speaking dominions, the center no longer held. Although largely

Scottish in their origins, British Canadians in the 1920s were aping the Americans: with its stock market, banks, and high-rise office buildings, Toronto resembled a medium-size city down in the States. Australians, proud of their role in the war and resentful of their sacrifices at Gallipoli, saw their island-continent as a brand-new world, free of British dominance. New Zealanders were becoming exotic, living in their beautiful, remote islands. Even the non-Boer South Africans were mutating into something distinctly non-British. High up on the veld, Johannesburg was a modern city of imposing buildings, broad streets arranged in a grid, and a rail line crossed by many bridges: Jo'burg, as it was called, looked brash, American.

Far from being an "experiment in empire-building," furthermore, the much-ballyhooed Statute of Westminster, passed by Parliament in 1931, gave the dominions their freedom in international affairs and the right unilaterally to change their constitutions. Apart from requiring allegiance to the crown, the statute set the dominions free as the "Commonwealth of Nations," whatever that meant.

Great Britain had granted that freedom voluntarily. Ireland's independence, though, did not come about so easily; it was the product of murder.

4

When the British cabinet in 1914 first learned of the Austro-Hungarian ultimatum to Serbia, Churchill wrote, "[t]he parishes of Fermanagh and Tyrone faded back into the mists and squalls of Ireland." By the early 1920s, however, Churchill envisioned "the dreary steeples of Fermanagh and Tyrone emerging once again."

Actually, they had never gone away. In the wake of the Easter Rebellion of 1916 (launched by Irish guerrillas and crushed by the British army), London had imposed the military draft upon all Catholic Ireland. But forced into British uniforms, young men had deserted in droves. "Irish conscription," Churchill later admitted, "was handled in such a fashion . . . that we had the worst of both worlds, all the resentment against compulsion and in the end no law and no men."

Churchill also distorted the truth. Ireland had its own law and its own men. Catholic loyalists formed a parliamentary body called the Dáil (pronounced "Doyle") Eireann, the "Irish Assembly," that authorized the creation of the Irish Republican Army and elected as its president the American-born Eamon De Valera. The British in response suppressed the Dáil and put De Valera in jail. In February 1919, however, Michael Collins, a cherubic-faced gunman of the Easter Rising and now general of the IRA, rescued De Valera and smuggled him across the ocean to New York. The British then put a price on Collins's head and he, going underground, initiated armed violence against the British army of occupation. His Majesty's officials in Dublin Castle, the symbol of British authority in Ireland, found themselves in a state of siege.

In the winter of 1919–1920, IRA gunmen murdered a good score of the resident English and even shot to death in plain daylight the British magistrate for Dublin. "This new Irish murder is very terrible," Clementine Churchill wrote to her husband. Responding, Churchill allowed that Irish assassins were "really getting very serious. . . . What a diabolical streak they have in their character! I expect it is that treacherous, conspiring trait which has done them in in bygone ages of history and prevented them from being a great responsible nation with stability and prosperity."

Churchill forgot, or chose to forget, that it had been nine centuries of English rule that had prevented Catholic Ireland from dwelling in "stability and prosperity." Wanting simply to crush what he called the "murder gang in Ireland," Churchill wrote in the *Illustrated Sunday Herald:* "No nation has ever established its title-deed by a campaign of assassination. The British nation, having come grimly through the slaughter of Armageddon, are certainly not going to be scared by the squalid scenes of sporadic warfare which are being enacted across the Irish Channel."

His wife cautioned him against such an excess of view: "Do my darling use your influence now for some sort of moderation or at any rate justice in Ireland. If you were ever leader you would not like to be cowed by severity & certainly not by reprisals which fall like rain from Heaven upon the Just & upon the Unjust. . . . It always makes me unhappy & disappointed when I see you inclined to take for granted that the rough, iron-fisted Hunnish way will prevail."

Churchill paid no attention; he believed it imperative to put out the uprising in the Emerald Isle before "flames of orange and green flash out of the Irish furnace." Yet he managed only to fight fire with petrol. Going to the cabinet, he secured permission to send eight thousand mercenaries to crush the Irish revolt. Because of their black belts and army surplus khaki uniforms, the force became known as the "Black and Tans." Unleashed in southern Ireland, they turned their guns on the civilian population. Defending them against charges of atrocities, Churchill wrote that "I cannot feel it right to punish the troops when, goaded in the most brutal manner and finding no redress, they take action on their own account."

Lloyd George backed him up. "We have murder by the throat," the prime minister declared. "[W]e had to reorganize the police [in Ireland], and when the government was ready we struck the terrorists and now the terrorists are complaining of terror."

But others, too, were complaining, especially after a blaze, allegedly set by the Black and Tans, in December 1920, nearly razed the city of Cork. Civilian Catholics in Ireland were outraged, as were Americans of Irish descent, along with the Labour Party, ever stronger on the British home front. Even some of the Conservatives were beginning to have misgivings.

Ever sensitive to the demands of his wartime coalition, therefore, Lloyd George turned the ship of state around. Inviting an Irish delegation, which included Michael Collins, to London shortly after the burning of Cork, he persuaded them to meet with Churchill. With Lloyd George his only political protector, Churchill had no choice but to cooperate.

The result of the negotiations, ratified by the House of Commons two days before Christmas 1920, was the Government of Ireland Act. Dividing Ireland into two parts, the six largely Protestant counties of the north and the almost wholly Catholic regions of the south, Eire, the measure provided that each could choose its own legislature. The act thus appeared to fulfill the old Irish dream of home rule.

As Churchill explained to the House, however, Great Britain would keep the naval base at Queenstown, the site of the *Lusitania* sinking; Eire would have no navy of its own nor, in any future war, would it remain neutral. Members of the Irish Parliament would be required to take an oath of allegiance to the British crown. For, Churchill declaimed, "we do not recognize the Irish Republic!"

The Irish crisis thus was far from over. In Dublin, De Valera, returned from America and deeply involved with the Irish Republican Army, refused to accept the London agreement. So bitter were the feelings of betrayal that, on August 22, 1921, IRA gunmen shot Michael Collins to death. And in the end, late in the 1930s, De Valera prevailed: the so-called Irish Free State became the Republic of Eire.

The Irish affair exposed the fatal flaw of the British Empire: without legitimacy, power was nothing. And so it was in another realm of Churchill's interest: the Middle East.

5

Among those present at the Paris peace talks had been a blue-eyed, blond, aristocratic Englishman, a linguist, archaeologist, and officer who had fought in the sands of Arabia for the defeat of Germany's ally Turkey. Although a young man, he was already famous. Lowell Thomas, the American impresario and later radio broadcaster, had marketed a best-selling slide show based on his supposed desert exploits: he was Colonel T. E. Lawrence, Lawrence of Arabia. Pro-Arab, he viewed with misgivings his government's determination to secure, under the aegis of a League of Nations mandate, the colonization of Palestine. Imposing such control on the Arabs, Lawrence believed, would lead the British Empire to shoulder an unbearable burden.

Lloyd George ignored Lawrence's pillar of wisdom; the prime minister had succumbed to the arrogance of power. With his party winning the election of 1918 overwhelmingly, he had stuffed his cabinet with out-and-out imperialists such as Viscount Milner, high commissioner of South Africa at the time of the Boer War, and Lord Curzon, once the viceroy of India. Lloyd George also had convinced himself that he could assure the Zionists a safe haven in Palestine.

He wanted more; he wanted to go down in history as the prime minister who finally brought the old Ottoman Empire to its end, opening its lands for Britannic expansion. With the cabinet imperialists—including Churchill, of course—cheering him on, Lloyd George in September 1922 sought to provoke a war with Turkey. But a Greek army, financed by Britain and sent over the Bosporus to do the job, was routed by the Turks. Unwilling to accept defeat, Lloyd George sent units of Britain's finest to Chanak, a coastal town on the Asiatic side of the Dardanelles. On September 23, 1922, British and Turkish soldiers faced each other across the barbed wire strung around Chanak.

Then Lloyd George had to back off. Failing to see Turkey as a threat to Europe as a whole, the dominions refused to send military aid, and the British public refused to endorse a new war. And in the middle of October, the commanders on the spot negotiated a truce; Lloyd George had no choice but to accept the arrangement. His reward was the end of his premiership.

Lloyd George did succeed in gaining Palestine and Mesopotamia. But he failed to topple the Bolsheviks; he failed to keep Ireland; he failed to defeat Turkey. And he fell, as he had risen, through a cabal. A gathering of Conservative back-benchers around Stanley Baldwin, a businessman from the provinces and a rising Tory star, was enough to undermine the wartime coalition government. The Lloyd George ministry broke up and, in the general election of October 1922, the Liberal Party received a defeat from which it never recovered.

Commenting on Lloyd George's downfall, Max Aitkin, the Canadian press magnate who became Lord Beaverbrook, wrote: "The Greeks told us of a man in high position, self-confident, so successful as to be overpowering to all others. Then his virtues turned to failings. He committed the crime of arrogance. His structure of self-confidence and success came tumbling down. He struggled against fate but he was doomed. So it was with Lloyd George." So it would be with Churchill.

As he fell, Lloyd George took Churchill down with him. Just before the 1922 election, Churchill underwent an operation for appendicitis; he was unable until the last four days of the campaign to show up at Dundee, his constituency. A Scottish town of ship-builders, linen weavers, and jute sackers, Dundee for more than a decade had been a safe seat for Churchill. Now, however, with unemployment rampant, the mood was prosocialist and anti-imperialist. When Clementine Churchill, pregnant with their last child, canvassed for her husband, she ran into a taunting mob that carried Irish Republican banners; the newspapers, she wrote back to Winston, were "vile." When Churchill himself, barely able to move, did appear onstage, hecklers shouted, "What about the Dardanelles?"

During one session, attended by a throng of yelling Labourites, he shouted back: "If about a hundred young men and women in the audience choose to spoil the meeting—if about a hundred of these young reptiles—"

The *Daily Telegraph* commented after the polling was finished, "[Churchill's] is perhaps the most sensational defeat of the whole election." Churchill himself was frank. He was, as he put it, "in the twinkling of an eye without an office, without a seat, without a party, and without an appendix."

Ever resilient, to be sure, Churchill soon switched back to the Conservative Party, and in 1924, granted a new constituency that was largely Tory, he emerged as chancellor of the exchequer. Finance bored him, however, and he took office just in time to observe, from inside the cabinet, the collapse of British power in yet another part of the empire—indeed, the "jewel in the crown," India.

6

The British government had taken special care to preserve its role in India. In 1921, it had sent the prince of Wales out on a royal tour of the Raj. The visit, however, was an insult to Indian sensibilities. Only two years before, British authorities in India had perpetrated an atrocity not to be forgotten anywhere in South Asia.

"The [train] compartment I entered was almost full and all the berths, except the upper one, were occupied by sleeping passengers." The writer was Jawaharlal Nehru, a disciple of Gandhi and future prime minister of India. In October 1919 he was taking a night train to Delhi from Amritsar in the Punjab, where recently Sir Reginald Dyer, a British general, had been responsible for the massacre of hundreds of Hindus. "I took the vacant upper berth," Nehru went on. "In the morning I discovered that all my fellow passengers were [British] military officers. They conversed with each other in loud voices which I could not help overhearing. One of them was holding forth in an aggressive and triumphant tone and soon I discovered that he was Dyer . . . and he was describing his Amritsar experience. He pointed out how he had the whole town at his mercy and he felt like reducing the rebellious city to a heap of ashes, but he took pity on it and refrained. He was evidently coming back from Lahore after giving his evidence before [a committee of inquiry]. I was greatly shocked to hear his conversation and to observe his callous manner. He descended at Delhi in pyjamas with bright pink stripes, and a dressing gown."

India had contributed heavily to the British war effort: abroad, thousands of Indians had died in the trenches; at home, the populace had endured the scarcity of food and the spiraling of inflation. All this had been endured with little complaint because, in the 1915 Defence of India Act, London had promised home rule, raising hopes of national independence.

In March 23, 1919, however, Parliament had passed the Rowlatt Act, a measure rescinding home rule. Headquartered in an ashram near Bombay, Mohandas K. Gandhi in response organized a national day of mourning and abstinence from work. Throughout India, on April 6, 1919, shopkeepers closed their doors. The British in turn arrested Gandhi, and violence soon spread. It reached its culmination in Amritsar.

With the city already rumbling with revolt, the British had deported some of the most extreme agitators. After Gandhi's arrest, then, residents rioted. British soldiers opened fire on them. Going wild, the mob murdered several Britons and burned banks, churches, and the railway station, all symbols of British authority. Three days later, General Dyer showed up, commanding a force of a thousand men. In a message spread by the beat of drums, he prohibited all public gatherings.

The following morning, Dyer received word that a great crowd was collecting in the Jallianwalla Bagh (*Bagh* meaning garden). Without hesitation, he led armed soldiers into the area, an enclosure within the city's bazaar. Preceded by two policemen on horseback and followed by two armored cars, and with ninety men on foot, Dyer rode in an open automobile, clattering through the sunbaked streets. Halfway into the bazaar, Dyer ordered the column to halt. Nearby, the shopfronts formed a narrow lane, contracting within a few yards into a cramped passageway. At Dyer's command, soldiers marched in a double file into the passageway. From beyond the corridor came the buzz of a restless crowd; overhead droned an airplane, a sign of British might. Debouching from the passageway, the soldiers mounted a narrow platform. Before them stretched several acres of ground almost totally enclosed by the walls of adjoining buildings. Filling the area, a vast crowd of Hindus, squatting, was listening to a speaker as he gesticulated on a stage. The British soldiers crouched, leveling their rifles. An officer ordered them to fire, high. The speaker jumped down, running forward with a white handkerchief in his hand. Then Dyer appeared and shouted another order: "Fire low, for what else have you been brought here?"

An Indian witness later told a committee of the Congress, the political party of Gandhi and Nehru that was striving for independence,

> the worst part of the whole thing was that the firing was directed toward the gates through which the people were running out. There were small outlets, four or five in all, and the bullets actually rained over the people at all these gates. Shots were also fired into the thick of the meeting. There was not a corner left of the garden facing the firing line where people did not die in large numbers. Many got trampled under the feet of the rushing crowds and thus lost their lives. Blood was pouring in profusion. Even those who lay flat on the ground were shot.

The "crowd was so dense," Dyer himself testified—this was just before he was on the train with Nehru—

> that if a determined rush had been made at any time, arms or no arms, my small force must instantly have been overpowered and consequently I was very careful of not giving the mob a chance to organize. I sometimes ceased fire and redirected my fire where the crowd was collecting more thickly. I fired and continued to fire until the crowd dispersed. . . . If more troops had been at hand the casualties would have been greater. . . . It was no longer a question of merely dispersing the crowd, but one of producing a sufficient moral effect . . . not only on those who were present, but especially throughout the Punjab. There could be no question of undue severity.

Ending his testimony, Dyer called the massacre "merciful."

The firing lasted about ten minutes. When it was over, at least fifteen hundred Indian subjects of King George V, emperor of the Raj, lay writhing from their wounds or dead.

All around Amritsar, the Punjab remained restless for another week. Guerrillas derailed trains, cut telegraph lines, and paralyzed the movement of rail freight. Then the disturbances ended. The news of Amritsar, claimed Sir Michael O'Dwyer, the British governor of the Punjab, had frightened the agitators into submission.

Stunned by the violence as well as by the failure of the resistance, Gandhi soon devised a new tactic. Abandoning for the moment the idea of another nationwide strike, he chose to launch a one-man campaign: he would break the law. The British authorities had ordered him to stay in the Bombay district. By himself, however, dressed simply in a *dhoti* and a handspun cloth cap, he left the region, walking and sleeping in fields. He kept the British notified of all his movements.

Arresting him, they fell into his trap. On March 18, 1922, guards dragged him from his cell to a Bombay courtroom. Tried for sedition, he was found guilty and sentenced to prison—a judgment that, as he had hoped, reignited the flames of Indian nationalism. By incarcerating the tiny, spindle-legged Gandhi, the British were acknowledging the ineffectiveness of their rule.

7

After his release in 1924 from prison, on the ground of ill health, Gandhi turned away from political agitation, concentrating instead on a campaign for the spinning of cloth by hand; thus he would end India's reliance on cotton clothing manufactured by machine in England. Otherwise he was out of the public view. He seemed weak and defeated. His hopes for Indian independence were stagnating with the rise of Hindu-Muslim tensions; mutual insults and harassments went on daily, and self-seeking politicians on both sides incited further ethnic hatred. C. R. Das, a Hindu who during Gandhi's imprisonment had taken over the leadership of the Congress Party, furthermore, was hinting at the possibility of reconciliation with Great Britain; Congress itself was splitting apart. Indeed, late in 1927, the British-controlled *Times of India* chortled over the "completeness of the Congress collapse, the utter futility of the Congress creed, and the total absence among Congress supporters of a single political idea."

Yet just at that moment, Indian nationalism bounded forward in seven-league boots; the British brought it on themselves. *Mother India*, a book published in 1927, scornfully indicted Hinduism and all its ways. Although the author, Katherine Mayo, was an American, Indian nationalists learned that the British government had subsidized the publication. British authorities in Kenya, furthermore, had chosen to discriminate against Indians and to forbid their immigration. In November 1927, finally, the British government set up an entity called the Indian Statutory Commission to study India's "fitness for self-government." When the members of the commission landed in Bombay in February 1928, hostile demonstrators appeared at pierside. Strikes broke out in jute and steel mills and when, after a scuffle with the police, a popular leader died of a heart attack, Indians blamed his death on the British.

The commission's report, issued in early 1930, was a disaster. Although it recommended a degree of self-rule in the provinces, it strongly urged that central power remain securely in British hands. In India, moderates and radicals alike denounced the document.

The leaders of Congress then decided to demand nothing less than full independence. So, on January 26, 1930, at gatherings all over India, people raised the Congress tricolor and orators read out a declaration of independence. And Gandhi reemerged at the fore-front of Indian politics.

To activate the people, he hit upon a symbol both commonplace and dramatic. He would break the law again, and in a most telling manner.

During evening prayers at his Bombay ashram, on March 11, 1930, Gandhi spoke to a small group of followers. What he intended, he explained, was nothing less than to bring about the end of the Raj. How to achieve that goal? The making of salt was the key! He would go to the sea and make salt!

Without salt in hot countries such as India, people would die; in India, however, the manufacture of salt was a government monopoly. Furthermore, the British laid taxes on all purchases of salt. The British monopoly, therefore, was a symbol of colonial harshness. "Our cause is just," Gandhi declared at the end of his talk. "Our means are strong and God is with us."

Early in the morning of March 12, 1930, Gandhi, followed by some eighty volunteers, all dressed in white homespun clothing, set out for a seacoast village below Bombay. Although sixty-one years old, Gandhi was lithe and vigorous. He wore a simple *dhoti* with cloth drawn up between his legs and he carried a staff of thick, iron-tipped bamboo. Ranged behind him, his original column soon became a procession of thousands. At the head of the march strode the little figure of Gandhi; as if he were a military conqueror, peasants along the roadside strewed green leaves about his feet. Under a broiling sun, Gandhi walked ten to fifteen miles a day, and each day brought rising excitement. News of the march was spreading across India and indeed beyond. Foreign press agencies sent correspondents and newsreel cameras. Movie theaters throughout the world showed clips of a tiny, elderly man striding along the dusty roads of India to do battle with the power and glory of the British Empire. By the time he had reached the coast, two weeks after he had started, Gandhi had become a world figure. British oppression had made him into the Mahatma, the holy one.

After a night of prayer, Gandhi walked into the sea in a ritual act of purification. Then, from the beach, he picked up some natural salt, squeezing it into a ball.

That was all, but within a week all India seemed to be violating the salt monopoly: violent attacks on British-owned salt depots became frequent. The authorities arrested Gandhi again, and along with him more than sixty thousand others. People were receiving seven-year prison sentences just for carrying Congress flags. India was careening out of control.

Realizing that something had to change, Edward Wood (Lord Irwin) ordered Gandhi released from jail. Later, as Lord Halifax, Wood would become the foreign secretary and then, early in 1941, Great Britain's ambassador to the United States. At the time of his writing to the king, he was the viceroy of the Raj. An imposing six feet, five inches tall, high-crowned, grave, wealthy (he had inherited vast estates in Yorkshire), and born into the nobility, Lord Irwin wore the imperial ermine as if it were his by birthright.

He saw himself as enlightened, too, and on February 17, 1931, talked with Gandhi at the viceregal palace in Delhi. Lord Irwin found Gandhi impressive. "I think that most people upon meeting him," Irwin wrote to King George V, "would be conscious, as I was conscious, of a very powerful personality, and this, independent of physical endowment, which indeed is unfavourable. Small, wizened, rather emaciated, no front teeth, it is a personality very poorly adorned with this world's trappings. And yet you cannot help feeling the force of character behind the sharp little eyes and immensely active and acutely working mind."

Mutually respectful, Gandhi and Irwin reached a truce. Gandhi for the moment would call off civil disobedience; Irwin would persuade the British government—Labour, at the time—at the end of the year to convene Round-Table Talks, negotiations over India's constitutional status. Accordingly, on August 27, 1931, Gandhi left Bombay, boarding the steamer *Rajputana* for Marseilles.

As Gandhi reached London two weeks later, taking a bed in a Friends' settlement house in the East End, news cameras began to track him constantly. They followed him when he inspected the slums of Lancashire; when he attended a ceremonial planting of trees; when on raw mornings he walked along the banks of the Thames where barges melted into the autumnal fogs; when, dressed merely in a loincloth and shawl, he took tea at Buckingham Palace; and when, shivering, he walked on bare feet through the arched doorway of St. James's Palace for the start of the Round-Table Talks.

The British government had planned the talks carefully, inviting fifty-six other Indian leaders, including Muslims, and more than a dozen native Indian princes. For Whitehall, the princes were crucial. Rather than espouse independence, they proposed an Indian federation, one that would leave them their own zones of autonomy, and the British in command of the government in Delhi. The presence of the Muslims, moreover, advertised differences among Indians themselves; it symbolized Great Britain's imperial strategy called "divide and conquer."

By their adjournment on December 1, 1931, thus, the first Round-Table Talks had done nothing to further Gandhi's goal. Upon his return to India at the end of the year, then, he learned that Lord Willington, Irwin's successor as viceroy, had ordered the arrest of most Congress leaders. "Christmas gifts," the Mahatma commented, "from Lord Willington, our Christian viceroy."

The longer the British stalled, however, the more difficult became their objective of holding on to India as a colony. On into the 1930s, India was in constant turmoil and, to the British treasury, the sheer cost of maintaining power was proving exorbitant.

8

Churchill refused to face such a fact of life. His view of any and all concessions to Indian nationalism was apocalyptic. Great Britain should not allow itself "to be edged, pushed, talked, and cozened out of India," he declaimed in the House of Commons early in 1931. Britons, after all, had earned "rights of our own in India." Think of the English women and children "in hourly peril amidst the Indian multitudes," he urged his fellow members of Parliament, and of the future to which, "step by step and day by day, we are being remorselessly and fatuously conducted."

There was more. The negotiations between Gandhi and Lord Irwin, Churchill fulminated in print in September 1931, would produce "nothing but further surrenders of British authority." For lacking British control and guidance, he asserted, India would revert to heathenism, "with its palaces and temples, its shrines and its burning gnats, its priests and ascetics, its mysterious practices and multiform ritual . . . unchanged through the centuries, untouched by the West." Thus, Churchill indicated, India would deprive itself of its rank of the most treasured colony in the British Empire, "from which all blessings flow."

He sneered at the Mahatma. When Gandhi reached the imperial headquarters in Delhi, Churchill spluttered: "It is alarming and also nauseating to see Mr. Gandhi, a seditious Middle Temple lawyer, now posing as a fakir of a type well known in the East, striding half naked up the steps of the viceregal palace, while he is still organizing and conducting a defiant campaign of civil disobedience to parley on equal terms with the representative of the king-emperor [George V]."

When transmitted to India, Churchill's choice of words only aggravated Indian ill will; at home, it only magnified Churchill's reputation for being foolish and fractious. Not surprisingly, therefore, in the cabinet of the so-called national government—the Labour-Conservative coalition of the early 1930s—Churchill had no place. Even when the Conservative Stanley Baldwin assumed the premiership in mid-1935, Churchill was merely a back bencher. His beloved British Empire was slipping away and, through his own words and deeds, Churchill now had entered into the political wilderness. To most observers in Great Britain, his political career was over.

CHAPTER 8

The Resurgence
of Roosevelt

1

The sun that never set on the British Empire was especially kind on the morning of July 21, 1932, for the opening in Ottawa, the charming capital of Canada, of the Imperial Economic Conference. The sky was bright, the thousands of flowers around the town were in full bloom, and the waters of the Rideau Canal and the Ottawa River, where they met at the base of Parliament Hill, were sparkling and clear. Long before 11:00 AM, the hour set for the opening of the gathering, the spacious lawn that stretched down from the Parliament buildings was filled with spectators, many of them Americans. The American flag flew on the new U.S. legation that faced back up the slope from right across Wellington Street; the Stars and Stripes were a reminder to Canadians (as if they needed reminding) of the proximity of the republic just to the south. Adding other touches of color were the scarlet coats of the Royal Canadian Mounted Police, who were standing stiffly on duty throughout the grounds or directing traffic and keeping the crowds in order.

Just a few minutes before eleven, the carillon in the Peace Tower, added to the center of the Houses of Parliament in 1927 as a monument to Canadians killed in World War I, chimed out Elgar's "Land of Hope and Glory." The crowds then heard the boom of guns and the martial strains of the approaching band of the

Canadian governor-general, the earl of Bessborough. Heads turned to watch as the crimson-coated guard of honor marched along Wellington Street from the east and on into the parliamentary grounds. Moments later, the lances of the mounted Dragoon Guards were seen approaching, glistening in the sunshine. Entering Parliament Square through the central gate, the horsemen assembled at the right and to the front of the Houses of Parliament. Following them, the governor-general stepped down from a gilded carriage, with red-coated footmen standing erect by each side of the landau's door. At a barked command, the band played "God Save the King."

Accompanied by two aides, the governor-general, in morning attire, entered the House of Commons. There he read a message of welcome from King George V and departed. Cheered by the throngs, he rode back to Government House, up on the bank of the Ottawa River.

The ceremony marked a memorable occasion for Canada, initiator and host of the conference, and indeed for much of the British Empire. For the first time, instead of the dominions going to Great Britain to confer on the issues of the day, Great Britain was going to one of the dominions. Stanley Baldwin led the British delegation; traveling with him was another important Conservative, Neville Chamberlain. Other delegations came from Newfoundland (not yet part of Canada), Australia, New Zealand, South Africa, Southern Rhodesia (now Zimbabwe), India, and Ireland. As they convened, they entered the chamber of the Canadian House of Commons, paneled to its lofty ceiling with the native stone of Manitoba. The seating arrangement was the same as that of the British House of Commons and the other legislative halls of the empire, with the government of the day and its parliamentary supporters sitting to the right of the Speaker and the Opposition on the left. The seats assigned to the Canadians were on the government side, and along with them were the Australians, New Zealanders, South Africans, Newfoundlanders, and Southern Rhodesians. The British delegation, which included seven cabinet ministers, sat across the aisle, beside the Indians and the Irish. To the relief of all, neither the Indians nor the Irish made any trouble.

Richard B. Bennett, the Canadian prime minister, stood before the central table and opened the negotiations. "Today," he said, "we are coming together tested by tribulation, wiser through experience, bound one to the other as joint heirs of a great past and of a great future to be built upon the foundations of a new and enduring plan of empire cooperation." Insisting that the work of the meeting be enduring, he stated: "This is not the time for ephemeral treaties. We must decide our course and follow it unswervingly. An arrangement terminable on short notice would, I fear, have but the effect of increasing the instability of conditions. And trade stability is essential to our recovery."

Bennett was referring to the economic crisis wrought by the Great Depression. The downturn had proved disastrous for all the advanced economies, but its ill effects had been aggravated by the American Smoot-Hawley tariff, passed by Congress and signed by President Hoover in 1930. The highest barrier to imports in American history, the measure had been intended to protect U.S. jobs by walling out foreign competition. Swiftly, however, other countries in retaliation had begun to raise their own protection, the result becoming worldwide policies of "beggar thy neighbor" and the shutdown of trade everywhere.

Canada in particular had felt aggrieved by limits placed on its lumber exports to the "mother country," Great Britain. But the other dominions, too, such as wool-shearing Australia, had been similarly frustrated; and Britain had experienced a diminution of its manufactured exports to the nations of the Commonwealth. All had agreed, therefore, to seek a formula for cooperation.

The cooperative spirit produced a series of arrangements collectively called the "Ottawa Agreements," and they opened the way to a wide-reaching policy of "imperial preference." The underlying principle was that Great Britain rescinded its nearly century-old ban on the taxation of food imports and adopted the slogan "home producers first, empire producers second, and foreign producers last." Since Britain's own farmers could not feed its population, the accords reached at Ottawa meant that Canada could ship its logs and beef, Ireland its potatoes, India its rice, New Zealand its butter, and Australia its mutton and wool to the "mother country" without having to pay duties. Great Britain in turn gained the right to export its factory-made products along with investment funds without discrimination.

But "foreign producers last"? The Ottawa negotiations raised tariff and other trade barriers to wheat from the Ukraine; consumer goods from Germany; and, above all, just about everything from the economic colossus of the world, the United States. Commonwealth leaders asserted loudly that they were not discriminating against America. But, of course, they were doing so, and indeed in response to America's own discrimination against them: "beggar thy neighbor."

In turn, Americans of nearly all political persuasions began to demand an end to the British imperial preferences. The demand was the one point on which Herbert Hoover and Franklin Roosevelt could agree during the presidential campaign of 1932. The clamor may have been hypocritical, but it also reflected the hardships brought about by the Great Depression in every quarter of the United States.

2

On another sunny day, this one in Washington fewer than four years before the Ottawa conference, Herbert Hoover stood on the inaugural stand outside the Capitol to take the presidential oath of office. In his muffled, droning voice, he declared: "I have no fears for the future of our country. It is bright with hope. . . . In no nation are the fruits of accomplishment more secure."

Eight months later, on Black Tuesday, October 29, 1929, stock prices on Wall Street fell, producing the most disastrous day in the history of the market. The next day, Wednesday, brought hope, for prices held firm throughout the trading session. To prevent further panic, Richard Whitney, vice president of the exchange, canceled all bidding for the rest of the week. When Wall Street reopened on

Monday, November 4, however, prices continued to tumble. By Christmas 1929, stocks listed in New York had lost 40 percent of their value: $26 billion of President Hoover's "fruits of accomplishment" were gone.

Publicly at first, Hoover refused to recognize the existence of a crisis. "Our joint undertaking," he told the U.S. Chamber of Commerce on May 1, 1930, "has succeeded to a remarkable degree." The extent of the collapse "has been greatly diminished. I am convinced we have now passed the worst and with continued unity of effort we shall rapidly recover." Hoover's was a vision of renewed housing construction, diminished joblessness, and expanded business confidence —and it clashed directly with what was taking place in the streets of America.

Agriculture had been in a depression throughout the 1920s, but now the distress had reached the industrial sector: even as Hoover spoke to the Chamber of Commerce, some 4 million American workers had no jobs. All over America, breadlines snaked around city blocks; men in ragged coats and grimy caps shuffled forward and reached their hands for crusts of bread and cups of coffee. Shelters for the poor were overcrowded, and New York City had to allow homeless men to sleep on municipal barges, docked at night at piers along the East River. In Detroit, reported William Green, president of the American Federation of Labor (AFL), "the men are sitting in the parks all day long and all night long, hundreds and thousands of them, muttering to themselves, out of work, seeking work."

The search for work was disheartening. At first came slowdowns, with the workweek reduced from six or five days to three or two. Then followed the layoffs. The quest for a new job uncovered nothing. Clothes and shoes began to wear out. Savings ended and borrowing began: loans from life insurance, family, and friends, extensions from landlords, and credit from merchants. Jewelry was pawned and furniture was sold. Hungry families moved into cheap rooms. Every night in the autumn of 1930, men gathered at the lower level of Wacker Drive, where Lake Michigan met the Chicago River, in the words of a historian of the Depression, "feeding fires with stray pieces of wood, their coat collars turned up against the cold, their caps pulled down over their ears, staring without expression at the black river, while above the automobiles sped comfortably along, bearing well-fed men to warm and well-lit homes."

Although President Hoover asserted that "voluntary organizations and community service" could take care of those without work, 1931 proved even worse. Almost every city in America came to be ringed with shacks, often made of cardboard and tarpaper and known as "Hoovervilles." People scrounged for food in garbage cans. Unemployment grew—from 4 million in March 1930 to 8 million in March 1931. With tax revenues drying up, states and municipalities found it ever more difficult to provide relief. Hoover appointed committees to study the matter and urged Congress to balance the budget.

With the crisis still worse in the spring of 1932, Edward F. McGrady, speaking for the AFL, testified before a committee of Congress that the "leaders of our organization have been preaching patience . . . [but] I say to you gentlemen . . . that if something is not done and starvation is going to continue the doors of revolution in this country are going to be thrown open." Stop trying to balance the budget, he entreated his listeners: "There are another two B's besides balancing the budget, and that is to provide bread and butter."

In fairness to Hoover, it must be said that probably no previous president had worked harder. Up early every morning for exercise, he was invariably at his desk by eight-thirty. There he worked from breakfast to bedtime as lines of worry deepened along his face. His eyes became bloodshot. "I am so tired," people heard him say, "that every bone in my body aches."

His dismal mood mirrored the nation's sense of gloom. Pacing about the White House, he stared through the servants as if they did not exist: "never a good-morning or even a nod of the head," wrote Ike Hoover, the White House usher. If someone ventured to speak to him, his reply was a grudging moan. He neither conversed nor relaxed. "There was always a frown on his face and a look of worry," Ike Hoover remembered; the president never laughed. A secretary asked why he took no time to chat. "I have other things to do," he replied, "when a nation is on fire."

•   •   •

Hoover was right about one thing: the nation was on fire. In 1932, unemployment rose to 12 million. That figure meant that almost one of every four American workers was out of a job. Statistics like that went on and on. In 1932, net investment (measured in 1929 prices) fell from minus $358 million the year before to a stunning minus $5.8 billion. According to the index of the Federal Reserve Board, manufacturing production dropped from 110 in 1929 to 57 in 1932; total wage payments fell by almost half. More specifically, in July 1932, the Pennsylvania Department of Labor calculated that in the field of building contracting wages had fallen to 7.5 cents an hour, in brick and tile manufacturing to 6 cents an hour, and in the sawmills to 5 cents an hour. Women in Tennessee textile mills were earning $2.39 for 50-hour weeks. Girls working in Connecticut sweatshops were making as little as 60 cents for 55-hour weeks. Workers lucky enough to have jobs were crying out for the right to bring home a "living wage."

Such were the numbers; what mattered were the people. In New York, people were living in huts in Central Park. In Chicago, city workers went for months without pay. In the coal fields of Pennsylvania, miners ate weeds and dandelions. In Kentucky, children went to school without coats or shoes. In Oakland, California, a four-year-old girl who had been abandoned among garbage cans died of starvation. In Northampton, Massachusetts, a father of eight, bereft of hope, committed suicide.

Early in May 1932, in Portland, Oregon, a group of veterans of World War I concluded that bonus money for their military service, due them by an act of Congress in 1945, might as well be paid up in 1932. They were hungry, and their children were emaciated. Led by a former sergeant named Walter W. Waters, they set out for Washington, riding the rails and accepting handouts. Joined by other veterans along the route, they called themselves the "Bonus Expeditionary Force," a derisive reference to the wartime British Expeditionary Force. Reaching the nation's capital, they encamped on the marshy flats along the Anacostia River where it flowed into the Potomac. Wearing their old uniforms, they erected army surplus tents, stood in line for chow, and rose and slept to the call of a bugle, just as they had done in the fields of France.

Hoping to shame Congress into granting the money, the men of the Bonus Army were a military force in all respects save one: they had no weapons. In late July 1932, nonetheless, President Hoover had had enough of their presence, almost in view of the White House. Upon his orders, a contingent of U.S. Army cavalry, tanks, and infantry with fixed bayonets descended on the Anacostia flats, with the intent of dispersing the embarrassing veterans. In command of the attack was General Douglas MacArthur; his principal aide was Major Dwight D. Eisenhower. Reaching the flats, the contingent fired off tear-gas canisters, set fire to the tents, and at rifle-point sent the Bonus Army fleeing into the countryside. President Herbert Hoover had used U.S. soldiers against American citizens assembled peaceably, as was their right under the First Amendment of the Constitution of the United States of America.

Hoover's dispersal of the veterans in Washington coincided exactly with the convening of the Imperial Economic Conference in Ottawa. On the surface, the two events had nothing to do with each other. In reality, they were intimately connected. Both were responses to the hardships wrought worldwide by the Great Depression. The Britannic reaction was to repress free trade; Hoover's reaction was to repress what he saw as revolution.

Yet one man at least understood that repression was no solution to anything. Although probably the least ideological person on the face of the earth, he believed by background, education, and instinct that the only road to recovery lay in freedom: freedom at home and freedom abroad. And if the world had to be forced to be free, so be it. He was the governor of New York, Franklin Delano Roosevelt.

3

After the failure of the Democratic ticket in the presidential election of 1920, Roosevelt returned to New York, dabbling in a Wall Street legal practice. He was resolved to wait until, as he put it in a letter to a friend, "this bunch in Washington show either that they can make good or that they are hopeless failures." To keep himself in the public eye, Roosevelt helped to organize the Woodrow Wilson Foundation, raised funds for the construction of the Cathedral of St. John the Divine in New York City, served as a trustee for Vassar College and Harvard University, became chairman of the Navy Club, and chaired the New York branch of the Boy Scouts of America.

"Thank the Lord," he wrote to Stephen Early, his advance man in the 1920 campaign, "we are both comparatively youthful!"

Then disaster struck.

On a bright, warm day in the middle of August 1921, while vacationing with his family at the cottage his mother owned at Campobello, an island in southwestern New Brunswick, Canada, near the coast of Maine, Roosevelt slipped off his sailboat. Since he was an experienced sailor, this had never happened before. Although he felt a chill, he paid it no attention. After more sailing and swimming the next day, he sat on the beach in a wet bathing suit, going through the mail. Feeling even colder than before, he went back to the cottage and, not wanting to infect his children with what seemed to be some kind of influenza, he went upstairs to bed. Franklin Delano Roosevelt never walked again.

Unable to move his toes or even to sit up, Roosevelt, in terrible pain and flat on his back in bed, spent weeks in agony. At last a doctor from Boston diagnosed the problem. The situation was perfectly plain: the disease was poliomyelitis, infantile paralysis.

Desperate to believe that Roosevelt could still pursue a political career, the ever-faithful Louis Howe told reporters that there would be no lasting paralysis. He even managed to slip Roosevelt, unseen by the press, down to New York's Presbyterian Hospital. Every turn and jerk of the train along the way racked Roosevelt with pain. Even after weeks of medical attention it seemed likely to many that Roosevelt's life in government was over.

He soon regained the use of his upper body, but his mother thought the best thing for him was to come home to Hyde Park and live as an invalid, much as his elderly father once had lived. She would take care of him. He could survive as a member of the landed gentry, pursuing old interests such as print and stamp collecting. But, according to Sara, he would have to give up any participation in the affairs of the world.

Eleanor Roosevelt would have none of it. Although shy, self-effacing, and self-doubting, and wounded irrevocably by the affair Franklin had pursued with her social secretary, Lucy Mercer, back in Washington, she confronted her mother-in-law for the first time. Franklin someday would be able to get out of the house, Eleanor insisted, speaking again to audiences and taking up his career where perforce he had left it off. Her willpower and discipline were staggering. Even while Franklin was still convalescing, she became his source of inspiration, ever trying to pull him back from the depths of depression.

His life nonetheless was in limbo, and a year and a half after his seizure, his doctors told him that he would never regain the use of his legs. Roosevelt, however, was an American aristocrat, and bred into his blue blood was the conviction that the rules that bound others did not apply to him. Refusing to accept the prognosis, he worked assiduously at every kind of exercise that seemed to promise improvement. Nothing worked, but true to the aristocratic code, he never complained. He did not even mention his paralysis. In the presence of his wife, mother, and children in the Hyde Park mansion, he always made sure to maintain a cheerful façade.

It was a façade nonetheless. By 1924 Roosevelt had come to regard Hyde Park as a trap, a luxurious prison from which he needed by all means to escape. That year, he bought a houseboat he named the *Larooco* and headed south. With the craft lazing off the coast of Florida, he swam, fished, joked with old friends, and filled his days with endless good times. He took in the sunshine, which he had persuaded himself would be beneficial, and he exercised constantly in the sand and the surf.

Yet there were many days aboard the *Larooco* when it would be noon before he could bear to drag himself forth from his cabin and face the others aboard the craft. These people, friends from prep school and college, and the years in Washington, were sympathetic, encouraging, even loving, but their support brought no improvement.

Roosevelt, however, refused to give up hope. Someday, some-how, he was determined, he would be back on the national scene.

To prepare for that return, Louis Howe persuaded Eleanor Roo-sevelt to keep her husband's name before the public eye. Under Howe's tutelage, she transformed herself from a woman of morbid shyness to a speaker who could equal anyone before an audience. Learning to talk with ease on almost any topic, she became a force in her own right in the women's division of the New York State Democratic Party. Running meetings, she discovered that she had a talent for organizing and dealing with people.

And for helping people, particularly from her position of pri-vilege. Embracing the major reform causes of the day, such as pub-lic housing and workers' compensation, she found within herself a power she had never supposed to exist. Yet she reminded New York voters constantly that her husband intended to be back with them soon.

His return had to wait. In 1924 the national Democrats invited Roo-sevelt to attend their nominating convention, and he delivered a speech but played no further part in the campaign. In the autumn, while he was at home, some New York Democrats asked him to run for governor. He quickly rejected the idea.

Still searching for a cure, Roosevelt abandoned Hyde Park again. He had heard that at Warm Springs, a village in western Georgia, minerals in the nearby waters possessed miraculous restorative powers. Such at least was the local legend. It was not so. Nonetheless, the temperature of the water gushing out of the side of a mountain was as high as ninety degrees, and mineral salts made the water buoyant, allowing for easy swimming and other aquatic exercise.

After making the journey to Warm Springs, Roosevelt found a new purpose in life. With money borrowed from his mother and taken from his own fortune, he bought on the edge of town a hotel and a row of cottages that were a once-famous and now run-down spa. Roosevelt saw the chance to turn the place into a modern rehabilitation center for those with polio. Refurbishing the cottages and constructing a swimming pool, he made the establishment the first such institution in the United States. Soon hundreds of polio victims from all over the nation were joining Roosevelt in the piney woods of Georgia.

Roosevelt biographers have discussed at length whether the polio affected his character, making him less frivolous and more patient than before, or whether the passing of years alone gave him maturity. This much is clear: at Warm Springs, Roosevelt for the first time in his life gave himself to helping others. Whether or not people at Warm Springs actually got better, they felt better, and they believed that with "Dr. Roosevelt" cavorting with them in the pool, anything was possible. Roosevelt delivered hope.

The simple white cottage he built in Warm Springs became for Roosevelt a symbol of liberation. Outfitting a Ford Model A with hand brakes and accelerator, he frequently made his way into the countryside, driving fast, feeling emancipated. He visited with the people, the hardscrabble farmers, the kinds of Americans he had never met before. Everywhere he went, he saw the shanties, heard the stories about the lack of electricity, learned about the low prices for crops. He was encountering the depths of poverty, and he did not sneer at it. No matter how lowly a farmer's status, Roosevelt had a kind word, a smile, a wave. Rural Georgians in turn loved Roosevelt. The years in Warm Springs were preparing him for his reentry into politics.

At Warm Springs, furthermore, Roosevelt could bide his time. In the presidential election of 1924, John W. Davis, the lackluster and nearly unknown lawyer whom the Democrats chose as their candidate, went down to ignominious defeat. Trying to recover his health in Warm Springs, Roosevelt was not associated with the loss, and no one could blame him for staying out of the fray.

He was out of sight but not out of mind. While at Warm Springs and during occasional visits to Hyde Park, Roosevelt, with the help of Louis Howe, maintained a filing system of thousands of index cards in dozens of shoe boxes. On those cards were the names and addresses of Democrats throughout the country, along with any available pieces of information about them: Democrats Roosevelt had met at Albany, Washington, and during his vice-presidential campaign; Democratic labor leaders he had met by taking the *Larooco* into Miami; southern Democrats who had visited him in Warm Springs; Democrats written about in the newspapers to which Roosevelt subscribed nationwide; Democrats to whom he could write letters of congratulation if they had won office, and messages of condolence and encouragement if they had lost. If he could travel little, he could write much, maintaining political friendships back in New York.

In 1926 the New York Democratic Party offered him the nomination to run for the U.S. Senate. Pleading ill health, he turned it down. In the Senate he would have to cast votes that would antagonize someone somewhere. Besides, in the Senate, Roosevelt would have been merely one among ninety-five other colleagues, and a freshman at that. Roosevelt had no intention of being subordinate to anyone.

The year 1928, however, was different. As their candidate for the presidency that year the Democrats nominated Al Smith, the whiskey-drinking, cigar-chewing Roman Catholic politician from Manhattan's Lower East Side and governor of New York. This time Roosevelt plunged into the campaign, delivering the nominating speech in which he christened Smith the "happy warrior" and using his network of contacts to build support for Smith. Smith in turn offered Roosevelt the New York gubernatorial nomination. Back in Warm Springs, Roosevelt feigned reluctance. Desperate for patronage, the New York Democrats nominated him anyway.

Smith, of course, lost the presidential election but Roosevelt, barely, won the governorship. So on the first day of 1929, amid the booming of guns and the playing of martial music, Franklin Roosevelt took the oath of office of governor of the state of New York. Theodore Roosevelt had taken the same oath of office; Franklin Roosevelt was now back on track.

By tradition, the governorship of New York had been an apprenticeship for the presidency of the United States. By 1929, Albany had already produced five presidents: Martin Van Buren, Millard Fillmore, Chester A. Arthur, Grover Cleveland, and the Republican Roosevelt. Such prominence in national politics was hardly accidental. New York was the biggest state in just about everything: electoral votes, population, industry, commerce, banking and investment, farming, and, compared to the rest of the Northeast, area. But size was not the only measure of New York; it called itself the "Empire State." In an America of growing imperial ambitions, New York City was fast becoming the cultural center of the world.

By the 1920s it also had become the center of the latest medium of mass communications, the radio. Based in New York City, the radio networks provided Governor Roosevelt with an ideal soundstage from which to run for the White House. While in Albany, Roosevelt honed to perfection the art of speaking through a microphone. A natural aristocrat, he felt no need to talk in jargon or grandiloquent language. His broadcasts to the people of New York were direct, plain, and easily comprehensible. His idiom was that of the King James Bible and the Book of Common Prayer; it enabled him to appeal directly to the American people as they suffered through the Great Depression.

The day after Roosevelt's landslide reelection in 1930, Louis Howe and James A. Farley, the quintessential political operator who had aligned himself with the governor, announced Roosevelt's intention to run for the presidency. Roosevelt's chances of victory seemed great. His background had earned him popularity in the cities and countryside alike. He was a northerner who had planted deep roots in the South. He bore the magic name of Roosevelt and, speaking on the radio, he was the great communicator of his era. He also was not Herbert Hoover. By the early spring of 1932, Roosevelt's claim on the White House had taken on all the characteristics of the classic political bandwagon.

Supporters were eager to jump aboard: the New York financier Herbert H. Lehman; Henry Morgenthau Jr., Roosevelt's Hyde Park neighbor and son of another New York financier who had worked for Woodrow Wilson; and yet another financier, with ties in New York and Boston, Joseph P. Kennedy. Lesser figures, too, clambered on, and their variety mirrored modern America: professors and business-men; Ku Klux Klan members and African Americans; populists and progressives; southerners and northerners; easterners and westerners. A cross section of America reposed its hopes in the governor of New York, and the Roosevelt nomination appeared a sure thing.

Late in the spring, however, the Roosevelt march slowed to a crawl. Supposedly finished in politics, Al Smith overwhelmed Roosevelt in the Massachusetts primary. In the California primary, Roosevelt fell behind the white-haired, blue-eyed, cigar-smoking Speaker of the U.S. House of Representatives from Uvalde, Texas, John Nance Garner. Thus as the Democrats convened in the Chicago Auditorium Building late in June 1932, the delegates were divided among the big-city anti-Prohibitionist Smith; the rural Pro-hibitionist Garner; and Roosevelt, the patrician who had positioned himself in the middle.

But the middle was right where Roosevelt wanted to be, and his strategy of inclusiveness, along with promises to Democratic con-servatives to balance the budget, paid off in the end. In the swelter-ing heat of July 3, the Democrats nominated Roosevelt to run against Hoover.

Roosevelt responded to the nomination with precedent-breaking drama. By tradition, the nominees of both parties had stayed away from their conventions, waiting at home for a committee of dele-gates to come with their formal offers. Roosevelt instead went to the convention.

The flight from Albany was rough. Privately chartered, the tri-motored airplane was lightweight, bounced around by winds as it skirted Lake Erie and southern Michigan. Since the fuselage was unheated, Eleanor Roosevelt; Sam Rosenman, an aide; and others shivered in the cold. Seated in the tail of the plane, John, the youngest Roosevelt son, was airsick.

However, the trip from the Chicago airfield to the stage of the Auditorium Building, where the Democrats were waiting late at night on July 3, was a triumphal procession. Roosevelt had been planning for this moment for years. Having spend a decade of doing exercises to strengthen his upper body, he had developed a grip of iron. So by holding the handle of a cane in one hand and with the other clamping onto the forearm of someone else, often James, his oldest son, and thus swinging his braced legs forward, Roosevelt had learned to create the illusion of walking. Since this mode of loco-motion was slow and painful, he sustained the illusion by forcing himself to chat amiably with the other person, or with people at the front of a crowd, as if he had all the time in the world. Even so, he and his aides had to plan his entrance onto a stage with care. Any jostling by well-wishers would cause him to topple over. He had to have a clear path to the podium. The podium itself had to be fas-tened securely to the floor, because the only way he could stand to speak was by holding on to an edge of the lectern; otherwise he would be in free fall. Thus did Roosevelt, in the greatest victory of his personal life to that point as the band played "Happy Days Are Here Again," reach the podium on the stage of the Chicago Audi-torium Building.

Accepting the nomination and gesticulating with his free right hand, he launched into his address. "Ours must be a party of liberal thought, of planned action, of enlightened international outlook, and of the greatest good to the greatest number of our citizens," he declared. Attacking the Hoover administration for its failure to engender economic recovery, he endorsed the liberal Democratic platform "100 percent." At the end he concluded: "I pledge you, I pledge myself" to give the American people "a new deal."

The next day, Roosevelt spoke to the Democratic National Com-mittee. "The campaign," he stated, "starts . . . tonight."

Was Roosevelt himself to take part in the campaign? Given his physical infirmity, his mother and wife begged him to stay at Hyde Park, give a few addresses on the radio, and confine himself to the front-porch strategy, in the manner of McKinley and Harding.

Roosevelt would have none of it. In an age in which families kept their crippled members stuck away in back rooms, with the shades drawn, as if paralysis were a kind of shame, Roosevelt believed it imperative that he show himself in public, proving to skeptics that he was vigorous, fully capable of performing the duties of president. Besides, he was fully confident of his ability to run an arousing campaign.

"There are two great actors in America," Roosevelt is supposed to have said once to the Hollywood star Orson Welles, "and you're the other one." Perhaps by instinct but more likely once again in emulation of Theodore Roosevelt, Franklin was about to prove himself the master of political stagecraft. Some of this was luck: like TR succeeding McKinley, FDR had in Hoover a good act to follow. Like TR, FDR knew the importance of a grand opening: hence the flight to Chicago. He also understood the need of a good supporting cast: TR had had his rambunctious boys and the princess of the age, his daughter Alice; standing before crowds, FDR would get laughs by introducing the towering James as "my little boy Jimmy." Traveling in trains covered with American flags and red, white, and blue bunting, and huge photographs of the famed TR teeth and pince-nez, Theodore had shown that the visual beats the verbal every time. Franklin outfitted his campaign train the same way and, holding on to the railing at the back of the rear carriage, would electrify onlookers with the toss of his head and his magnetic smile. Although aristocrats, both Roosevelts spoke plainly, using the concrete language their audiences could understand. Both insisted that their trains keep to schedule, departing from stations abruptly and leaving the onlookers wanting more. Most important, like TR, who had kept himself at center stage by portraying himself as the good guy who flayed the bad guy (the monopolist J. Pierpont Morgan), FDR offered America little by way of programs and a lot by way of picturing Hoover as the villain of the century.

Opening the campaign in August at Columbus, Ohio, Franklin Roosevelt launched a scathing indictment of Hooverian economics. In mid-September, in Topeka, Kansas, he dwelt at length on the failures of Hoover's farm policies. At Salt Lake City he lit into Hoover's refusal to countenance the regulation of railroad rates. At Portland, Oregon, he charged Hoover with allowing power companies to gouge the public. Returning to the Midwest, Roosevelt stopped at Sioux City, Iowa, to lambaste Hoover and the Smoot-Hawley tariff.

Throughout this swing around the West and Midwest, people turned out in huge numbers, in railroad yards behind the train, in auditoriums in the cities, in open fields in the farmland, eager to hear what this new Roosevelt had to say. He offered them not programs but showmanship. As a Roosevelt biographer described it, "[p]eople began to look for the Roosevelt characteristics: the up-thrust head; the confident look with the eyebrows arched when he let fly a gibe at the opposition, followed by the slow grin as the audience caught on; the sly mockery; the biting scorn; the righteous wrath." Played before spectators all across the country, Roosevelt's was a sold-out performance.

Henry Adams, historian and descendant of two American presidents, had deemed Theodore Roosevelt to be "pure act." So it was with Franklin Roosevelt.

In the middle of October, with the trees from Washington to Boston turning scarlet and gold, Hoover at last tried to strike back. He, too, went to the country to make speeches, but his style was dry and his substance was self-defensive. On the last day of October he appeared at Madison Square Garden and gave exactly the sort of speech Roosevelt had hoped he would deliver. The campaign was "a contest between two philosophies of government." Roosevelt, Hoover charged, was "proposing changes and so-called new deals which would destroy the very foundations of our American system." But those foundations were already on the verge of destruction, and Hoover was only acknowledging his own defeat.

On the night before the election in November, Roosevelt spoke by radio from Hyde Park and broadcast his final lines: "You may not have universally agreed with me, but you have universally been kind and friendly to me. The great understanding and tolerance of America came out to meet me everywhere; for all this you have my heartfelt gratitude." He concluded: "Out of this unity that I have seen we may build the strongest strand to lift ourselves out of this Depression."

The next day Americans went to the polls. President Hoover had repaired to his mansion in Palo Alto, California, with Lou Henry, his wife, and virtually no one else. Roosevelt stayed in a room beside the Democratic headquarters on the first floor of the Biltmore Hotel in New York City. Unlike Hoover, he was hardly alone: Eleanor and the children were present, as were Sam Rosenman; Henry Morgenthau; and Roosevelt's top economic adviser, Raymond Moley. James A. Farley came and went, scurrying about with reports. Louis Howe kept away, hardly daring to hear the returns.

The early results were mixed. Massachusetts and Rhode Island were going for Roosevelt; the rest of New England was with Hoover. Not surprisingly, New York was in Roosevelt's camp. But Pennsylvania and Delaware were voting Republican. The mood in the Biltmore was tense in the extreme. Then the fear turned to joy. The tallies from the South, solidly Democratic ever since the Civil War, came in for Roosevelt. The rest was a Democratic landslide.

Two decades before, in Albany, Louis Howe had purchased a bottle of sherry, putting it away for the day that Franklin D. Roosevelt would be elected to the White House. Now, showing up at last in the Biltmore, he uncorked the bottle; filled glasses; and, raising his own, addressed himself to the crippled man seated in an armchair, saying, "To the next president of the United States!"

4

Saturday, March 4, 1933, was Inauguration Day. Leaving his suite in the Mayflower Hotel at L Street and Connecticut Avenue in Washington, Roosevelt rode the short distance to attend a morning service at St. John's Episcopal Church, the house of worship on the edge of Lafayette Square. As the Roosevelt family moved into a red-cushioned pew, the organ and the choir filled the little sanctuary with the majesty of an ancient Protestant hymn:

> Our God, our Help in ages past,
> Our Hope for years to come.
> Our Shelter from the stormy blast,
> And our eternal Home.

Frances Perkins, the New York social worker appointed by Roosevelt as the secretary of labor, described the moment: "The economy was at a standstill. If ever a man wanted to pray, that was the day." Roosevelt did want to pray, and he wanted the American people to pray for him.

Under a bleak and cheerless sky, an open limousine took Roosevelt around the park and came to a halt under the North Portico of the White House. Hoover took a seat beside the president-elect. During the ride to the Capitol, Hoover sat glum and mute, and Roosevelt, thinking he had to do something, began to wave his silk top hat to the crowds, and he kept waving it until he got to the entrance of the House of Representatives.

As he made his way to the podium on the inaugural stand, Roosevelt appeared to be walking, but in fact he was pressing down on James's arm with his powerful grip. Below and beyond the platform, a vast crowd waited in silence. Coming into their view, Roosevelt turned to face the chief justice of the United States, appointed by Hoover in 1930, Charles Evans Hughes.

Repeating the oath of office, President Franklin Delano Roosevelt addressed the multitude gathered on the Capitol Plaza and the millions of Americans gathered by their radios throughout the land. The wind tossed the pages of his speech.

"This is a day of national consecration," he began. "This is pre-eminently the time to speak the truth, the whole truth, frankly and boldly. Nor need we shrink from honestly facing conditions in our country today. This great nation will endure as it has endured, will revive and prosper."

The huge crowd was still silent and still waiting. "So first of all, let me assert my firm belief that the only thing we have to fear is fear itself."

Roosevelt's chin was outthrust and his face was grave. "If I read the temper of our people correctly, we now realize as we have never realized before our interdependence on each other . . . ; that if we are to go forward, we must move as a trained and loyal army willing to sacrifice for the good of a common discipline. . . . We are, I know, ready and willing to submit our lives and our property to such discipline, because it makes possible a leadership which aims at a larger good. This I propose to offer. . . . I shall ask the Congress for . . . broad executive power to wage a war against the emergency, as great as the power that would be given to me if we were in fact invaded by a foreign foe."

Roosevelt closed with a prayer. Then he waved to the crowd, flashed his dazzling smile, and left for the White House.

When President Roosevelt entered the executive mansion that afternoon, the United States of America was without hope. Its farms had long since failed; its factories more recently had failed; and now its banks were about to fail. The American financial engine that ever since World War I had fueled the economy of the world had run out of gas. The military machine that had secured the salvation of the Allies a decade and a half before was reduced to the size of the army of Guatemala. And the inspiring words of Woodrow Wilson, that soaring vision of a world remade in the image of America, had disintegrated into the grumbling and mumbling of Herbert Hoover.

A dozen years later, with the end of World War II, all would be different. The American economy would become the envy of people around the world. The American military would come to have at its disposal the greatest might in the history of humanity. And the American president, Franklin D. Roosevelt, would have wrought the most significant transformation of international relations since the fall of Napoleon Bonaparte, the transference of world leadership from the *Pax Britannica* to the *Pax Americana*.

CHAPTER 9

The British Declaration of War

1

In his inaugural address, Roosevelt had made his priorities clear. "I shall spare no effort to restore world trade by international economic adjustment," he had declared, "but the emergency at home cannot wait on that accomplishment."

Confronted by the Great Depression, all the major powers had turned to protectionism. The United States had its Smoot-Hawley tariff and Great Britain had mounted its system of imperial preferences. But France, too, had sought to surround itself and its colonies in Africa and Southeast Asia with obstacles to competition. Then, denied access to the markets of America, Japan in 1931 had seized Manchuria, renamed it Manchukuo (Manchu Country), and used it to create a zone of political and commercial autonomy. And, taking power in Germany only days before Roosevelt's inauguration, Adolf Hitler and his Nazi minions dreamed of *Lebensraum* (living space), a realm to the south and east in which Germany would reign supreme and secure itself against the buffeting of the global crisis.

This division of the world into separate, walled-off blocs took place in deliberate defiance of the principle of free trade. In his famous tome *The Wealth of Nations*, the eighteenth-century Scottish economist Adam Smith had put forth the rationale of unhampered commerce. He had used the example of trade between Great Britain and Portugal. With its temperate, rainy climate, which meant that sheep could safely graze, Britain was well suited for the manufacture of woolen cloth. Hotter and dryer, with sandy soil, Portugal was a natural producer of wine. So Britain could ship cloth to Portugal, and Portugal sherry and port to Britain, and both countries would profit. But suppose that tariffs and other governmentally imposed barriers to free commerce blocked such exchanges. Britain would have to make its own wine, Portugal its own wool, and since neither could do so efficiently, if at all, the costs would be prohibitive. With tariffs, both would lose; without tariffs, both would win.

Roosevelt and at least many of his advisers understood this analogy. They also knew well that when Great Britain in the 1840s had repealed its Corn Laws, or grain tariffs, subjecting British agriculture to foreign competition, world trade had begun its greatest expansion ever.

Theory and history were one thing, however, and immediate political pressures were another. First and foremost, Roosevelt had to produce the domestic relief measures promised in his inaugural address.

In the four months between his election and his inauguration, Roosevelt by and large had kept silent, not revealing plans and so keeping expectations down. Once in office, though, ever the actor, he threw off the guise of passivity and hurled himself into the drama of the first hundred days.

Before anything else, Roosevelt had to deal with the crisis in banking. By the day he became president, nearly half of the nation's banks had closed and more were on the verge of going under. What to do? On the morning of March 5, awakening for the first time in the White House, Roosevelt had himself wheeled to the Oval Office. Soon reporters assembled, expecting to see a president like Hoover, despondent and despairing. Rather, one Washington journalist wrote, "looking across under the shaded desk lamp sat the president, in a blue serge business suit. Sturdy-shouldered, smiling, calm, talking pleasantly with an occasional humorous sally, he was the picture of ease and confidence. As he talked, he deliberately inserted a fresh cigarette in an ivory holder. It was as if he was considering whether to sign a bill for a bridge in some faraway rural county."

Instead, Roosevelt signed a proclamation declaring that until Congress could meet (not until March 9, which was the earliest date that senators and representatives from the Pacific Coast could reach Washington), all banks would be closed. Then, with Congress in session, Roosevelt introduced a bill that would put federal dollars into financial institutions known for their worthiness. Added to this step was the creation of the Federal Deposit Insurance Corporation, intended to restore popular confidence in the banks.

So it went in those first hundred days: the creation of the Civilian Conservation Corps (an army of employment for youths); the Securities and Exchange Commission (intended to regulate Wall Street and chaired by the most skilled stock manipulator of the era, Joseph P. Kennedy); the Tennessee Valley Authority (designed to provide electricity to the rural poor); and above all, the National Recovery Administration (whose bureaucrats were to negotiate price floors in the various sectors of the economy and thus halt the collapse of prices and investment). Things were getting done, or such was the impression given out to the American people.

The Roosevelt White House certainly was a picture of cheer. Roosevelt would begin each day with breakfast in bed—coffee, toast, orange juice, and scrambled eggs from a tray laid across his lap. While eating, he would peruse the dozen or so newspapers to which he subscribed from across the country. After giving instructions to various advisers, he would have himself dressed and wheeled out of the bedroom, sometimes to the sunny, yellow-wallpapered second-story Oval Room, but usually to the Oval Office down the elevator and over in the West Wing. Behind his desk and receiving visitors, he was endlessly chatty and full of jokes.

By the late summer of 1933, however, not even Roosevelt could deny a fundamental point: his programs, collectively called the New Deal, were not lifting the nation out of the Depression, for the economic crisis hardly existed in one country alone. It was worldwide and, Roosevelt at last had to admit, its solution had to be worldwide.

And pushing the president always in the direction of that global relief was his secretary of state, Cordell Hull.

Hull was a "handsome man," wrote Dean Acheson, himself an eventual secretary of state. "He looked like a statesman in the classic American tradition—the tradition of the great Virginia dynasty, of Henry Clay, of Daniel Webster (but much handsomer, more like Warren Harding). His well-structured face was sad and thoughtful, his speech was slow and gentle." Formerly a representative and senator from Tennessee, Hull conveyed the air of a southern gentleman, and with his slight speech defect—he sometimes referred to a "wecipwocal twade agweement pwogwam to weduce tawiffs"—some people thought him meek and mild. That was a mistake. A suspicious man, he brooded over what he considered to be various indignities. The brooding led, Acheson noted, "in accordance with Tennessee-mountain traditions, to feuds. His hatreds were implacable —not hot hatreds, but long, cold ones. In no hurry to 'get' his enemy, 'get' him he usually did."

The greatest of Hull's enemies, at least until the advent of World War II, were those who had signed the Ottawa trade agreements. The imperial wall erected in Canada was, to Hull, the "king of evils," as he said repeatedly; it was the "largest single underlying cause of the present panic."

On taking office, Roosevelt was not fully convinced; he frequently disparaged Hull's persistent advocacy of free trade. In no way a systematic thinker, FDR had indeed accepted Hoover's protectionism without much reflection. Nevertheless, a major part of Roosevelt's political genius was his flexibility. During his years of struggle with polio, he had adopted the attitude that if one cure did not work, he would try another. So by 1934, with the New Deal propagating a host of agencies but not alleviating the nation's economic woes, Roosevelt was prepared to try something new. He finally agreed with Hull.

With his views shaped by his idol Woodrow Wilson, Hull was a quiet evangelist for the idea that "unhampered trade dovetailed with peace; high tariffs, trade barriers, and unfair economic competition [were conducive to] war," he wrote in his memoirs. Hull emphasized that by raising everyone's living standard, a "freer flow of goods eliminated the economic dissatisfaction that breeds war."

Dorothy Thompson, a popular newspaper columnist, described Hull as a "backwoods Tennessean, who looks very much like a gentle and long-suffering saint. . . . Yet this quiet man is a person of considerable force; this restrained man is capable of complete and almost fanatical devotion to an idea [the liberation of world trade] he believes in."

Once converted to Hull's point of view, Roosevelt decided that the way to end the Great Depression at home was to push American goods into markets abroad. To that end, Roosevelt and Hull forged two weapons still in the American arsenal: the Export-Import Bank (Ex-Im) and the Reciprocal Trade Act (RTA).

Ex-Im started off in a small-scale way, helping to finance trade with the Soviet Union (recognized by FDR in 1933) and with Cuba. But angry over the resistance of France and Great Britain to repaying their loans from World War I—Sir Ronald Lindsay, the British ambassador to the United States in the early 1930s, begged the United States to "forgive us our debts," but to no avail—Congress allowed Ex-Im to expand its aid to Americans seeking to invest in the French and British Empires.

The RTA, passed in June 1934, bore the full imprint of Cordell Hull. Granting the president the authority to reduce American tariffs by as much as 50 percent on another country's imports, as long as the country reciprocated, allowing American access to its own markets, the measure gave Roosevelt vast new powers to expand U.S. trade abroad. As Hull had conceived it, the RTA was a wrecking ball with which to knock down foreign tariff walls. And the major walls to be demolished were those of the British Empire.

2

The British Empire was facing other pressures as well. Indian agitation for independence was not about to be stilled. In Palestine, a territory acquired under the League of Nations mandate, for British authorities the problems caused by Jewish-Arab violence were proving insoluble. In East Asia, the 1931 Japanese invasion of Manchuria brought an end to the two-decade-long Anglo-Japanese alliance: clearly Great Britain's days as the preeminent foreign power along the China coast were numbered. And early in 1933, Adolf Hitler came to power in Germany.

On the evening of February 27, 1933, Hitler, recently elected as Germany's chancellor, was having dinner in a Berlin suburb with Josef Goebbels, propaganda chief of the Nazi Party. Relaxing with the Goebbels family, they were telling stories and listening to music on the record player. Suddenly, Goebbels would write in his diary, the telephone rang. On the line was Ernst Hanfstängl, a wealthy German who had gone to Harvard College and later attached himself to the Nazis as a sort of in-house intellectual. Hanfstängl seemed hysterical. "The Reichstag [the German parliament building] is on fire!" he blurted out. "I was sure that he was telling a tall tale," Goebbels explained, "and declined even to mention it to the Führer." In the center of Berlin, however, inside the exclusive Herrenklub on Vossstrasse, just around the corner from the Reichstag, President Paul von Hindenburg, the elderly general from World War I, and Franz von Papen, a civilian politician who at the moment was vice chancellor, also were dining together. While they were at the table, Papen recorded in his diary, "we noticed a red glow through the windows and heard sounds of shouting in the street. One of the servants came hurrying up and whispered, 'The Reichstag is on fire!' which I repeated to the president. He got up and from the window we could see the dome of the Reichstag looking as though it were illuminated by searchlights. Every now and then a burst of flame and a swirl of smoke blurred the outline."

After driving the elderly Hindenburg to his home, Papen steered back toward the burning building. In the meantime Goebbels had mulled over the telephone message, made some calls of his own, and learned of the fire. Soon he and Hitler were careening along the Charlottenburger Chaussée to, in Goebbels's words, "the scene of the crime."

Was the burning of the Reichstag an act of arson? The truth has never become clear. Goebbels nonetheless blamed the fire on Marinus van der Lubbe, a mentally retarded laborer with a possible Communist affiliation. Broadcasting the charge throughout Germany, Goebbels, Hitler, and others in the Nazi top echelon used the allegation to justify their complete takeover of the government.

Brilliantly cloaking the naked coup, Goebbels staged the transference of authority from Hindenburg to Hitler in the Garrison Chapel at Potsdam, the temple of Prussian militarism. There lay buried the bones of Frederick the Great; there Kaiser Wilhelm II and his royal ancestors had worshiped; and there Hindenburg himself, as a young officer fresh from Bismarck's war with Austria, the conflict that had launched Germany on its road to unification, had taken off his pointed helmet and bowed his head in prayer. The date Goebbels chose to mount the ceremony—March 21, 1933—also conjured up the Prussian past: it was the anniversary of the day when, in 1871, Otto von Bismarck, the Iron Chancellor, had officially opened the first parliamentary proceedings of the Second Reich. Now, at Potsdam, just outside Berlin, Hitler would proclaim the advent of the Third Reich.

Goebbels designed the event with consummate craft. Resplendent in uniforms from the days of Wilhelmine Germany, elderly generals and admirals filled the pews of the little Lutheran church. One seat remained empty: the box off the gallery once reserved for Kaiser Wilhelm II. As the service got under way, with a pastor present to render prayers, Hitler and Hindenburg, side by side, processed up the nave. Hitler was clad in a formal cutaway suit; Hindenburg was attired in a too-tight uniform of field gray, carrying his field marshal's baton in one hand and his spiked helmet in the other. Passing before the kaiser's empty place, they paused. Then they reached the altar. There the ancient general bestowed his blessing on the new regime of Adolf Hitler.

Scripted by Goebbels, Hitler's response linked the past with the present: "Neither the Kaiser nor the government nor the nation wanted the war. It was only the collapse of the nation which compelled a weakened race to take upon itself, against its most sacred convictions, the guilt for this war [World War I]." Then, facing Hindenburg, who was seated in the front pew, Hitler added: "By a unique upheaval in the last few weeks our national honor has been restored and, thanks to your understanding, *Herr Generalfeldmarschall*, the union between the symbols of the old greatness and the new strength has been celebrated. We pay you homage."

Stepping down from the altar, Hitler bowed low before Hindenburg and shook the hand of the ancient field marshal. Newsreel cameras that Goebbels had placed around the sanctuary recorded the moment, so that movie theaters around Germany could display the handclasp of the field marshal, and the former corporal, the continuity of the old Germany and the new.

Two days later, at the Kroll Opera House, where the deputies of the Reichstag had convened, Hitler introduced the "Law for Removing the Distress of People and Country." It was the enabling statute for the establishment of the Nazi totalitarian state.

Hitler's first objective in 1933 was the Nazification of Germany. This consolidation of power entailed the elimination of the individual states, largely self-governing in the decades since Bismarck; the destruction of the Communist Party and even middle-class organs such as the Catholic Bavarian People's Party; the dissolution of the labor and trade unions; the imposition of state control over both Catholic and Protestant churches; the early persecutions of Jews; and the crushing of part of the Nazi movement itself.

Tensions ran high between Hitler and Ernst Röhm, head of the SA (for Sturmabteilung, or Storm Division) and its 5½ million Brownshirts. In the "Night of the Long Knives," the Nazi term for the event, June 30, 1934, the Gestapo murdered Röhm and his top aides, eliminating the SA as a rival source of political power. Hitler then turned his attention to the world outside the Third Reich.

In 1933 and 1934, Germany's standing in the world was one of isolation and impotence. Alarmed by Hitler's rise to power, Marshal Józef Pilsudski, the dictator of Poland, approached the French and suggested a joint preventive war to oust Hitler. Nothing came of the initiative. But because of the anti-Communist purge in Germany, the Soviet Union, too, was hostile, and even Italy's Benito Mussolini looked with misgivings on Hitler's rise to power. Friendless, Nazi Germany possessed no military might, or certainly little in comparison with its immediate neighbors.

Given such weakness, Hitler set out to alleviate suspicions abroad. On May 17, 1933, Hitler appeared before the deputies of the Reichstag and responded with apparent enthusiasm to a call by President Roosevelt for universal disarmament. In the course of his speech, the Führer termed Germany "prepared to agree to any solemn pact of nonaggression, because she does not think of attacking but only of acquiring security." The British papers were impressed. The right-wing *Spectator* believed that Hitler had offered hope to a troubled world; the left-wing *Daily Herald* admired Hitler's "sincerity"; and the quasi-official *Times* considered Hitler's desire for security to be right and just. All ignored the warning buried in Hitler's text: that if Germany were not granted equality with the other great powers, it would strive to achieve that equality.

Equality for Hitler meant the removal of the restrictions placed on Germany by the Versailles Treaty: its strictures against German rearmament; its neutralization of the Rhineland; its prohibition of any union between Germany and adjacent German-speaking areas; and its separation of East Prussia from Germany proper, making Danzig a free city and granting Poland a corridor to the Baltic. Since neither Paris nor London nor Washington made any moves to eliminate these limitations, Hitler on October 14, 1933, withdrew Germany from the League of Nations. He took another step as well: he ordered General Werner von Blomberg, the minister of defense, to prepare Germany's token army against an armed attack from the outside.

None of the powers, though, had been about to attack Germany. As Hitler had calculated correctly, all were too preoccupied with the problems imposed by the Great Depression to concern themselves overly with what was going on inside the Third Reich.

What was taking place inside the Third Reich—besides the perse-cution of the churches, the imposition of Nazi ideals on the nation's institutions of education and culture, the censorship of the press, the enslavement of labor, and the abolition of an independent judiciary, in short, the creation of a full-fledged totalitarian state plus the ris-ing persecution of the Jews—was the beginning of Hitler's efforts to breach the Versailles Treaty. All patriotic Germans, even many Jews, regarded the terms of the treaty as unjust.

The first step in Hitler's campaign was rearmament. With the Röhm business settled in mid-1934, Hitler directed General Ludwig Beck, chief of the general staff, to increase the size of his army from one hundred thousand to three hundred thousand. Hitler also autho-rized Admiral Erich Räder, the naval chieftain, to start the building of two battle cruisers (known eventually as the *Scharnhorst* and the *Gneisenau*), at twenty-six thousand tons each almost twice as large as permitted by the Versailles Treaty. Hitler further allowed Räder at the Kiel naval base to assemble submarines, the parts of which the government of the preceding Weimar Republic had been construct-ing covertly in the shipyards of Spain, Finland, and Holland.

Hitler's own military buildup forged ahead in the strictest pos-sible secrecy. Since the Versailles Treaty had forbidden the very existence of a German general staff, Goebbels kept any mention of General Beck's organization out of the papers. All references to the work of the navy, too, were rigidly censored. The silence was designed to lull the European powers into quiescence, as well as to allow Hitler, with his instinct for the dramatic moment, to spring a Saturday surprise.

The Saturday in question was that of March 16, 1935: on that day, Hitler announced universal military service and the creation of an army of nearly 500,000 soldiers. He thus ended the military lim-itations imposed on Germany by the Versailles Treaty. As he had bet, the governments of France and Great Britain did nothing.

Sunday, March 17, 1935, was the *Heldengedenktag*, the Day of the Remembrance of Heroes. Attending the ceremony in the Kroll Opera House was William Shirer, an American reporter in Berlin and later the author of the best-selling *Rise and Fall of the Third Reich*.

The "entire lower floor was a sea of military uniforms," he wrote, "the faded gray uniforms and spiked helmets of the old imperial army mingling with the attire of the new army, including the sky-blue uniforms of the Luftwaffe, which few had seen before. At Hitler's side was Field Marshal [Hans Georg] von Mackesen, the last surviving field marshal of the kaiser's army, colorfully attired in the uniform of the Death's-Head Hussars. Strong lights played on the stage, where young officers stood like marble statues holding upright the nation's war flags. Behind them on an enormous curtain hung an immense silver-and-black Iron Cross."

Ostensibly the ceremony was a commemoration of those Germans who had died in World War I. Actually it was a celebration of the death of the Versailles Treaty and the rebirth of German military might, for Hitler's next target was the Rhineland.

In April 1935 Jean Dobler, the French consul in Cologne, noticed that everywhere he walked or drove—through the narrow, medieval streets; high along the banks of the Rhine; or out into the fertile countryside—he saw swarms of Germans erecting barracks, building depots, and laying out airfields, just what the Rhineland would need to shelter a Nazi army of occupation. Dobler informed the Quai d'Orsay in Paris of what he had seen, but the French government paid little attention.

Articles 42 and 43 of the Versailles Treaty had forbidden the emplacement of German forces and fortifications in the Rhineland, both on the left bank and in a zone extending fifty kilometers (thirty-one miles) to the east of the right bank. The prohibition had given France a measure of security, but in Germany it had created bitterness and resentment. So in the spring of 1935, while publicly promising to respect the territorial provisions of the treaty, Hitler was secretly planning to reoccupy the Rhineland and fill it once more with German arms and troops. He called his plan Operation Schulung (meaning "schooling" or "training"), to be executed as a surprise blow carried out with "lightning speed."

He made his preparations slowly, however, for his top generals feared an Allied counterattack. Finally, early on the morning of

Saturday, March 7, 1936—when, according to German intelligence Stanley Baldwin (again the British prime minister) and the rest of the cabinet had left London for the weekend in the countryside— Hitler struck.

The German advance guard consisted only of three soldiers on bicycles, as they pedaled over the mist-shrouded Hohenzollern Bridge at Cologne. As they reached the cathedral square, onlookers clapped in approval. Then the clapping turned into thunderous applause: following directly behind the bicycles marched line after line of German infantrymen, goose-stepping in perfect unison. As the soldiers passed before a reviewing stand for inspection by their general, the people for the moment fell silent: a little blond girl gave the general a bouquet of red carnations. With that, the crowd erupted with joy. A once-dignified German gentleman cried out: "The first soldier I get my hands on is going to get as cockeyed drunk at my expense as I did when I was a soldier in 1914—and I'm going to get cockeyed with him! *Heil* Hitler! Thanks be to God! *Deutschland über Alles!*"

The French government considered sending a force into the Rhineland, then reconsidered, simply filing a protest with the League of Nations. The British did not even contemplate action. A week after the Rhineland invasion, during a dinner party in London, Baldwin told Pierre Flandin, France's new foreign minister, that "if there is even one chance in a hundred that war would follow [a counterattack along the Rhine] I have not the right to commit England." The *Times* of London added a rationale. It was not as if Hitler were invading a foreign country: "He is only going into his own back garden."

Had the French and the British even budged, Hitler admitted, "we would have had to withdraw with our tails between our legs." In command of the invasion, General Alfred Jodl added: "Considering the situation we were in, the French covering army could have blown us to bits."

Emboldened, Hitler set his sights next on another territorial restriction of the Versailles Treaty, the prohibition against a union of Germany and Austria; for Austria also could be considered Germany's "back garden."

Not surprisingly, since it had been the land of Hitler's birth, Austria had its own, homegrown Nazi Party. Indeed, barely a year after the Reichstag fire, the Austrian Nazis had tried to mount their own coup d'état, bombing a power station outside Vienna and paralyzing the capital's bus-and-streetcar network. Austria's chancellor, Engelbert Dollfuss (a tiny man whom the Viennese had nicknamed *"Millimetternich,"* a miniature version of the nineteenth-century statesman Prince Klement von Metternich), had tried to suppress the insurgency. On July 25, 1934, however, a gang of Nazi gunmen burst in on Dollfuss while he was meeting with his cabinet and pumped him full of bullets. Then they laid him out on a settee where, clad only in shoes and trousers, he bled to death.

Nonetheless, the attempted takeover failed. Army officers loyal to Dollfuss quickly arrested the assassins and brought order to the streets of Vienna. Austria furthermore soon acquired a new chancellor, Kurt von Schuschnigg, the former minister of education who for the moment enjoyed the blessings of foreign support. Headlines in New York blazoned "war scare." The *Times* of London declared that the Dollfuss murder "makes the name of Nazi stink in the nostrils of the world." And Benito Mussolini, a personal friend of Dollfuss, ordered fifty thousand soldiers to the Brenner Pass, on Italy's frontier with Austria.

Stunned by the reaction, Hitler disavowed any connection with the Dollfuss affair. He only wanted, he avowed, to establish Germany's relations with Austria along "normal and friendly paths."

Hitler's apparent respect for Austria as an independent state, however, proved short-lived. On the afternoon of November 5, 1937, he met in his monumental Berlin office with some of the highest officials of the realm: Field Marshal Werner von Blomberg, who had become the minister of war; General Werner von Fritsch, commander of the army; Admiral Erich Räder, chief of the navy; General Hermann Göring, leader of the air force; and Baron Konstantin von Neurath, the foreign minister.

Also present was Colonel Friedrich Hossbach, Hitler's aide-de-camp. Hossbach served as stenographer.

As the officials took their seats around a large circular table, Hitler launched into a virtual monologue. Germany, he claimed, had to expand: the German people had the right to *Lebensraum*, living space beyond their existing borders, with the right to migrate into the countries to the east and to control food sources there, and to enjoy the blessings of a Greater Germany with frontiers more secure than they were at the moment.

Hitler's lecture went on from late afternoon until well after dark. When he finished, Hossbach rushed out to type the transcript of the meeting.

Nine years later, at the postwar Nuremberg trials, the prosecution introduced the "Hossbach Memorandum" as proof that Hitler at the meeting had stated his intention of starting a Europe-wide war. As the late British historian A. J. P. Taylor pointed out, however, such was not the case. Hitler hoped, rather, that Germany could achieve its expansionist aims without a great war. Nevertheless, Hitler's reason for calling the meeting was to persuade his listeners of the need for further rearmament, even at the cost of running a budgetary deficit. To Hitler, France and Great Britain were "hateful enemies" to whom "a strong German colossus in the center of Europe would be intolerable."

3

That statement by Hitler takes us to a great legend of modern international relations: the myth of appeasement, the "Munich analogy," the idea that Great Britain failed to stand up to Hitler's expansionism. In the decades since, the analogy has enjoyed great appeal, especially with American leaders. It is, however, false.

What, then, is true? In early 1938 Hitler's forces at last marched into Austria—to the jubilation of the native population—and the British and the French took no military action. In mid-September 1938 Hitler demanded the unification of the German-speaking part of Czechoslovakia, the Sudetenland, with the Third Reich. Neville Chamberlain (who had succeeded Stanley Baldwin as Britain's prime minister the year before) in early October 1938 met with Hitler at Munich, extracting a pledge on paper "that the method of consultation shall be the method adopted to deal with any . . . questions that may concern our two countries." On his return to Ten Downing Street, Chamberlain appeared at a window and exulted to the crowd gathered below: "My friends . . . there has come back from Germany peace with honour. I believe there is peace for our time." And in March 1939, having already annexed the Sudetenland, Hitler imposed "protectorates" on Bohemia and Moravia and overran Prague.

The American diplomat George F. Kennan was assigned to Prague and bore witness to the German entry on March 15, 1939, into the Czech capital. At about 4:30 AM he received a telephone call from a "terrified acquaintance" who said that the German occupation was about to get under way. After daybreak, Kennan drove around the city:

> A full blizzard was blowing . . . and the snow was staying on the streets. The downtown section was crowded, partly by the normal early-morning traffic of people going to work but partly by people running about and making last-minute preparations of all sorts. The news was widely spread by this time, and many of the women were weeping into their handkerchiefs as they walked. . . . For the rest of the day, the [German] motorized units pounded and roared over the cobblestone streets, hundreds and hundreds of vehicles plastered with snow, the faces of their occupants red with what some thought was shame but what I fear was in most cases merely the cold. By evening the occupation was complete, and the people were chased off the streets by an eight o'clock curfew. . . . It was strange to see those Prague streets, usually so animated, now completely empty and deserted. . . . [W]e were all acutely conscious that . . . the curfew had indeed tolled the knell of a long and distinctly tragic day.

So goes the story of Neville Chamberlain's appeasement of Adolf Hitler: in violation of his Munich agreement, Hitler did, without question, overrun Czechoslovakia and then made preparations for the reunification of East Prussia with the main body of Germany—and that step involved the conquest of Poland.

This far, however, the story is incomplete. Almost from the moment of Hitler's rise to power, the British government, recognizing its conventional military weakness, had been laying plans for economic warfare against Nazi Germany. "Economic warfare," a then classified document stated, "is a military operation, comparable to the operations of the three services in that its object is the defeat of the enemy, and complementary to them in that its function is to deprive the enemy of the material means of resistance. But, unlike the operations of the armed forces, its results are secured not only by direct attack upon the enemy but also by bringing pressure to bear upon those neutral countries from which the enemy draws his supplies." For the British government, economic warfare was a direct lineal descendant of the naval blockade imposed on Germany during World War I; its purpose was through diplomatic and financial pressures to stop neutral countries from shipping resources to Germany.

A contingency plan, of course, is one thing, and action is another. What was the British record in the period of the Munich conference itself? Within the limits of its power, to contain German eastward and southeastward expansion, the British government fired off "silver bullets": trade agreements, orchestrated by the Ministry of Economic Warfare and intended to keep Poland, Romania, Hungary, and the nations of the Balkans out of the German commercial zone.

And after Munich? The record shows that in the first three quarters of 1939, London assiduously sought trade agreements with Turkey, Romania, Greece, Bulgaria, and Yugoslavia, negotiations that pointed toward the economic isolation of Germany.

Before, during, and after the Munich conference, rather than seeking to appease Hitler, the British government sought to contain Nazi Germany through what amounted to the World War I–era economic blockade. Thus Great Britain in the 1930s was in the classic situation of a declining power trying however it could to fight off the challenge of a stronger power; the last thing Chamberlain and his colleagues wanted to see was a major redistribution of power in Europe. And the implication of these facts, a British historian has written, is that the old thesis of "Hitler's unique responsibility for the Second World War is undermined. Instead of a German war of aggrandizement, the war becomes one of Anglo-German rivalry for power and influence, the culmination of the struggle for the right to determine the future configuration of Europe." In that struggle, the British government took upon itself much of the responsibility for the actual war that followed and the disaster that befell Great Britain.

Far from appeasing Nazi Germany, Chamberlain stood up to Hitler. Just before 3:00 PM on March 31, 1939, Prime Minister Chamberlain spoke to the House of Commons and made a fateful announcement. Harold Nicolson, writer and member of Parliament, provided us with a vivid portrayal of the moment: "Chamberlain arrives looking gaunt and ill. The skin above his high cheek bones is parchment yellow. He drops wearily into his place. . . . [T]he P.M. rises. . . . He reads his statement very slowly with a bent grey head. It is most impressive. The House does not cheer his explanatory part beyond a vague murmur of assent. But when he says he will support Poland, there are real live cheers from all parts of the House."

For Chamberlain had declared: "I now have to inform the House that . . . in the event of any action [by Germany] which clearly threatens Polish independence . . . , His Majesty's government would feel themselves bound at once to lend the Polish government all support in their power."

Here was no appeasement. Here was an unconditional guarantee of support by the British government to the Polish state.

The British guarantee to Poland of March 31, 1939, flowed directly from the British declaration of war on Germany on August 4, 1914. From the fall of Napoleon onward, British statesmen had regarded the maintenance of a balance of power on mainland Europe as essential to the preservation of their empire; if no one power dominated the Continent, then no one power could use the resources of the Continent to challenge Great Britain's supremacy beyond the water's edge.

Why, then, the assurance to Poland? A quick glance at the map of Europe, as it was drawn in 1939, reveals the reason. Once in control of Poland, Hitler would have easy access to the oil of Romania and the wheat of Ukraine. Then, positioned in southeastern Europe, he could have reached, as in time he nearly did, that British holy of holies, the Suez Canal. The Chamberlain government therefore drew the line at Poland.

But could it maintain that line? Indeed, 1939 was not 1914. In 1914, Great Britain went to war rich, and had to borrow most of the war costs from the United States; in 1939, Great Britain would have to go to war poor. So even more than in 1914, once committed to the support of Poland, Great Britain was obliged to beg for its own support from the United States. Chamberlain and his colleagues saw little choice: to save the empire, Great Britain would have to go begging again to the very country that wanted to dismantle that empire.

4

As the special train with its blue and silver central car started over the Niagara bridge, the young couple inside pressed their faces to the window. He was fine-boned; she was plump but pretty. Peering out at the floodlights at the crest of the falls, he felt a thrill, for he had not seen that sight since his days as a fledgling British officer. His wife was Queen Elizabeth and he was King George VI, and on this, the night of June 7, 1939, he was about to be the first British monarch to set foot on American soil.

Newly crowned in the wake of the abdication of his older brother, Edward VIII, who had relinquished the throne to marry Mrs. Wallis Warfield Simpson, George VI had planned an official visit to Canada. Learning of the trip, President Roosevelt had extended an invitation to the royal couple to come down to the United States. In London, the prime minister urged the king to accept: desperate to win American goodwill, Chamberlain was eager to put the winsome royal husband and wife on public display. Leaving their small daughters, Elizabeth and Margaret, in good care in Britain, the king and queen set out for their visit to the New World.

Guns boomed forth as the train reached the station on the American side of the St. Lawrence River. A red carpet stretched to the edge of the platform; Secretary of State and Mrs. Cordell Hull stood at midcarpet, waiting. The train came to a halt. As flashbulbs popped, the king, followed three paces behind by the queen, stepped down from the car. Shaking hands with the monarch, Hull extended a formal welcome. The king bowed and the queen curtsied. Joined by the Hulls and William Lyon Mackenzie King, the Canadian prime minister, the royal couple mounted the steps of the railroad car again, and the train left the station, heading for Washington.

Just before 11:00 AM the next day, a Thursday, the presidential limousines reached Union Station, pulling onto the platform. Standing beside Mrs. Roosevelt, the president balanced himself on the arm of General Edwin Watson, a White House aide. The train arrived and the distinguished visitors alighted.

As they shook hands all around, the Marine Band played "God Save the King" and "The Star-Spangled Banner." The president and the king then entered one limousine, Mrs. Roosevelt and the queen another, and, preceded and followed by Secret Service automobiles, the motorcade left Union Station, going down along First Street. Right in front of the Capitol flew two huge American flags. King George VI snapped off a salute, and the crowds of American onlookers went wild. The procession then drove on to the White House.

The next morning, the Roosevelts accompanied the royal couple to Mount Vernon, where the British monarch laid a wreath on George Washington's tomb. The American press loved it: the king of England was paying tribute to the leader of the American Revolution!

The king and queen finished their American sojourn at Hyde Park, and there they spent an all-American Sunday afternoon. Following services just up the road at St. James's Episcopal Church, the president took them for a spin in his shiny new blue Ford convertible. As he sped along the lanes around his estate, he chattered away at a steady pace, often throwing his head backward with laughter. No accident occurred.

Back at the house, the king and queen strolled to the edge of the bluff, from which they could look up and down the Hudson River. Then they joined Mackenzie King and the Roosevelts, including the president's mother, for a picnic on the lawn. Crowded behind barriers, onlookers could scarcely believe their eyes. There, right in front of them, seated in a weathered wooden armchair, King George VI was eating a hot dog, drinking a beer, and asking for seconds of both.

Late in the afternoon, the king and queen boarded their train once more and, as it pulled out of the Hyde Park siding, started their journey back home. Their American visit was over.

It had been a smashing success, and in one way the public knew nothing about. On Saturday night, Roosevelt had chatted with the king and the prime minister in the library of the Hyde Park mansion. Two days later, George VI described the talk in his diary. Roosevelt had promised no alliance. "If London was bombed," however, the president had told the king, "the USA would come in."

5

Assured of eventual American support, His Majesty's government soon ran the biggest risk in the history of the British Empire. Early on the morning of September 1, 1939, Hitler's armies moved into Poland and, in conjunction with France, Great Britain sent an ultimatum to Berlin: if Germany did not withdraw its forces from Poland by eleven in the morning, Greenwich time (noon in Berlin), September 3, 1939, the British government would consider itself in a state of war with Nazi Germany. Berlin did not respond.

CHAPTER 10

The Horrible Year

1

In inviting the king and queen to the United States, President Roosevelt had gauged correctly the contradictions in America's public opinion. For many Americans, the England of titles, rituals, and empire still inspired awe; hence the fascination with the abdication of King Edward VIII and his obsession with Wallis Simpson. Yet the Great Depression also had spawned antiforeign resentments, of which Great Britain seemed the major recipient. Most Americans had no comprehension of Secretary Hull's theories of international trade. They just knew, or thought they knew, that Great Britain was backward-looking, obsolete, and interested only in hanging on with its lion claws to the tatters of its empire. So why, many asked, remembering the trench fighting of World War I, should the United States go off once again to the defense of that empire?

With that question in mind, Roosevelt early in 1938 had appointed as the new American ambassador to Great Britain a figure who by his birthright had no love at all for the British. In making the assignment, Roosevelt was at last repaying an old political debt, for the appointee had contributed heavily to the Democratic presidential campaign of 1932. Presidents often choose their envoys for reasons of politics, with few attendant problems. This choice, however, as the richest man of Irish descent in the world, was bound to be controversial. In selecting this man, from among a host of others who would have gone to the Court of St. James's, Roosevelt was implying that while he might come to the aid of the British, he also saw through their motives. The nominee was Joseph P. Kennedy.

Although the nomination sailed through the Senate, Kennedy had to delay his leaving for several weeks: Rose Kennedy suffered an attack of appendicitis and had to enter a Boston hospital for an operation. Since her recovery took longer than expected, he decided to precede his family across the Atlantic. Just before departure time, on February 23, 1938, as reporters crowded into his stateroom aboard the liner *Manhattan*, docked alongside a pier by the Hudson River, Kennedy wisecracked: "I'm just a babe being thrown into—." A newsman finished the sentence for him: "the lion's mouth?"

Not quite. Kennedy left for the London embassy determined to represent the United States in thought, word, and deed.

Donated to the United States by J. P. Morgan, the palatial American embassy stood at Prince's Gate on Grosvenor Square, just below Oxford Street. Most of its occupants had aped the British aristocracy, donning tweeds, going off for weekends in the country, and posing as men of polish. Never Kennedy. He swore profusely, referred to Queen Elizabeth as a "cute trick," and gave press conferences in his embassy office chewing gum and with his feet up on the desk. The papers at first portrayed him as an American authentic.

In the spring of 1938, his ambassadorship was in its honeymoon. When Rose and the nine children finally arrived, they were the darlings of the tabloids. At royal receptions, news photographers ignored the nobility and trained their cameras instead on the photogenic Kennedys.

The goodwill soon came to an end. The British aristocracy had come to dislike Kennedy intensely. One member of the nobility considered the ambassador a "tycoon who . . . combine[s] all the disagreeable traits of all the very rich men I [have] met with hardly any of their virtues." Another thought that Kennedy's chief merit "seems to be that he has nine children." And in his diary, Harold Ickes, Roosevelt's secretary of the interior, after a conversation with Sir Josiah Wedgwood, of the Wedgwood china family, wrote: "At a time when we should be sending the best we have to Great Britain, we have not done so. We have sent a rich man, untrained in diplomacy, unlearned in history and politics, who is a great publicity seeker and who is apparently ambitious to be the first Catholic president of the United States."

By 1939, Britons by and large had come to see Kennedy as a most undiplomatic diplomat, pro-American, anti-British, above all an isolationist, and they had plenty of reasons to view him thus. In one of his speeches, he offended his Britannic audience by stating: "It is true that the democratic and dictator countries have important and fundamental divergences of outlook, which in certain areas go deeper than politics. But there is simply no sense, common or otherwise, in letting those differences grow into unrelenting antagonisms. After all, we have to live together in the same world, whether we like it or not." Even after the British declaration of war, he declared publicly that the conflict would bring about the "collapse of capitalism" and the "destruction of democracy." He added that "there is no justification for the U.S. to enter the war." During a brief vacation back home in Boston, Kennedy made his point clear: "This is not our fight."

In Great Britain (and in the White House) Kennedy by late 1939 was well on the way to becoming persona non grata; 1940 would be his last year at the Court of St. James's. Nevertheless, at about the time of the British declaration of war, Prime Minister Chamberlain showed Kennedy the government's secret balance sheets. The outlook was grim: already in shaky economic condition, London faced the specter of bankruptcy if it went to war. The leaders of the government did not "want to be finished economically, financially, politically, and socially," Kennedy wrote to Roosevelt in September 1939, "which they are beginning to suspect will be their fate if the war goes on very long."

Kennedy thought the British were crazy to have gone to war, and he did not mind telling them so. But why were they doing it? "The real fact," Kennedy submitted to Roosevelt, "is that England is fighting for her possessions and her place in the sun."

2

My dear Churchill;

It is because you and I occupied similar positions in the World War that I want you to know how glad I am that you are back again at the Admiralty. Your problems are, I realize, complicated by new factors but the essential is not very different. What I want you and the prime minister to know is that I shall at all times welcome it if you will keep in touch with me personally with anything you want me to know about. You can always send sealed letters through your pouch or my pouch.

I am glad you did the Marlboro [*sic*] volumes before this thing started—and I much enjoyed reading them.

The reference in the last sentence was to the fourth and final volume of Winston S. Churchill's *Marlborough: His Life and Times*. The author of the letter, dated September 11, 1939, just eight days after the British declaration of war on Germany, was Franklin D. Roosevelt. And the occasion was the appointment by Prime Minister Chamberlain of Churchill to his old rank, first lord of the Admiralty.

Ever since Hitler's rise to power, Churchill had been demanding action against the Third Reich. Although only a back bencher, he had gathered about himself a coterie of like-minded bureaucrats, young politicians, and press magnates, an anti-Nazi lobby based at Chartwell and prepared to see England sally forth against Germany at all possible costs. Churchill and his associates had publicized their cause with skill, and such had been the political pressure on Chamberlain that on September 1, the date of the German invasion of Poland, he had taken Churchill back into the ministry. On September 3, Churchill had attended his first cabinet meeting in nearly a decade.

As soon as the session was over, Churchill, clad in a dark suit with vest, a gold chain across his by now ample middle, wearing a dark bow tie, and black homburg, strode across the Horse Guards Parade to the Admiralty. Met at a private entrance by a naval captain, Churchill rushed up the steps to his old office. It was almost the same as before, the sofa, the charts, the ship models, and the desk. Meeting in the evening with the brass in the boardroom, Churchill was filled with emotion. Then, his nostalgia under control, he said, "Gentlemen, to your tasks and duties."

In popular memory, the German invasion of Poland (Germany being joined in that operation by the Soviet Union), was followed by the "phony war," or *drôle de guerre*, or *Sitzkrieg*, a war that was not a war at all. The terms seemed apt, at least for a while, because during the winter of 1939–1940, little if any active fighting took place. On the planning tables of Berlin, Paris, and London, however, the two sides were mapping out a race that both believed could determine the outcome of the war. The goal of the race was the northern Norwegian port of Narvik.

For decades, Germany's industrial prowess had rested on the productivity of the valley of the Ruhr, famed for centuries as the anvil of Germany. Nearby coal deposits had enabled weapons manufacturers, such as the Krupp cartel, to flourish. But Germany had suffered one critical shortage: the lack of iron ore. A great power, of course, can import what it needs, and Germany's source of the ore had lain in mines in northern Sweden. Extracted from the earth, the ore had been hauled by train across the Swedish-Norwegian border to Narvik, then shipped down along the channel formed by offshore islands to Stavanger, thence along the Danish coastline to Germany. For Germany, the importation of iron ore from Sweden through Narvik was an economic necessity, and the British and the French knew it.

On February 5, 1940, therefore, the Admiralty in London hosted a meeting of the Allied Supreme Command—top military and civilian officials of France and Great Britain—and the session was marked by an extraordinary Anglo-Franco accord. "Everybody," noted General Sir Edmund Ironside, commander in chief of the British army, "was purring." What they decided seemed so simple. They would send a joint naval expedition up the North Sea, seize Narvik and the Swedish iron mines, and bring Hitler's military production to a halt.

The understanding was a triumph of concurrence over good sense. When General Henry Pownall, the chief of staff of the British Expeditionary Force (BEF) in France, learned of the Narvik scheme, he was outraged. "For five months we have been struggling to make fit for action in the spring a force that last September was dangerously under-equipped and untrained," he wrote in his diary. "There were signs that we were getting some reasonable way to our goal. . . . If this business [the attack at Narvik] goes through (and the saving grace is that I don't believe it can) we shall be cut by thirty percent. It is a most disheartening business. . . . Of all the hare-brained projects I have heard of, this is the most foolish."

The originator of this "harebrained project" was Churchill. From the moment of his occupying his office in the Admiralty, Churchill had begun casting about for ways of outflanking Germany; so he had done in World War I when his eye had lit upon the Dardanelles. At one point he considered sending a British fleet into the Baltic. With Poland defeated and the Danzig harbor in German hands, however, Hitler was in a good position to defend the Baltic littoral. Churchill later talked about mining the waters along the Norwegian coastline; Chamberlain was more concerned about the state of British air defenses. Finally, Churchill hit on the idea of seizing Narvik.

To Churchill, the prospect was so alluring that he wanted to move at once, in September 1939. Since he did not yet wield the power of the prime ministership, however, his project had to run the gauntlet of seemingly endless committees and subcommittees. Questions inevitably arose. Would Norway, a neutral, assent to a landing on its own soil? Would Sweden demand compensation for the loss of iron ore sales to Germany? Could Britain afford to divert resources from the BEF in France? As the days and then the weeks went by, officials in Whitehall quibbled, shuffled papers, and did nothing: in the backs of their minds always was the remembrance of Churchill's failure at Gallipoli.

Suddenly, however, a new element entered the equation: on November 29, 1939, the Soviet Union invaded Finland. The world was horrified, then amazed. In the depths of the winter, the Finns actually hurled the Soviets backward.

The Soviet retreat (which turned out to be temporary) offered Churchill the opening he needed. On January 20, 1940, he spoke on the BBC: "Only Finland—superb, nay, sublime—in the jaws of peril—Finland shows what free men can do," Churchill said. "The service rendered by Finland to mankind is magnificent. They have exposed, for all the world to see, the military incapacity of the Red Army and of the Red Air Force. . . . We cannot tell what the fate of Finland may be, but no more mournful spectacle could be presented to what is left to civilized mankind than that this splendid northern race should at last be worn down and reduced to servitude." The implication of Churchill's address was that the Western powers should go to the aid of the Finns. To do so, they would have to pass through Narvik and northern Sweden, not by coincidence depriving the Third Reich of its Scandinavian iron ore.

Churchill's speech impelled the Allies at last to action. On February 5, the British and French high commands decided to send four divisions to Norway, including two British ones earlier scheduled to go to France. Churchill was getting his wish.

Yet as one inside observer noted, an "air of unreality pervades the proceedings." The lack of realism included "underestimation of the administrative difficulties of such a campaign, the slight regard paid to the danger of provoking Soviet hostility, the miscalculation of German efficiency and resource, and the wishful thinking, which discounts the determination of the neutral governments to maintain their neutrality."

Then the Soviets eliminated Churchill's pretext for action. By early March, the Red Army had finally overwhelmed the Finns. Forced to surrender, Finland ceded to the Soviet Union a vast stretch of territory along the Russian frontier. With Finland defeated, London could no longer justify an attack on Narvik on humanitarian grounds.

By the end of March, nonetheless, the ice in the harbor at Narvik was melting, and the shipments of iron ore to Germany were about to resume. Then came another delay, this caused by Churchill himself. Besides taking Narvik, he asked the British and French brass, why not also drop mines into the Rhine? In that way, Germany would be deprived not only of its iron ore but also of its internal water transport. Ever inventive, Churchill even had a code name for the proposed maneuver: Operation Royal Marine. The Allied Supreme Command considered the idea, but the French vetoed it. Nothing, Paris believed, would so surely provoke a German attack on France as the implementation of Operation Royal Marine. The debate postponed the scheduled Narvik landing to April 8.

The most amazing thing about the Narvik operation is that neither the British nor the French seemed to have an inkling that Hitler might know what they were up to. Actually, Hitler had an informant, an ambitious Norwegian politician named Vidkun Quisling. A graduate of Norway's War Academy, Quisling in the early 1930s had served as minister of defense, then organized Norway's version of a Nazi Party. Traveling frequently to Berlin, he had warned the Führer that British reconnaissance planes had been spotted over Narvik and that they presaged an Allied invasion. Late in 1939, accordingly, Hitler had told his own brass to prepare a preemptive occupation of the whole of Norway.

While German staff officers were drawing up their plans, a scuffle in the North Sea led Hitler to believe that he had to move fast. A German ship, the *Altmark*, had picked up some three hundred British sailors, whose ships had gone under in various skirmishes, and had been trying to transport them to Germany as prisoners of war. With a pack of British destroyers in close pursuit, the *Altmark*, under cover of fog, had ducked into a Norwegian fjord. When the air cleared, however, British pilots located the ship, and a British boarding party had swarmed onto the deck, freeing the captured seamen. Since the British action had taken place in Norwegian territorial waters, Oslo had sent London a vehement protest.

But the Norwegian government had taken no action and, Hitler concluded, was unlikely to actively oppose an Allied grab for Narvik. He ordered Germany's attack to start on April 9.

Shortly before dawn that day, German forces swept up through Denmark and landed at Oslo. The Norwegian resistance was minimal. So when the Allied force reached Narvik a week later, the Germans were already in the port, well dug in and impossible to dislodge. By early May, the result of the race for Narvik had become clear: France and Great Britain had suffered a humiliating defeat.

The press and Parliament alike laid the blame for the failure at the door of 10 Downing Street; Chamberlain had been the man in charge. Leading the attack in the House of Commons was a Conservative back bencher, Leopold Amery. Rising on the afternoon of May 7, he began his speech with an anecdote, the tale of a young man who set out to hunt a lion in Africa: "He secured a sleeping car on the railway and had it detached from the train at a siding near where he expected to find a certain man-eating lion. He went to rest and dreamed of hunting lion in the morning. Unfortunately, the lion was out man-hunting that night. He clambered onto the rear of the car, scrabbled open the sliding door, and ate my friend. That in brief is the story of our initiative over Norway."

After roundly denouncing the government for the Narvik debacle, Amery borrowed a line from Oliver Cromwell when he had dissolved Parliament in 1653. Turning toward Chamberlain, Amery demanded: "You have sat too long here for any good you have been doing. Depart, I say, and let us have done with you. In the name of God, go!"

Three days later, Churchill received a summons to Buckingham Palace. Believing that he could no longer function as prime minister, Chamberlain had notified the king of his intention to resign. Lord Halifax, who had been serving as the foreign secretary, was reluctant to move up. The king therefore turned to Churchill.

"I suppose you don't know why I have sent for you?" George VI asked by way of starting the conversation.

"Sir," Churchill replied, "I simply could not imagine."

But, of course, Churchill knew why he was in the palace. Throughout the rest of the day, he made certain that he had the backing of the Conservative Party, then enlisted the support of the Labour Party. By nightfall he was able to inform the king that he would accept the premiership.

That night in 10 Downing Street, Churchill wrote, he felt as if he were "walking with destiny, and all my past life had been but a preparation for this hour and for this trial." A trial it would be: on May 10, 1940, the very day that Churchill received the summons from King George, the Germans opened their offensive through the Low Countries and into France.

3

From a point in the Maginot Line, just outside Strasbourg in France, a pair of young French sentries hunched their heads down to glance through the slot in their concrete pillbox. It was shortly before dawn on May 10. The sun was about to peek over the hills of Germany to the east; the air would become dry and clear, and the day would grow bright and warm. As soon as they saw the first band of daylight, the sentries knew that they would soon be relieved, free to go to the barracks below, assured of a peaceful sleep.

Before dawn that same day, the tanks of the German Nineteenth Armored Corps, under the command of General Heinz Guderian, were rumbling along with their lights extinguished through the Eifel Mountains of Germany, just east of Luxembourg and just north of the top end of the Maginot Line. Right behind the tanks came armored cars and reinforced motorcycles; next came troop trucks, heavy artillery, and the supply echelons; finally, stretching fifty miles to the rear, came columns of German athletes, the elite corps of the Nazi infantry, the blond supermen of the Third Reich.

Luftwaffe crews, too, were up and about, tumbling from their bunks, scrambling into their flight jackets, and racing to reach their briefing sessions on time. Even before sunrise, German bombers were in the air, most of them droning off toward Holland and Belgium, hoping to divert the attention of the French and the British from where the main armored forces were headed.

When the Germans invaded France in 1914, they had swung their columns down from northern Belgium in a giant sicklelike sweep. The strategy had failed because the French and the British had rushed enough forces into Flanders to stop the German advance. In 1940, however, Hitler decided to reverse the direction of the sweep, encircling the Allies from the south. But where in the south? Through the Ardennes Forest, Hitler had contended. Impossible, the generals had argued; the forest was impenetrable. Hitler had been willing to gamble, nonetheless, that his armored units could indeed cross the terrain and that the Allies could be lured up into Belgium.

Events proved Hitler right. After sunrise on May 10, General Guderian drove his lead tank across a bridge into Luxembourg, keeping an eye on the brightening sky for any signs of approaching Allied aircraft. None appeared. By ten o'clock in the morning he had crossed the thirtysome miles of Luxembourg and had reached the Ardennes Forest, at the southwestern corner of Belgium.

There the Belgians had thrown trees and wooden barricades across the roads and had dynamited the bridges so thoroughly that the Germans had to rely entirely on their pontoon system to get across the rivers. And Guderian's engines sometimes broke down. A tank would stall or run out of gas, forcing the vehicles in the columns behind to spend precious minutes pushing it aside. Guderian found such delays nerve-racking. The more delays his armor encountered, the more inviting it seemed to become targets for planes of the French air force.

To his relief, the only aircraft he saw that day bore the black crosses of the Luftwaffe; at nightfall he was encamped on the wooded slopes of the Ardennes Forest. The next day, Guderian's forces made their way through the Ardennes, as Hitler had bet they would do, and crossed the frontier into France, right above the Maginot Line.

Still nervous, though, even before dawn on May 12, Guderian was standing in the turret of his tank, shouting out to his units to go faster and faster toward Sedan, an ancient town in northeastern France. Now he did run into trouble, for French and British fighters appeared overhead. But their German counterparts soon cleared the skies, and the German columns on the ground kept moving. At the end of the afternoon Guderian stopped on a hillside from which he could see the medieval spires of Sedan. With a yell and a wave, he led his tanks down the slope and out across the valley of the Meuse toward the town.

On May 13, Guderian forded the Meuse. On May 14, he broke through the defenses around Sedan. And on May 15, he set out again, leading the way into northeastern France, where his armored units began to close a trap on the Allied divisions higher up, in Belgium.

Churchill wrote to Roosevelt on May 15:

Although I have changed my office, I am sure you would not wish me to discontinue our . . . correspondence. As you are no doubt aware, the scene has darkened swiftly. The enemy have a marked preponderance in the air. . . . The small countries [Luxembourg, Holland, and Belgium] are simply smashed up, one by one like matchwood. . . . If necessary, we shall continue the war alone and we are not afraid of that. But I hope you realize, Mr. President, that the voice and force of the United States may count for nothing if they are withheld too long. . . . All I ask now is that you should proclaim non-belligerency, which would mean that you would help us with everything short of actually engaging armed forces. Immediate needs are: first of all, the loan of forty or fifty of your older destroyers to bridge the gap between what we have now and the large new construction we put in hand at the beginning of the war.

Roosevelt replied the next day:

I have just received your message and I am sure it is unnecessary for me to say that I am most happy to continue our private correspondence. . . . I am, of course, giving every possible consideration to the suggestions made in your message. . . . [W]ith regard to the possible loan of forty or fifty of our older destroyers: As you know a step of that kind could not be taken except with the specific authorization of the Congress and I am not certain that it would be wise for that suggestion to be made to the Congress at this moment.

In the neutrality acts of the late 1930s, Congress had forbidden the president to help the belligerents in Europe and Asia. Still, in

1936, the Supreme Court had given Roosevelt command of foreign policy. With the *Curtiss-Wright* case, which had dealt with the president's right to block the shipment of matériel to Paraguay and Bolivia, fighting the so-called Chaco War, the Court had stated: "In this vast external realm [of foreign affairs], with its important, complicated, delicate, and manifold problems, the president alone has the power to speak or listen as a representative of the nation. . . . Congressional legislation . . . must . . . accord to the president a degree of discretion and freedom from statutory restriction which would not be admissible were domestic affairs alone involved."

Roosevelt could have invoked the *Curtiss-Wright* language to justify lending Churchill the destroyers. In the spring of 1940, however, he chose not to do so. Why not? It is hard to escape the conclusion that the president was waiting, waiting until Churchill was even more desperate than he was in mid-May 1940, waiting until Great Britain and its empire had something valuable to offer by way of collateral. Roosevelt was playing the loan shark.

On May 24, 1940, only eight days after Roosevelt's reply, four hundred thousand Allied soldiers, some French, a few Belgian, but mostly British, found themselves pinned against the coast of France at the port of Dunkirk. Guderian's tank columns were barely ten miles away and advancing fast. The Allied forces seemed doomed.

Between May 27 and June 3, however, there took place the rescue that became legendary and mythic. The myth is that hundreds of tugs, skiffs, schooners, and other small craft sailed by civilian volunteers made their way from Dover to Dunkirk, evacuating to British soil more than three hundred thousand of those trapped. In truth, a good two-thirds of those saved were lifted from the eastern mole of the Dunkirk harbor onto ships of the Royal Navy; and those acts of salvation succeeded only because a cloud cover prevented attacks by German aircraft. Only on the evening of May 30, when nearly three-quarters of the BEF had been shipped back to England, did the British government call for volunteers. The small boats, furthermore, accounted for no more than 8 percent of those brought out of Dunkirk. The British press at the time and accounts of the

Dunkirk "miracle" ever since, finally, portrayed the escapees as heroes. In fact, in their race to get to the ships, large numbers of British officers deserted their men; Britons of all ranks were involved in kicking Frenchmen off the ships. Once back in England, the disillusioned soldiers threw rifles and helmets out the windows of their railway carriages; some, telephoning their wives to bring civilian clothes, dumped their uniforms and walked home. In private, Churchill confessed that Dunkirk had been "the greatest British military defeat for many centuries."

In public, of course, all was different. Churchill told the House on June 4, the day after Dunkirk fell to the Germans:

> We shall go on to the end. We shall fight in France, we shall fight in the seas and the oceans, we shall fight with growing confidence and growing strength in the air, we shall defend our island, whatever the cost may be, we shall fight on the beaches, we shall fight on the landing grounds, we shall fight in the fields and in the streets, we shall fight in the hills; we shall never surrender, and even if, which I do not for a moment believe, this island or a large part of it were subjugated and starving, then our empire beyond the seas, armed and guarded by the British fleet, would carry on the struggle, until, in God's good time, the New World, with all its power and might, step forth to the rescue and liberation of the Old.

This was Churchill's most famous speech, and by all accounts the members of the House of Commons received these words of defiance with cheers of jubilation. But just what had Churchill really said? From where were the "growing confidence and growing strength in the air" to come? What assurance did he provide that the English people would not surrender? How could he be certain that the "empire beyond the seas" would come to the aid of the "mother country"? Churchill provided no answers, but then his speech was not an academic dissertation. It was a sales pitch aimed at one person, the president of the United States.

With Dunkirk, the economic and military power of Great Britain had collapsed. Churchill had only one hope: "the New World . . . step[ping] forth to the rescue and liberation of the Old."

"We all listened to you last night and were fortified by the grand scope of your declaration," Churchill wrote to Roosevelt a week later. In a speech to the graduating class of the University of Virginia, on June 10, Roosevelt had stated that in "our American unity . . . we will extend to the opponents of [Nazi] force the material resources of this nation."

"Everything must be done to keep France in the fight and to prevent any idea of the fall of Paris," Churchill continued. For if France fell, then the German submarine fleet, based in Brest and other such ports, would have easy access to the Atlantic. "To such a possibility the only counter is destroyers. . . . Nothing is so important as for us to have thirty or forty old destroyers. . . . Not a day should be lost."

On that same day, June 11, Churchill flew across the Channel to bolster the morale of the French leaders. As he feared, France was about to fall.

4

The controller in the airfield tower outside London was having a busy time. He had already sent six Hurricane fighters into the air, and he could see six more lining up along the runway for takeoff. But he was more concerned with the big Flamingo passenger plane revving up its motors on the landing strip just below. Inside its cabin were several British officials, including General Edward Spears, bilingual in English and French and Churchill's personal representative to Paul Reynaud, the French premier. Anthony Eden, the minister of war, also was aboard, cool as always and elegantly dressed. But the controller knew that someone else was seated in that plane: the stooped, potbellied, black-suited figure of Winston S. Churchill.

The controller gave the signal, and the Flamingo roared down the runway behind the first six Hurricanes. The other six followed immediately behind.

Churchill's destination was a château near Briare, a hundred miles southeast of Paris, where General Maxine Weygand, commander in chief of the retreating French army, had established his temporary headquarters; the Germans had already taken Paris. Churchill wished to persuade Weygand and the French cabinet, which was present, to set up a defensive line behind which they could escape, through Bordeaux, to North Africa. From Morocco and Algeria, Churchill hoped, France could stay in the war.

Upon landing, however, Churchill saw that he hoped in vain. The château, General Spears wrote, was a "monstrosity of red lobster-coloured brick and stone the hue of ripe camembert." Inside things were even worse: "It was like walking into a house thinking one was expected," Spears went on, "to find one had been invited for the following week. Our presence was not really desired."

The hostility did not deter Churchill. Meeting with the French leaders, Spears wrote, Churchill "found wonderful flashing words with which to express his fiery eloquence. They came in torrents, French and English phrases tumbling over each other like waves racing for the shore when driven by a storm." Whatever happened, the British would "fight on and on and on, *toujours*, all the time, everywhere, *partout, pas de grâce*, no mercy. *Puis la victoire.*"

Would the French also fight on? The stricken faces in the building gave Churchill his answer. The next day he returned to London and the French government renewed its retreat, this time to Tours in the valley of the Loire.

Churchill nonetheless still cherished the dream that someone in the French army or government would carry on the fight. He asked Spears to go back to France to try to locate such an official.

Tours was only a way station. Late in the afternoon of June 14, an exhausted Premier Reynaud drove into Bordeaux with his mistress. Once inside the city, they inched through the refugee-packed streets in search of the district military headquarters; there Reynaud set up his formal residence.

Two nights later, having flown to Bordeaux, General Spears, burly, uniformed, and carrying the swagger stick of a British officer, entered the residence. Perhaps Reynaud would go on with the war. While looking for Reynaud's office, Spears, still in the gloom of the hallway, heard someone call his name. He recognized a tall figure wedged behind one of the columns, a brigadier general he had encountered in Briare: Charles de Gaulle.

De Gaulle had a request: could Spears fly him to London, where he could organize a resistance? After checking with Churchill by telephone, Spears gave his assent.

The next morning, June 17, Spears drove de Gaulle from a hotel to the Bordeaux airport. De Gaulle's profile, the prominent nose, the clipped mustache, the pouting lips, and the receding chin were not yet famous, so the guard at the airport gate failed to recognize him. After a delay caused by the need to lash down a trunk of official papers de Gaulle had brought along, Spears's airplane took off, the vineyards and pine trees around the Bordeaux airport swaying below.

On the afternoon of June 18, de Gaulle spoke in French over the BBC: "I, General de Gaulle, now in London, call on all French officers and men who are at present on British soil [the few who had escaped from Dunkirk], or may be in the future, with or without their arms; I call on all engineers and skilled workmen from the armaments factories. . . . Whatever happens, the flame of French resistance must not and shall not die!"

Churchill agreed to support de Gaulle's tiny organization, La France Libre. For the British government, however, the fall of France (Reynaud's ministry surrendered to Germany on June 18) was a staggering blow. Despite Churchill's brave words, it forced him and his colleagues to consider seriously whether to seek an armistice from Germany.

We now know that several in the cabinet were prepared to sue for peace. They made a potent argument: in 1939, the Treasury had estimated that Great Britain's reserves of dollars and gold might last for three years; after the fall of France, however, the count dropped to two years. And if Britain fought on, the probability of bankruptcy loomed for the very near future.

In the end, in July 1940, Churchill persuaded the ministers to choose continued war. Yet he knew well that Britain could go on fighting only if America came to the rescue. The next question, therefore, one that the government certainly did not present to the British public, was: what price would America charge for its aid?

5

July 31, 1940

Dear Mr. President;

It is some time since I ventured to cable personally to you and many things both good and bad have happened in between. It has now become most urgent for you to let us have the destroyers . . . for which we have asked. The Germans have the whole French coast-line from which to launch U-boats, dive-bomber attacks upon our trade and food, and in addition we must be constantly prepared to repel by sea action threatened invasion in the narrow water [the English Channel], and also to deal with breakouts from Norway towards Ireland, Iceland, Shetlands, and Faroes. Besides this we have to keep control of the exit from the Mediterranean, and if possible the command of that inland sea itself, and thus to prevent the war spreading seriously into Africa.

This is a frank account of our present situation and I am confident, now that you know exactly how we stand, that you will leave nothing undone to ensure that 50 or 60 of your oldest destroyers are sent to me at once. I can . . . use them against the U-boats on the western approaches and so keep the more modern and better-gunned craft for the narrow seas against invasion.

Mr. President, with great respect I must tell you that in the long history of the world, this is a thing to do now.

In this letter to Roosevelt, Churchill promised a "frank account of our present situation." He did no such thing. He did not tell Roosevelt that despite Germany's success on the land against Denmark and Norway, Hitler had lost about half of his fleet in the North Sea naval battles. He did not inform the president that British production of fighter planes was two and a half times that of Germany. And he withheld from the White House the information that the Third Reich possessed only about thirty usable submarines, hardly enough to stop Great Britain's seaborne trade.

So why Churchill's plea for the destroyers? With the collapse of the French republic, all the problems that had beset Great Britain from 1914 onward came to a head. Sprawled across the globe, the British Empire was overextended and faced the nightmare of having to deal with three enemies—Germany, Italy, and Japan—at the same time and without allies. At home, Britain's industrial base was antiquated and its financial resources were dwindling fast. Only with the destroyers did Churchill have any hope of keeping Great Britain great, let alone preserving the empire.

If Churchill thought Roosevelt would extend the loan without requiring collateral, however, he was sorely mistaken. Churchill might have taken the hint. Between the middle of May and the middle of June 1940 he had sent ten messages to Roosevelt and received only three replies. The first had dismissed out of hand the prime minister's plea for help; the second had been merely a copy of a noncommittal message from Roosevelt to Premier Reynaud; and the third had made clear that the United States was sticking to its neutrality. After the third missive from the White House, Ambassador Kennedy had advised Churchill to drop the subject of the destroyers until the Democrats had renominated Roosevelt for president.

So Churchill did not write to Roosevelt again until July 31. Even then, he did not have another message from Roosevelt again until August 13. In it FDR spelled out what he wanted in exchange for the destroyers.

Roosevelt's lack of responsiveness was the result—in part, at least—of a tricky problem: how to reconcile a transfer of destroyers with the neutrality laws, which forbade the president's giving aid to the belligerents. Dean Acheson, the tall, elegant, mustachioed Washington lawyer who at the time was in private practice, came to the rescue.

"It has been suggested that fresh legislative authority is required to permit the executive branch of the government to release these old destroyers for sale to Great Britain. We should like to place on record our own legal opinion that this is not the case."

So began a letter signed by Acheson and three other attorneys and published in the *New York Times* on August 11, 1940. It is worth noting that Acheson referred to a sale, not a loan, of the destroyers.

The letter was long, going on for three and a half columns. In all probability, most readers of the *Times* scarcely bothered to wade through it; at a press conference, Roosevelt himself confessed that he had only skimmed the piece. But the sheer density of the letter was precisely the point. Acheson had shown its early versions to Secretary of War Henry L. Stimson, Justice Felix Frankfurter, and Secretary of the Navy Frank Knox, and after several drafts had produced what reflected a mountainlike consensus. The thesis of the letter was that the deal would violate no law if the transfer of destroyers would serve the interests of America's defense—and if the British in exchange were willing to hand over their naval bases in the Western Hemisphere.

Seated in a low-backed chair aboard the presidential train, Roosevelt on September 3, 1940, was returning to Washington from the Tennessee border, where he had just dedicated the Chicamauga Dam, a project of the Tennessee Valley Authority (TVA). He invited the reporters who were aboard to gather around for an informal press conference. That very morning, FDR announced, Congress would receive "notes exchanged between the British ambassador at Washington [Lord Lothian] and the secretary of state . . . under which this government has acquired the right to lease naval and air bases in Newfoundland, and in the islands of Bermuda, the Bahamas, Jamaica, St. Lucia . . . Trinidad and in British Guiana. . . . The right to bases in Newfoundland and Bermuda are gifts—generously given and gladly received. . . . The other bases have been acquired in exchange for fifty of our overage destroyers."

In the late summer of 1940, as the Luftwaffe was starting to drop its bombs on the East End of London, Roosevelt had driven quite a deal with Churchill. The destroyers sent over were not just "overage," they were also obsolete. In return, the United States got control of all the British naval bases in the Western Hemisphere, from New-foundland to the Caribbean. What Roosevelt had demanded, and got, as Churchill complained in a letter to FDR on August 25, 1940, was a "blank cheque on the whole of our transatlantic possessions."

The bases-for-destroyers agreement marked the end of British independence in world affairs. By 1941, the year in which the United States officially entered World War II, Great Britain, the hub of the empire, had already become an American client state. The events of the great conflict to come only underlined this great transformation of international relations.

But it was Lord Lothian, the ambassador, who best expressed the state of affairs. "Well, boys," he said to reporters at the end of November, "Britain's broke; it's your money we want."

Part III
The Grand Alliance

CHAPTER 11

The Atlantic Charter

1

Late in January 1941, Great Britain's new ambassador reached the United States. The previous envoy, Lord Lothian, a Christian Scientist, had died of untreated uremic poisoning. The new diplomat, foreign secretary under Prime Minister Chamberlain, was a scion of the British aristocracy and the owner of vast estates in Yorkshire. He was Edward Frederick Lindley Wood, Lord Halifax.

Taller always it seemed than anyone else around him, Halifax possessed a long, mournful, but shrewd face that made him look at once religious and crafty; his nickname was "Lord Holy-Fox." Ambassador Kennedy had been less subtle: after one session in the Foreign Office on Downing Street, he had left screaming about "Halifax and all that God stuff!" Halifax certainly had little charm, as was well known in British ruling circles. Harold Laski, a professor at the London School of Economics, had sent a transatlantic warning. "There is something of the genuine saint" about Halifax, Laski had written in a letter to the *Washington Post*. It was "this quality that made so vivid an appeal to Mr. Gandhi."

It may have been this saintly quality, or the sense of duty to God, king, and country ingrained in the British nobility, that had led Halifax to accept the ambassadorship to the United States. The assignment certainly had been a step down from the position of foreign secretary. Churchill had tried to persuade him otherwise: "The business we now have with the United States," Churchill had written him on December 19, 1940, "can only be handled by one who knows the whole policy of the government, and is in constant direct relation with us. If New York and Washington were as near as Paris used to be, all important affairs would be transacted by personal meetings between prime ministers and foreign secretaries on both sides. The Atlantic requires that this intimacy should be achieved by other processes, and you are, I am sure, the one person best qualified for this permanent duty." If anyone could lead Roosevelt to regard Great Britain as an equal partner, Churchill had implied, it was Halifax.

Halifax had had his doubts. "I felt as if my roots had been suddenly pulled up or much as a fish must feel when suddenly pulled out on to a bank," he had confided to his diary. Fearing, quite sensibly, that Churchill had wanted him, a political rival, out of London and safely across the Atlantic, Halifax had demanded to know: "How far should we change our policy here because the United States sent us Cordell Hull?"

Gloomily, Halifax had accepted the assignment. He and Lady Halifax left King's Cross Station on January 14, 1941, traveling by a special train to board the newly commissioned battleship *King George V* at Scapa Flow.

Winston and Clementine Churchill traveled with them, as did Harry Hopkins, the onetime social worker who had become Roosevelt's personal representative to London. As the train pulled out of the city, it passed by the rubble of bomb sites. In the morning, high in Scotland, they all awoke to a world white with snow. The sky was as pale as steel and the sea was black, churned up by a bitter northeaster. Lord and Lady Halifax nonetheless got onto the battleship without accident. Departing the vast bay at Scapa Flow, the warship rounded a headland and entered into the Atlantic Ocean, following a zigzag course to evade German submarines.

Fast, powerful, riding low in the water, and surrounded by a convoy of destroyers, the huge battleship seethed across the gray of the Atlantic. Close to Boston, the escorting ships dropped off and the *King George V* plowed on alone. In the cold mist of the morning of

January 23, 1941, it started up from the mouth of the Chesapeake Bay. "Except that it was smooth," Halifax wrote in his diary, "we might have been in mid-Atlantic, for the fog prevented us seeing any land. . . . We anchored about two o'clock and for some time nothing seemed to happen except that it poured with rain."

Suddenly, however, the ship received electrifying news. In an unprecedented step, the American president was coming to greet the British ambassador. Churchill three days before had notified Roosevelt of Halifax's arrival and had invited FDR to meet the *King George V* at Annapolis; Roosevelt almost immediately had expressed the desire to do so. Now it was clear that he was coming.

Back in Washington and just after lunchtime on January 24, a five-car presidential motorcade sped out of the White House, raced through the intersections to New York Avenue, hurtled onto U.S. 50—now a broad thoroughfare but then a road through piney woods and swamps—and twisted along the curves until it reached the pier at the Naval Academy.

The rain had turned into a downpour, and aboard the battleship Halifax could see nothing but the wet. The captain and he nevertheless decided that they would "receive the president with all the honors due to a sovereign."

Accompanying the president, Secretary of the Navy Frank Knox, Chief of Naval Operations Admiral Harold Stark, White House aide General Edwin M. Watson, and eight Secret Service agents got out of their automobiles at dockside. Roosevelt was helped into a launch, then lifted aboard the presidential yacht *Potomac*, waiting at anchor in the basin of the Severn River. Officers and midshipmen snapped to attention; the executive flag broke out from the foremast, and as pipers played traditional naval tunes, the *Potomac* raised anchor. Despite the squall, it put out in the direction of the British battleship.

The yacht at last materialized out of the storm, and as it started to circle the ship, the *King George V* boomed out a twenty-one-gun salute. The launch left the yacht for the side of the battleship and, well protected with raingear and umbrellas, Lord and Lady Halifax went aboard the yacht. They did so just in time for tea.

Knox and Watson met them in the companionway, taking them straight to the dining saloon. Roosevelt was seated behind a table. In just one moment, Halifax wrote in his diary, "he put us completely at our ease, and we were chatting away as if we had known each other all our lives. Nothing could have been more friendly, and he said he regarded this as dispensing with any formal business of presentation of credentials. Much talk over tea—quite easy and intimate, and at times pleasantly indiscreet."

After tea they kept on talking, discussing "everything under the sun, and I liked him very much. He spoke a great deal about his experiences in Europe at the end of the last war and about various common friends. Finally, he told me that he hoped that I should feel myself free to ring up the White House at any time and ask to see him, and be prepared myself to be called by him at any time."

Night came, and although the rain had diminished, reporters clustered along the Annapolis quay were shivering in the dark. Then a beam cut the blackness, swinging back and forth in the night: the *Potomac*'s light was searching out the pier.

As the presidential yacht pulled alongside, the journalists could see into the saloon, where Roosevelt and his aristocratic guests were seated at dinner. *Time* described the scene:

> The saloon was warm and brightly lit; there was a bowl of pink roses on the table; President Roosevelt was talking animatedly and laughing while Lord Halifax listened. Photographers mobbed Lord and Lady Halifax when they appeared on deck, snapped their pictures as the ambassador apologized for keeping them waiting in such miserable weather. He read a brief statement to the correspondents who were standing along the cold, windswept pier: "Lady Halifax and I are very glad to be here . . . and now the president has done my country the great honour of coming to greet us on arrival. . . . I have come here, as a member of the war cabinet serving as His Majesty's ambassador to make known to the government and the people of the United States . . . in what ways, if they are willing, they can best give us the help we need."

Then, slipping into the presidential limousine, Lord and Lady Halifax sped to the British embassy, a Queen Anne–style red-brick establishment high on Massachusetts Avenue in Washington. Out in the night, the *King George V* was streaking back to sea.

2

Despite Roosevelt's graciousness in making the drive to Annapolis, the diplomatic reality was clear. Lord Halifax had come to the United States as a supplicant, and his specific task was to lend his prestige to ensuring passage through Congress of a huge aid package for Great Britain, the legislation popularly known as Lend-Lease.

The term *Lend-Lease* had its origins in a press conference Roosevelt had held on the afternoon of December 17. Calling reporters into the Oval Office, the president greeted them from behind a desk cluttered with pens, clocks, ashtrays, papers, little flags, and other knick-knacks. Putting a cigarette in his holder at its usual jaunty angle, he told the "boys" that he had no real news. Then, contradicting himself with a wink, he admitted that there might be one item worth bringing up. Ridiculing "a great deal of nonsense" put out by people who thought of finance in "traditional terms," he decried the very thought that Great Britain had asked for money. Britain had been making purchases in the United States, to be sure, and had to pay for them, but he had thought only of "encouraging" such expenditures.

What kind of encouragement? someone asked. "Something brand new in the thoughts of practically everybody in this room," Roosevelt answered.

He used an analogy. If your neighbor's house is on fire, he said, you will gladly lend him your garden hose. When the fire is put out, he will return the hose.

Just how your neighbor was supposed to put out the blaze with a mere garden hose, Roosevelt did not explain. Nor did he say how the British were ever going to return shot-down airplanes and burned-out tanks. Nonetheless, the press conference gave rise to the term *Lend-Lease*: a bankrupt Britain could get American military assistance and only later replace it or produce the funds for payment.

"Give us the tools and we will finish the job," Churchill had pleaded over the radio. Lobbied by Halifax, Congress passed the Lend-Lease Act (patriotically numbered H.R. 1776), providing the tools. Signed by Roosevelt on March 11, 1941, the measure was all-encompassing. The law started with the term "defense article." "Defense article" meant "any weapon, munitions, aircraft, vessel, or boat." "Any law to the contrary," the act went on, referring to the earlier neutrality legislation, the president could authorize the head of "any . . . department or agency" to contract for "any defense article . . . the president deems vital," to "sell . . . , exchange, lease, lend, or otherwise dispose of . . . any defense article to any friendly government," to "communicate to any such government any defense information pertaining to any defense article furnished to such government." In short, President Roosevelt could order the production of anything he wanted, share intelligence with anyone he wanted, and unleash any kind of clandestine operation he wanted.

The Lend-Lease Act of March 1941 thus fulfilled the promise of the *Curtiss-Wright* decision of 1936. In the "vast external realm of foreign affairs," President Roosevelt was free at last of the shackles of the neutrality laws.

Churchill greeted the passage of the Lend-Lease Act with a public show of gratitude. In a speech to the House of Commons he deemed the measure "the most unsordid act in the history of any nation."

But was it so? Although convinced, as were most Americans, that Nazi Germany posed a threat to Western democracy, Roosevelt and his administration were not in the business of trying to save the British Empire. Secretary of the Treasury Henry Morgenthau Jr.— tall, balding, mournful of mien, and nicknamed by Roosevelt "Henry the Morgue"—insisted that to pay for the matériel Great Britain had to use every available source of dollars and gold; and that meant handing over the reserves the U.S. Treasury was certain were stashed away in the empire and the commonwealth. The elderly secretary of war, Henry L. Stimson, rammed American-type weapons down the throats of the reluctant British brass. And Secretary of State Hull demanded that Great Britain post collateral: a pledge to dismantle its system of imperial preferences.

Despite Churchill's oratory, British historians would come to dispute the true meaning of Lend-Lease. One condemned the United States for its unwillingness to pool fully its financial resources with those of Great Britain. Another described Britain's role in accepting Lend-Lease as the "poverty of the poor relation." A. J. P. Taylor contended that Great Britain had sacrificed its role as a great power; Lend-Lease, he argued, ruined Britain as an exporting nation and stripped it of its remaining dollars.

Hitler mocked the British for allowing the Americans to take advantage of their financial woes. We can dismiss such statements as propaganda. But in conversations with Spanish and Soviet diplomats, the Führer seemed honestly to believe that, to receive Lend-Lease aid, Great Britain was obliged to subordinate itself to America's imperialistic aims.

He missed the point. Lots of Americans, certainly, were delighted to take advantage of the British; Roosevelt was hardly immune to such thinking. Yet he was cautious. A destitute Britain might well give up and turn to Hitler in surrender. Committed to the defeat of Nazi Germany, the president saw Great Britain as a launching pad for an eventual invasion of the European continent. Britain was useful and might even serve as an adjunct to the American military machine that Roosevelt already envisioned.

All the same, the Germans did have a point. In a cable to Berlin dated March 9, 1941, Hans Thomsen, Hitler's chargé d'affaires in Washington, concluded that with the enactment of Lend-Lease, Great Britain had become America's "paid vassal."

3

With the passage of Lend-Lease, the United States laid the legislative foundation for its coming war with Germany. What remained was a formal, if covert, declaration of its participation in that conflict.

Shortly after Halifax's arrival in Washington, British officers who had come on the *King George V*, along with their Canadian and American counterparts, all dressed in mufti and, meeting secretly in the old Public Health Building on Constitution Avenue, began to negotiate a clandestine agreement. In the United States, only Roosevelt and his secretaries of state, war, and navy, along with the negotiators and the Joint Chiefs of Staff, were to have knowledge of this, the ABC (American-British-Canadian) Agreement. Completed on March 27, 1941, it committed the United States to engaging in economic warfare against the Third Reich. The document explained:

12. The strategic concept includes . . . as the principal offensive policies against the Axis powers:
    a. Application of economic pressure by naval, land, and air forces and all other means, including the control of commodities at their source by diplomatic and financial measures.
    b. A sustained air offensive against German military power, supplemented by air offensive against other regions under enemy control which contribute to that power.
    c. The early elimination of Italy as an active partner in the Axis.
    d. The employment of the air, land, and naval forces of the Associated Powers [President Wilson's term for the United States], at every opportunity, in raids and minor offensives against Axis military strength.
    e. The support of neutrals, and of allies of the United Kingdom, associates of the United States, and populations in Axis-occupied territory in resistance to the Axis Powers.
    f. The building up of the necessary forces for an eventual offensive against Germany.
    g. The capture of positions from which to launch the eventual offensive.

Roosevelt withheld the ABC Agreement from the Congress, where the forces of isolation still had strength. Nonetheless, it amounted to a treaty whereby the United States pledged to join in the struggle against the power of the Third Reich. So the ABC Agreement, and not the congressional declaration of war against Japan on the day after the bombing of Pearl Harbor, marked America's actual entry into World War II.

With the agreement, albeit a secret one, in place, the president's men swung into action. They were starting to close the vise on Nazi Germany.

Harry Hopkins, Roosevelt's closest aide, took off for London. Ostensibly he was to serve as interim ambassador, running the embassy until the former governor of New Hampshire, John G. Winant, could win Senate confirmation; Kennedy had resigned the post. Actually, Hopkins's job was to get to know Churchill and to prepare for a late summer summit meeting, when the prime minister and the president would promulgate their joint war aims.

William J. Donovan, international lawyer and coordinator of the Office of Information, precursor to the Office of Strategic Services and then the Central Intelligence Agency, was in the eastern Mediterranean, visiting Egypt, Greece, Bulgaria, and Yugoslavia, trying to build up a front against German expansion. Much in line with Chamberlain's prewar efforts, Donovan was intimating that cooperative countries would be eligible for American economic aid.

Admiral Harold Stark was positioning his forces for Atlantic warfare. Following the curve of the globe, his air patrols were flying as far up as Iceland, and his destroyers were escorting convoys as far over as Liverpool.

To Admiral Erich Räder, these moves presented Germany with the direct threat of war. He begged Hitler, hitherto reluctant to embroil the Third Reich with the United States, to strengthen Germany's forces in the Atlantic. In a limited way Hitler gave his assent: he unleashed the battleship *Bismarck*. Thus commenced the Battle of the Atlantic.

4

The war was raging elsewhere, too. The British faced yet another challenge, this in the desert sands of North Africa: General Erwin Rommel was on the loose. Kicking up towering clouds of dust, he, one of the heroes of the Battle of France and commander of Germany's Afrika Korps, went swirling into the Libyan desert. He had arrived in Tripoli in December 1940—the British had been on the brink of driving Germany's ally Italy out of North Africa altogether —and had taken a look around. The desert, he had realized, had been made just for him, for there, he wrote to his wife, "speed is the only thing that matters."

So early in April 1941, Rommel's tanks raced into Cyrenaica, the hump of Libya that lay east of the Gulf of Sidra, hurled out in every direction, confused the British, and seized at a whirlwind pace all the main strategic points. Within days, Rommel's armored divisions were crossing the border into Egypt, threatening soon to reach the Suez Canal.

Simultaneously, German forces were sweeping down through the Balkans. Yugoslavia fell early in April; next came Greece, during Easter Week in 1941. Last was Crete. German bombers reached that long, mountainous island southeast of Greece in the middle of May; there the occupying British had no cover.

Shortly after dawn on May 20, 1941, an observer in Crete looked up. Overhead, in the brightening sky, masses of bombers were approaching, flying so close together that their wingtips seemed to touch. Many of the planes trailed gliders, which soon descended. Then, from transport aircraft even higher, specks appeared, dots that soon turned into parachutes floating to earth and bearing German paratroopers. Crete fell, and as it did so, many thought the Third Reich unstoppable.

In the last week of May 1941, accompanied by the cruiser *Prinz Eugen*, the *Bismarck* moved out of Kiel. When Churchill learned of the departure he became, in the words of Anthony Eden, his new foreign secretary, "nervy and unreasonable." One can see why. The

Bismarck came equipped with more armor, bigger guns, and greater speed than any other ship afloat. What was worse, after a British reconnaissance plane spotted it off the coast of Norway, the *Bismarck* disappeared, obscuring itself in the fogs and mists of the North Atlantic. The threat the ship posed to convoys headed for Britain was immense.

It was sighted again at dawn on May 24, silhouetted against the gray of an iceberg, its guns aimed at the *Hood* and the *Prince of Wales*, two British battleships that had gone out in pursuit of the *Bismarck*. The *Hood* fired first, but its shells fell short, and the *Bismarck* sank it within minutes. The *Prince of Wales* drew out of range as fast as possible.

One of its shells, however, had reached the *Bismarck*. The blow was only minor, a rupture in one of the fuel tanks, yet enough to make the battleship trail oil. Its range reduced, the *Bismarck* made for the French port of Saint-Nazaire for repairs.

In passing down the Atlantic, Gunther Lutjens, the admiral in command, made a crucial mistake: he radioed Berlin an account of his sinking the *Hood*, and he did so at length. Listening in, Admiralty intelligence in London thus was able to determine the ship's approximate location. So informed, several British cruisers and the *Ark Royal*, an aircraft carrier, drew near.

Then, on the morning of May 26, a British seaplane spotted the *Bismarck* and, shortly before nightfall, a squadron of biplanes went up from the deck of the *Ark Royal*. As they approached the *Bismarck* in the fast-gathering darkness, its antiaircraft guns blazed away, scoring hit after hit on the obsolete British aircraft. In this instance, however, obsolescence had its merits. The airplanes were covered with canvas; although the shells from below tore numerous holes, they caused little real damage.

Torpedoes were fired. Many missed. One only bounced off the armor along the side of the ship. But another hit home. It crashed into the *Bismarck*'s engine room, jamming the steering mechanism. Its rudders stuck, the *Bismarck* could turn only to the right, away from Saint-Nazaire and toward the oncoming British flotilla. The *Bismarck* still could return fire, but it had lost its ability to maneuver.

It survived the night. By dawn, though, more and more of the British aircraft were finding their target. One shell destroyed a forward turret on the *Bismarck*; another demolished the fire control machinery. With the *Bismarck* soon ablaze, the *King George V,* the battleship that had borne Lord Halifax to the United States, came up to the scene, four miles away, two miles, and then at nearly point-blank range. Its shells were pouring onto the *Bismarck*.

Just after 10:00 AM, Gerhard Junack, the chief turbine engineer and one of the few to survive, made his way to the deck. "There was no electric light," he wrote, "only the red glow from numerous fires; smoke fumes bellowed everywhere; crushed doors littered the deck, and men were running here and there, apparently aimlessly."

Junack and about a hundred others were able to climb down into lifeboats. "Hardly were we free of the ship," he went on, "when it keeled over to port, rolling the deck-rail under and bringing the bilge-keel out of the water. A pause—then *Bismarck* turned keel-up, slowly, the bows rose in the air, and stern first *Bismarck* slid to the bottom."

Although wounded severely, the *Prinz Eugen* escaped to France. It played no further part in the Battle of the Atlantic.

The drama of the sinking of the *Bismarck* obscures the broader picture of what was taking place across the Atlantic. The Roosevelt-Churchill correspondence gives a sense of the larger events:

April 11, 1941

Dear Churchill;

This government proposes to extend the present so-called security zone and patrol areas which have been in effect since very early in the war to a line covering all North Atlantic waters west of about west longitude 25 degrees. [This extension, Secretary of War Stimson wrote in his diary, "midway between the westernmost bulge of Africa and the easternmost bulge of Brazil," stretched greatly the concept of the Western Hemisphere.] We propose to utilize aircraft and naval vessels working from Greenland, Newfoundland, Nova Scotia, the United States, Bermuda, and the West Indies.

On the very day of this letter from Roosevelt, the U.S. Navy fired its first shot in the struggle for control of the Atlantic. Rescuing men from a torpedoed merchant ship just inside the line Roosevelt had drawn, an American destroyer dropped depth charges intended for what sonar showed to be a submerged German submarine. The episode had little effect on the outcome of the battle, but with the new zone for "hemisphere defense," the United States was gunning for any German vessels west of the Azores.

May 29, 1941

Dear Churchill;

In our common interest . . . I am prepared to direct the Army and the Navy to assume full responsibility for the transfer of American-built aircraft from factory to the point of ultimate take-off and to supply maintenance and servicing facilities along the way and at the ultimate staging field. . . .

For example, the American Army and Navy could deliver planes at Botwood, Newfoundland, ready and serviced for the [Royal Air Force] to take them over and fly them across. Later and depending on developments we might be able to deliver them to your people in Iceland.

Because of the lengthening of daytime in the North Atlantic, American air patrols out of North America were spotting more and more U-boats and directing destroyers to them. Still, Roosevelt hoped to base aircraft in Iceland, where the British had maintained a force. Indeed, the president proposed to have American planes there replace British ones altogether.

May 29, 1941

Dear Mr. President;

We cordially welcome your taking over Iceland at the earliest possible moment, and will hold ourselves and all our resources there at your disposal. . . . It would liberate a British division for defence against invasion of the Middle East. It would enable us to concentrate our flying boats now there on northwestern approaches. If it could be done in the next three weeks or less, or even begun, it would have a moral effect even beyond its military importance. You have only to say the word and our staffs can get to work at once.

Hoping to avoid a German takeover, Iceland, formerly a Danish colony, had cut its ties with the crown in 1941. A week after receiving Churchill's letter, FDR decided to send the Marines ashore at Iceland (and, reluctantly welcomed by the Icelanders, they did so in July). A force based in Iceland could help guard the convoys and also provide a transfer point for ferrying aircraft from the United States to Great Britain. Besides, German airplanes had been spotted over Reykjavik, the capital, and FDR feared another Crete. As Morgenthau put it, Roosevelt was "getting [to Iceland] first."

At almost the same time, on May 28, Roosevelt made another decision with regard to the Atlantic. He instructed the army and the navy to prepare an American occupation of the Azores.

A broad pattern had thus emerged. In 1939 Roosevelt had extended the Monroe Doctrine to Canada, making the United States and no longer Great Britain Canada's protector. In 1940, the bases-for-destroyers deal had given the United States effective possession of British naval bases all along the North American littoral. Now, in 1941, American forces were replacing the British in Greenland, Iceland, and the Azores, a possession of Portugal, a traditional British ally.

By midsummer 1941, Uncle Sam had taken over from John Bull control of all the important strategic points in the Mid- and North Atlantic. Then Hitler made his last roll of the dice.

5

Winter hung on late in Russia in 1941, at least in Moscow and Leningrad; snow was on the ground even on May Day, and chilly fogs were rolling in from the shores of the Baltic well into June. Even the summer carried the promise of winter again, for late June was unseasonably cool. Despite such omens, however, Hitler plunged ahead.

Operation Barbarossa, his scheme for the defeat of the Soviet Union, started off in grand style. In July 1941, a force of 3 million German soldiers moved across the Polish frontier and progressed so swiftly that within a week German armored units were approaching Smolensk, more than three hundred miles into the Soviet Union. Pushing ever onward, General Heinz Guderian, the commanding officer, was heading for Moscow. He would capture Moscow as he had taken Paris, he believed, and then he would destroy the remnants of the Red Army.

But the distances were great, the German supply lines were stretched thin, and Soviet guerrillas were mounting deadly rearguard action. Despite the optimism of Guderian and Hitler, the Germans were slipping into a stalemate, a point being trumpeted in major American newspapers. Headlines alone told the story. July 21: "RUSSIANS REPORT NAZI DRIVES HALTED IN FOUR SECTORS WITH HEAVY LOSSES" (the *New York Times*). July 29: "NAZI DRIVE BROKEN, RED ARMY ON OFFENSIVE, RUSSIANS SAY" (the *Washington Post*). The news stories exaggerated, for the German drive was by no means broken. The advance nonetheless had slowed to a crawl.

Officials in Washington were taking note. Chief of Staff General George C. Marshall thought that inferior lubricating oil was wearing out the German tanks. Henry Stimson estimated that the Germans had suffered half a million casualties. Adolf Berle Jr., a high-ranking figure in the State Department, held that the German invasion of the Soviet Union was already a failure.

Henry Morgenthau spoke for the president. Now, he declared, was the "time to get Hitler."

6

By the beginning of August 1941, Washington was soggy, sweltering, and broiling. The heat, *Time* reported, was melting the asphalt on Massachusetts Avenue. Anyone who could flee the capital did so, and Roosevelt was no exception. Soon, the papers announced, he would leave for a vacation. He was just going to spend time aboard the *Potomac* during a cruise off the coast of New England.

Late on Saturday morning, August 2, the executive flag came down from over the White House and, accompanied by three aides, Roosevelt rode to Union Station. Leaving at 11:00 AM, the presidential train steamed northward, and by 8:15 PM it had reached New London, Connecticut. The station stood at the edge of the harbor; and as a crowd watched from around Nathan Hale's old schoolhouse and the Congregational Church up on the hill, Roosevelt was transferred to the yacht. In the last glow of the sunset, the *Potomac* slipped down the Thames River and into the ocean beyond. After dropping anchor off Point Judith by the base of Narragansett Bay, the vessel proceeded at dawn to South Dartmouth, Massachusetts, where Roosevelt welcomed aboard members of the Norwegian and Danish royal families in exile. Their presence aboard the *Potomac* made all the New England papers. Late in the afternoon, the yacht took off again, putting in at Martha's Vineyard.

The waters there were full of American warships: the destroyers *Madison*, *Moffett*, *Sampson*, *Winslow*, and *McDougal*, along with the cruisers *Tuscaloosa* and *Augusta*. Waiting aboard the *Augusta* were General Marshall; Admiral Stark; General Henry H. Arnold, head of the Army Air Corps; and Admiral Ernest J. King, commander in chief of the U.S. Atlantic Fleet.

Reporters on shore did not see these men. Nor did they see Roosevelt being moved to the *Augusta*. And they did not see the flotilla leave under the cover of darkness for Placentia Bay, by a fishing village called Argentia on the southeastern coast of Newfoundland.

There, in the waters of the North Atlantic, Roosevelt and Churchill were scheduled to join in their first summit meeting. The conference opened on the morning of August 9, 1941.

"How are you, Harry?"

"Harry" was Harry Hopkins. From London he had flown to Moscow to get a firsthand impression of the war between Nazi Germany and the Soviet Union. Ensconced in the Kremlin, the Soviet leaders had treated Hopkins well: long dinners with plenty of caviar and vodka; inside information about the state of the Soviet Union's defenses; a long conversation with Stalin. The Germans were strong, Stalin had acknowledged, but the snows were about to fall, and after the first of October Hitler's forces would bog down.

Hopkins had been impressed, for the Soviets seemed capable of slowing, even halting, the German advance. With that conviction in mind, he had flown back to Britain, to Scapa Flow, and from there had set sail with Churchill for Placentia Bay aboard the *Prince of Wales*. Once at the shores of Newfoundland, a special launch had transported Hopkins to the *Augusta*, where Roosevelt welcomed him back.

"Are you all right?" Roosevelt asked. "You look a little tired."

Exhausted and ailing, Hopkins waved the concern aside. He was intent on relaying to Roosevelt what he had gleaned in the Soviet Union.

At 11:00 AM Churchill followed Hopkins to the *Augusta*. Dressed in navy blue—as prime minister, he had the right to wear the nautical uniform of warden of the Cinque Ports—and surrounded by the highest brass of Britannia, resplendent in their ribbons, braids, and buttons, he lowered his corpulent body into a barge, which set out across the water.

Churchill could hardly miss the contrast between the *Augusta* and the battleship he had just left. "The *Prince of Wales* was camouflaged," an accompanying British reporter wrote; "her guns protruded from their turrets like rigid pythons. The American ships were uncamouflaged and shone in peacetime grey. We had been in action, and our brass was either painted or tarnished and our decks were not what they would have been in other days. The American ships were spotless. We admired the beautiful steps of their pinnaces, the gleaming brass, the pine-white woodwork, as those craft lay tossing in our grim shadow."

Dressed in a light Palm Beach suit, Roosevelt stood waiting under an awning, supporting himself on the arm of his son Elliott. The Joint Chiefs of Staff and a few top advisers were nearby; they held themselves at attention, and down by the railing the Marine Band struck up "God Save the King." Churchill had reached the deck.

The prime minister was "unmistakable," Elliott Roosevelt wrote: "short, rotund, . . . florid . . .—not an especially prepossessing figure at an instant's glance, yet a man whose calm, confident power required but a moment to make itself evident."

After the musicians had played "The Star-Spangled Banner," Churchill stepped forward. Approaching Roosevelt and making a formal bow, he presented the president with a letter of salutation from King George VI. Then Churchill and Roosevelt shook hands; officers and advisers introduced themselves to their counterparts; Churchill lit up a cigar; Roosevelt, lowered into his wheelchair, inserted a cigarette in his holder; and the two leaders went off for a tour of the ship. The Argentia Conference was under way.

Sunday morning brought a clear sky and a warm breeze. The hillsides around Argentia were bright green, and the waters of the bay were shimmering. Leaving the *Augusta* for a worship service aboard the *Prince of Wales*, Roosevelt, dressed in a double-breasted blue suit, crossed over on the destroyer *McDougal*. Once on the British battleship, helped by his cane and his son Elliott, Roosevelt made his way the entire length of the vessel to his chair of honor on the quarterdeck. Never since being afflicted with polio had he attempted a walk of such a distance. But he made it, and he took his chair beside Churchill for the start of the service.

Under the bright sunshine, each with a hymnbook in his hand, they jointly faced the makeshift altar. Just behind the two chairs stood the assembled officers and advisers. As two chaplains, one British and one American, stepped forward, a small organ introduced the first of the hymns.

"None who took part in it will forget the spectacle presented that sunlit morning on the crowded quarterdeck," Churchill wrote in his history of World War II, "the symbolism of the Union Jack and the Stars and Stripes draped side by side [behind] the pulpit; the American and British chaplains sharing in the reading of the prayers; the highest naval, military, and air officers of Britain and the United States grouped together behind the president and me; the close-packed ranks of British and American sailors, completely intermingled, sharing the same books and joining fervently together in the prayers familiar to both." Churchill himself had selected the hymns: "For Those in Peril on the Sea"; "Onward, Christian Soldiers"; and "Our God, Our Help in Ages Past," the last being, as Churchill knew, the hymn Roosevelt had chosen for the day of his first inauguration.

For Churchill, the service was to be the keystone of the Argentia Conference. By evoking all that Great Britain and America had in common, he could bind Roosevelt to the British imperial cause, he hoped.

Back on the *Augusta* that night, however, Roosevelt gave a dinner for Churchill, and Churchill's hopes soon evaporated. Elliott Roosevelt was present. "You sensed," he wrote, "that two men accustomed to leadership had sparred, had felt each other out, and were now readying themselves for outright challenge."

Conflict indeed soon erupted.

Father started it all by bringing up imperial preference. "Of course," he remarked, with a sly sort of assurance, "of course, after the war, one of the preconditions of any lasting peace will have to be the greatest possible freedom of trade."

He paused. The P.M.'s head was lowered; he was watching Father steadily, from under one eyebrow.

"No artificial barriers," Father pursued. "As few favored economic agreements as possible. Opportunities for expansion. Markets open for healthy competition." His eye wandered innocently around the room. . . .

Churchill's neck reddened and he crouched forward. "Mr. President, England does not propose for a moment to lose its favored position among the British Dominions."

"You see," said Father slowly, "it is along in here somewhere that there is likely to be some disagreement between you, Winston, and me. I am firmly of the belief that if we are to arrive at a stable world peace it must involve the development of backward countries. Backward peoples. . . . I can't believe that we are in a fight against fascist slavery, and at the same time not work to free people all over the world from a backward colonial policy."

Around the room, all of us were leaning forward attentively. Hopkins was grinning. Commander Thompson, Churchill's aide, was looking glum and alarmed. The P.M. himself was beginning to look apoplectic. Father ignored the danger signals.

"The peace," he concluded, "cannot include any continued despotism. The structure of the peace demands and will get equality of peoples."

Elliott Roosevelt may not have remembered the dialogue exactly. But his father's point was plain to everyone present: in the postwar world, America was going to make the rules, as became manifest in the language of the Atlantic Charter.

"The president of the United States of America and the prime minister, Mr. Churchill, . . . deem it right to make known certain common principles . . . on which they base their hopes for a better future for the world."

Thus began the preamble of the Atlantic Charter, signed by Roosevelt and Churchill aboard the *Prince of Wales* on the morning of Tuesday, August 12, 1941. The document continued:

First, their countries seek no aggrandizement, territorial or other.

Second, they desire to see no territorial changes that do not accord with the freely expressed wishes of the peoples concerned.

Third, they . . . wish to see the sovereign rights and self-government returned to those who have been forcibly deprived of them.

Fourth, they will endeavor . . . to further the enjoyment by all states, great or small, victor or vanquished, of access, on equal terms, to the trade and to the raw materials of the world which are needed for . . . prosperity.

Fifth, they desire to bring about the fullest collaboration between all nations in the economic field.

Sixth, after the final destruction of the Nazi tyranny, they hope to see established a peace which will afford . . . assurance that all men in all lands may live out their lives in freedom from fear and want.

Seventh, such a peace should enable all men to traverse the high seas and oceans without hindrance.

Eighth, they believe that all the nations of the world . . . must come to the abandonment of the use of force.

Having agreed to these aspirations, Roosevelt and Churchill took lunch together; afterward they went to the quarterdeck of the *Augusta* to express their formal farewells. As they parted, Roosevelt gave Churchill a copy of the poem "The Building of the Ship" by Henry Wadsworth Longfellow, which included these lines:

Sail on, O Ship of State!
Sail on, O Union, strong and great!
Humanity with all its fears,
With all the hopes of future years,
Is hanging breathless on thy fate!

The Atlantic Charter at last publicly committed the United States to the defeat of Nazi Germany. But it was also Wilsonian to the core. It called for the abolition of international aggression, the freedom of the seas, free trade, and the end of colonialism: "the sovereign rights and self-government restored to those who have been forcibly deprived of them."

Churchill had no choice but to sign the Atlantic Charter: Great Britain needed America's money. Yet the price he had to pay was the promise of the dissolution of the British Empire.

CHAPTER 12

The Turning of the Tide

1

With the conclusion of the Argentia Conference, the world seemed to be rushing toward a climax. Intelligence reports that reached London and Washington indicated that Japan was preparing a massive naval assault, probably into southeastern Asia; once back in Britain, Churchill dispatched the *Prince of Wales* to Singapore in the hope of giving that colony a measure of protection. Although snow fell on Moscow at the end of September, the German army was pushing ever farther into Russia. And with the September days growing shorter and with fewer and fewer daylight hours in the North Atlantic, the chances of a collision between a German submarine and an American vessel of war were ever greater. The "British," wrote Theodore Wilson, the major historian of the Argentia Conference, "understandably looked forward to such an occurrence." They had hardly forgotten the sinking of the *Lusitania*.

And another such incident took place, almost. Roosevelt had gone to Hyde Park, for his mother had died, and he had spent several days in seclusion. But on September 11 he went on the air to give an account of an incident concerning the American destroyer *Greer*.

An old vessel of World War I vintage, the *Greer* had gone out from Boston on a mail run to Reykjavik. Nearing Iceland on September 4, the captain had received word from a British patrol plane that a German submarine lay in its path. Under orders to track and locate any U-boats in the area, the destroyer had spent several hours on the search. Finding the U-boat at last, the *Greer* had informed the British of the submarine's whereabouts. With the German boat submerged, a Royal Air Force plane passed overhead, dropping depth charges. The U-boat had responded by firing two torpedoes at the *Greer*. Dodging them, the *Greer* had launched its own depth-charge attack. Then twilight had come and the submarine escaped.

Wearing a black armband and seated beside a poster that said, "Keep 'Em Flying," Roosevelt spoke into a microphone. He said nothing about the sequence that had led the submarine to open fire. He framed the issue differently: "[I]t is now clear that Hitler has begun his campaign to control the seas by ruthless force." Roosevelt told his radio audience that there "has now come a time when you and I must see the cold, inexorable necessity of saying to these inhuman, unrestrained seekers of world conquest: 'You shall go no further.' . . . When you see a rattlesnake poised to strike, you do not wait until he has struck before you crush him."

Driving through Tennessee near the Norris Dam, Samuel Rosenman, a White House speechwriter, was listening to the broadcast on his car radio. "The atmosphere was quiet and peaceful down there . . . on that still September night," Rosenman would recall. "It seemed so far away from the world of conflict and destruction . . . that the bold, resolute—almost belligerent—tones of the president seemed a little like a voice coming from another planet."

"Let this warning be clear," the voice went on. "From now on, if German or Italian vessels of war enter the waters the protection of which is necessary for American defense, they do so at their own peril."

In London, Churchill was hopeful. "Hitler will have to choose between losing the Battle of the Atlantic," he wrote, "or coming into frequent collision with United States ships."

The *Greer* episode, however, did not propel the United States formally into the war. Nor did the sinking by a U-boat of the *Reuben James*, a U.S. destroyer, off Ireland on October 31; 115 Americans drowned. On November 2 Churchill wrote Roosevelt: "I am grieved at the loss of life you have suffered with *Reuben James*. I salute the land of unending challenge!"

Churchill's words were not enough. Roosevelt still held back. Then . . .

December 7, 1941, 1:00 PM, Greenwich time, at Chequers, the prime minister's official country residence. Churchill was putting on a luncheon, and all his invited guests had arrived save one. The late-comer was John Winant, the U.S. ambassador, finally confirmed by the Senate. Winant wrote,

> When I reached Chequers, . . . the prime minister was walking up and down outside the entrance door—the others had gone on into lunch twenty minutes before. He asked me if I thought there was going to be war with Japan. I answered "Yes." With unusual vehemence he turned to me and said:
>   "If they declare war on you, we shall declare war on them within the hour."
>   "I understand, Prime Minister. You have stated that publicly."
>   "If they declare war on us, will you declare war on them?"
>   "I can't answer that, Prime Minister. Only the Congress has the right to declare war under the United States Constitution."
>   He didn't say anything for a minute, but I knew what was in his mind. He must have realized that if Japan attacked Siam [Thailand] or British territory it would force Great Britain into an Asiatic war. . . . He knew in that moment that his country might be "hanging on one turn of pitch and toss."
>   Nevertheless he turned to me with the charm of manner that I saw so often in difficult moments, and said, "We're late, you know. You get washed and we will go to lunch together."

The afternoon proceeded uneventfully; Churchill had his usual postluncheon nap. In time, all the guests, who included Averell Harriman, Roosevelt's immensely wealthy special envoy to Great Britain, dressed for dinner, which began well after sunset.

"The prime minister seemed tired and depressed," Harriman wrote. "He didn't have much to say throughout dinner and was immersed in his thoughts with his head in his hands part of the time."

Churchill himself would remember that "I turned on my small wireless set shortly after the nine o'clock news had started. There were a number of items about the fighting on the Russian front and on the British front in Libya, at the end of which some sentences were spoken regarding an attack by the Japanese on American shipping at Hawaii, and also Japanese attacks on British vessels in the Dutch East Indies."

The penultimate passage was vague, and Churchill at first paid it little attention. But Harriman pointed out that Americans apparently were under attack.

Then Frank Sawyers, Churchill's butler and valet, entered the dining room. He and other members of the Chequers staff also had heard the broadcast.

"It's quite true," he said, "we heard it outside. The Japanese have attacked the Americans."

Ambassador Winant recounted what happened next:

We looked at one another incredulously. Then Churchill jumped to his feet and started for the door with the announcement, "We shall declare war on Japan!" There is nothing half-hearted or unpositive about Churchill—certainly not when he is on the move. Without ceremony I too left the table and followed him out of the room.

"Good God," I said, "you can't declare war on a radio announcement."

He stopped and looked at me half-seriously, half-quizzically, and then said quietly, "What shall I do?" The question was asked not because he needed me to tell him what to do, but as a courtesy to the representative of the country attacked.

I said, "I will call up the president by telephone and ask him what the facts are."

And he added, "And I shall talk with him too."

We got through to the White House in a few minutes and the president told me very simply the story of the attack—so tragic in itself and yet the final mistake that was to end the power of the Axis. He could not, however, over the open transatlantic telephone, tell the extent of the crushing losses sustained by the fleet, or the heavy casualties. I said I had a friend with me who wanted to speak to him. I said, "You will know who it is as soon as you hear his voice."

Once Churchill got on the line, Roosevelt confirmed the news of the attack at Pearl Harbor; he added that the next day, December 8, he would ask Congress for a declaration of war against Japan. Great Britain's own declaration, Churchill said, would follow America's "within the hour."

On December 11, Germany and Italy formally declared war on the United States. A few hours later, the United States formally declared war on Germany and Italy.

Sure at last of America's official entry into the war, Churchill on December 12 cabled to Anthony Eden, the foreign secretary, who was en route to the Soviet Union: "The accession of the United States makes amends for all, and with time and patience will give certain victory." He also lost no time arranging another meeting with Roosevelt, this time in the White House, to discuss matters of joint strategy. So a week after the bombing of Pearl Harbor, Churchill and his military staff were aboard the *Duke of York*, bound for the United States.

Churchill could not travel again on the *Prince of Wales*. Along with a sister ship, the *Repulse*, the *Prince of Wales* on December 9 had steamed up the Malay Peninsula to intercept a reported Japanese landing. But a Japanese submarine had spotted the British ships and, late the next morning, aircraft from nearby Japanese carriers had descended on the vessels; with no fighter protection from Singapore, the battleships were doomed. Shortly after noon on December 10, both the *Repulse* and the *Prince of Wales* had gone under.

Still abed in Britain, Churchill had received the news in a telephone call from First Sea Lord Sir Dudley Pound. To the prime minister, who so recently had ridden on the ship, the sinking of the *Prince of Wales* had been the most shocking event of the war so far. Besides entailing the loss of more than two thousand lives, it had signaled to him the end of Great Britain's Far Eastern empire.

Weighed down by the sense of loss, Churchill went to Scapa Flow to board the *Duke of York*. And crossing the Atlantic, he brooded over what he foresaw as Great Britain's role as junior partner in the conflicts to come.

2

The *Duke of York* reached the mouth of Chesapeake Bay on December 22, 1941, but instead of proceeding to Annapolis, it entered Hampton Roads, the anchorage formed by the mouth of the James River; Churchill was impatient to get to Washington. While the rest of the British party proceeded northward by train, Churchill and Lord Moran, his personal physician, boarded a U.S. Navy Lockheed. The aircraft took off at dusk. As it approached Washington the Britons, accustomed to nightly blackouts, were astonished to see the blaze of lights below. After the plane had landed at National Airport, Churchill went down the ramp first. Following, Lord Moran noticed through the gloom that nearby a man was standing propped up against a large automobile. Churchill called the doctor over and introduced him to President Roosevelt. Churchill would write of that moment that "I clasped [Roosevelt's] strong hand with comfort and pleasure."

Upon reaching the White House, Churchill was ushered to the Northeast Suite, on the second floor at the opposite end of the gallery from the president's private rooms; the suite was soon filled with flowers, gifts from people all over the United States. Across the hall was the Monroe Room, which Roosevelt had reserved for Churchill's use as an office. Within a day the walls of the office were covered with maps, just as were the walls of Churchill's underground warren back in London; British naval and military officers with their red leather dispatch cases were in and out of the office so frequently that for all practical purposes the eastern end of the White House became the command post of the British Empire.

The disruptions left Harry Hopkins, who had a bed in the White House close to the Monroe Room, decidedly miffed. More flexible, Roosevelt adjusted to Churchill's eccentric routine. Churchill took long afternoon naps and then habitually worked, drank, and talked into the small hours of the morning. Roosevelt, who normally retired early but who did not want to miss a word of the Churchillian rhetoric, joined the prime minister in these late-night sessions.

And then there was the matter of the morning bath. According to the account left by Commander Thompson, the aide, this "was often quite a spectacular event. [Churchill] would fling himself under the water, and then surface again, blowing like a whale. When he emerged ... Sawyers [the valet] would be standing with an enormous towel, and, draped in this, the prime minister would pace to and fro, followed by Kenna [a stenographer] with notebook and pencil." On one such occasion, according to legend, Roosevelt wheeled himself into Churchill's suite and, just at that moment, the towel fell to the floor. "You see," Churchill stated, referring to American suspicions that the British government had secreted vast stores of wealth out in the Empire and Commonwealth, "I have nothing to conceal from the president of the United States."

Churchill without question was trying to sell the idea of Anglo-American unity. On Christmas Eve 1941 he and Roosevelt stood together on a balcony of the White House as the lights illuminated the huge conifer down on the Ellipse.

Thousands of spectators were crowded behind the fences. Churchill addressed them through a microphone:

Whether it be the ties of blood on my mother's side, or the friendships I have developed here over many years of active life, or the commanding sentiment of comradeship in the common cause of great peoples who speak the same language, who kneel at the same altars, and, to a very large extent, pursue the same ideals, I cannot feel myself a stranger here in the centre and at the summit of the United States. I feel a sense of unity and fra-

ternal association which, added to the kindliness of your welcome, convinces me that I have a right to sit at your fireside and
share your Christian joys.

Commenting on the sadness of that Christmas Eve with
war "raging and roaring over all the lands and seas," Churchill
concluded:

Let the children have their night of fun and laughter. Let the
gifts of Father Christmas delight their play. Let us grown-ups
share to the full in their unstinted pleasures before we turn
again to the stern task and the formidable years that lie before
us, resolved that, by our sacrifice and daring, these same children shall not be robbed of their inheritance or denied their
right to live in a free and decent world.

On Christmas Day, Roosevelt and Churchill attended an inter-
denominational church service. Although there were no children in
the White House, a host of adult Roosevelts showed up, forty or fifty
of them, and they all gathered for dinner. Throughout the meal,
Churchill was unusually quiet, preoccupied with the speech he was
scheduled to give the next day to Congress. Rather than stay with
the president, the first lady, and their familial guests to watch a post-
prandial movie, he returned to his suite. Leaving the table, he
explained that he must do his "homework."

Churchill was still at his "homework" in the middle of the morning
when White House aides told him that the time had come for him
to leave for the Capitol. Joined by Lord Moran, Churchill got into
a limousine at the back entrance of the White House, "dashing,"
Lord Moran wrote, "through the streets with siren wailing and two
G-men on each of the running boards, their pockets bulging with
revolvers, ready to jump off in a second if anything happened. A few
people lining the streets waved and cheered."
     Once at the Capitol, Churchill waited in a small room, compos-
ing his thoughts. "Do you realize we are making history?" he asked

the doctor. Then Churchill was ushered to the rostrum in the House of Representatives, there to address a joint session of Congress.

He got on good terms with them right away: "I cannot help reflecting," Churchill said, "that if my father had been American and my mother British, instead of the other way around, I might have got here on my own."

The laughter was great and the shouts of approval were even greater when, speaking of the Japanese, he asked: "What sort of people do they think we are?"

The mood in the House turned somber, however, when Churchill stated: "If we had kept together after the last war, if we had taken common measures for our safety, this renewal of the curse need never have fallen upon us."

The House chamber was silent when he then declared: "Five or six years ago, it would have been easy, without shedding a drop of blood, for the United States and Great Britain to have insisted on the fulfillment of the disarmament clauses of the treaties which Germany signed after the Great War." Continuing, he avowed that "there would have been the opportunity for assuring to Germany those raw materials which we declared in the Atlantic Charter should not be denied to any nation, victor or vanquished. That chance has passed. It is gone. Prodigious hammer-strokes have been needed to bring us together again."

Churchill finished by expressing his hope and faith, "sure and inviolate, that in the days to come the British and the American peoples will for their own safety and for the good of all walk together side by side in majesty, in justice, and in peace."

When Churchill finished, the members of Congress rose as one person, cheered loudly, and waved papers until he departed. Back at the White House, Churchill confided to Lord Moran that "I hit the target this time." Three days later, the prime minister flew to another rousing welcome, this time in Ottawa.

When Churchill's airplane landed at the Ottawa airfield late in the morning of December 29, he rode straight to Government House; the air was frigid and the streets were covered with snow. After a hot bath, he took lunch with MacKenzie King and the rest of the Canadian cabinet. After the inevitable long nap came a reception and a formal dinner; late in the evening Churchill retired to prepare yet another speech, this one to the Canadian Parliament.

Speaking in the great chamber the next morning, Churchill dwelt on one of his favorite themes, the unity of the English-speaking peoples: "We have not journeyed all this way across the centuries, across the oceans, across the mountains, across the prairies, because we are made of sugar candy. [Neither the length of the war] nor any form of severity, it may assume, shall make us weary, or shall make us quit."

He spat out contempt for the French, who had quit. While the French army was in retreat, Churchill told his Canadian audience, General Maxime Weygand had gone to France's cabinet and stated, "In three weeks England will have her neck wrung like a chicken."

Churchill paused.

Then to huge laughter and applause he said: "Some chicken! Some neck!"

On the morning of New Year's Eve, Churchill held a press conference in Government House. "Do you think Singapore can hold on?" a reporter asked; the Japanese had begun their push down the Malay Peninsula.

"I sure do," Churchill answered.

Later in the day, he took a train back to Washington. He arrived on the afternoon of January 1, 1942.

Once back in the White House, he learned news that contradicted his earlier optimism about Singapore: the Japanese were moving through the peninsula with hardly any opposition. Churchill became glum, and with Roosevelt he was no longer his usually voluble self. "[F]or the first time," Lord Moran wrote, "I have seen Winston content to listen. You could almost feel the importance he attaches to bringing the president along with him, and in that good cause he has become a very model of restraint and self-discipline; it is surely a new Winston who is sitting there quite silent. And when he does say anything it is always something likely to fall pleasantly on the president's ear."

In that spirit of harmony, Churchill on New Year's Day endorsed Roosevelt's draft declaration of the United Nations, which was to embrace the United States, Great Britain, the Soviet Union, and several of the nations under Nazi rule. The document called upon all the anti-Axis countries of the world to use their "full resources, military or economic," against Germany, Italy, and Japan, and not "to make a separate armistice or peace with the enemies." Only a total victory could lead to "life, liberty, independence, and religious freedom, and to . . . human rights and justice in their own lands as well as in other lands." The last passage reiterated a major principle of the Atlantic Charter, decolonization.

On January 5 Churchill flew from Washington to Florida, where he ensconced himself in a secluded bungalow near the beach at Pompano; he had not wished to give the impression of kowtowing too long at the foot of Roosevelt's throne. The weather was "balmy after the bitter cold of Ottawa," Lord Moran wrote, "oranges and pineapples grow here. And the blue ocean is so warm that Winston basks half-submerged in the water like a hippopotamus in a swamp." Nonetheless, duty called, and after five days of sun and surf, Churchill returned to Washington by train.

Along the route he was informed that the Japanese had made their first assault on the Dutch East Indies. Then, while back in the White House, came a report about Singapore's lack of defenses. "This is a shocking tale," he cabled to the British cabinet, "and everybody seems to blame. . . . These elements of deficiency must have been known . . . before the war broke out."

His worries pressing on him, Churchill on January 14, 1942, left for London, flying from Norfolk to Bermuda, and thence on to England. The Washington Conference was over.

What had been its results? Despite the triumphs of his speechmaking, his three weeks in North America had been ones largely of agony for Churchill. Against the advice of many of his aides, to be sure, Roosevelt had promised Churchill that, for the United States, the war in the Atlantic would take precedence over that in the

Pacific. Roosevelt furthermore had granted Churchill's request not to launch a cross-Channel invasion of the European continent in 1942; Churchill well remembered the horrors of trench warfare in the previous world war and believed that a premature effort to land on the beaches of France would lead to disaster. Roosevelt had warned Churchill nonetheless that "if the West fails to support Indian nationalism, Japan . . . is likely to inspire a full-fledged anti-Western revolt." Churchill also had argued long and passionately for separate military commands, or at least important decisionmakers situated in London. Counseled by General Marshall, however, Roosevelt had said no: the British and American commands would be unified, under the direction of the United States, and the locus of decisionmaking would be Washington. From the very outset of the Anglo-American war against the Axis powers, Great Britain would be the junior partner. With that point driven home, Churchill to his humiliation also had had to accede to Secretary Hull's demand for the destruction of British imperial preferences.

Already largely in control of the Atlantic, the American leaders in Washington had made their point clear. As far as they were concerned, the British Empire was to be a thing of the past, as was shown by the fall of Singapore.

3

On the day of Churchill's return to London, January 15, 1942, the docks of Singapore were ablaze. The British had provided the island colony with fearsome artillery, but the gun barrels had pointed out to sea, in anticipation of a Japanese naval assault. The warriors of the rising sun, however, had come the other way, down the Malay Peninsula, and by the middle of January they had pushed right up to the strait that separated Singapore from the mainland. There, capturing a Malay palace that stood on a hillock, they had set up their command post. From the tower of the palace, Yamashita Tomoyuki, the invaders' commanding general, now enjoyed a clear view of the three-mile-long Singapore harbor and the island's bomb-blasted airfield.

After bombing and shelling Singapore for two more weeks, attacks directed from his high point of vantage, Yamashita sent the first of his soldiers across the strait in rubber boats. The landing took place on the night of January 31, and it was undetected.

The morning of February 1 was hot and humid. The sky was a pale blue tufted with dazzling white clouds. As the sun rose, it pressed down like an iron, flattening the sea to a sheet of corrugated glass. The wharves baked underfoot, and the air by the waterfront reeked of wet rope, machine oil, and the stench of burning rubber. The effects of the previous night's bombing were everywhere. The docks were empty. The wreckage of the warehouses still smoldered. Offshore, a fuel tanker poured out a heavy column of dark smoke. Up by the Blue Funnel piers a freighter was on fire and burning. And in the hotels, clubs, and bungalows around the heights, word went around: not many boats were left on which to escape.

Even worse was to come. By early morning, February 10, the Japanese were coming ashore in large numbers, and the British-Australian defenders on the island were in headlong retreat. Groups of men became separated in the jungle that covered much of the island. Many became lost. Many died. A few managed to straggle into the city itself. Yamashita's forces now held nearly half the island, and A. E. Percival, the British commanding general, ordered his men to prepare the city for surrender, which meant setting fire to anything that might be of use to the enemy.

As the sun rose on Sunday, February 15, Singapore was burning. Even the ocean seemed to be blazing. Flames from a soap factory threw grotesque patterns on the walls of nearby buildings. Smoke from timber sheds reached as high as six hundred feet. Orbs of fire glimmered from nearby islands, where the British had kept their oil reserves; the impression was that of minor setting suns coming to rest upon the horizon.

But there was "no hope or help on the horizon," General Gordon Bennett, Percival's immediate subordinate, wrote in his diary. "The tropical sun is sending its steamy heat onto the dying city which is writhing in its agony." He added: "Silently and sadly we decided to surrender."

"I speak to you under the shadow of a heavy and far-reaching military defeat," Churchill broadcast to the British people on February 15, 1942,

> It is a British and imperial defeat. Singapore has fallen. All the Malay Peninsula has been overrun. Other dangers gather about us out there and none of the dangers which we have hitherto successfully withstood at home and in the East are in any way diminished.
>
> This, therefore, is one of those moments when the British race and nation can show their quality and their genius. This is one of those moments when it can draw from the heart of misfortune the vital impulses of victory.
>
> We must remember that we are no longer alone. We are in the midst of a great company. Three-quarters of the human race are now moving with us. The whole future of mankind may depend upon our action and upon our conduct. So far we have not failed. We shall not fail now. Let us move forward steadfastly together into the storm and through the storm.

The speech was not Churchill's finest hour. "I fear a slump in public opinion which will deprive Winston of his legend," Harold Nicolson wrote on February 16. "His broadcast last night was not liked. The country is too nervous and irritable to be fobbed off with fine phrases. Yet what else could he have said?"

Or done? Just about the only thing Churchill could do was to go to Washington again. This time, on June 17, he flew.

4

The Americans had already enjoyed considerable success, at least in the Pacific. In April 1942, Col. James H. Doolittle, with a squadron of sixteen bombers based on the carrier *Hornet*, had bombed Tokyo. In May, American naval and air forces had sunk a hundred thousand tons of Japanese shipping in the Battle of the Coral Sea, thus safeguarding

Australia. And in early June, American aircraft had played a decisive role in turning back a Japanese fleet during the Battle of Midway.

Such gains might have given Churchill a measure of confidence. They produced, rather, just the opposite. It had been, after all, Japan and not Germany that had attacked the United States. What was to prevent the Americans, full of the desire for revenge against Japan, from throwing their resources into the Pacific and ignoring the Atlantic Theater? Roosevelt had promised to put victory in Europe first, but could the president be trusted? Churchill flew back to America in a most uneasy state of mind.

After his flying boat landed on the Potomac late on June 18, Churchill spent the night in the British embassy; Lord Halifax was his host. In the morning, the prime minister flew northward to meet with Roosevelt at Hyde Park. "He welcomed me with great cordiality," Churchill wrote in his history of World War II, "and, driving the car himself, took me to the majestic bluffs over the Hudson River. . . . The president drove me all over the estate, showing me its splendid views." The next day, Roosevelt and Churchill returned to Washington on the presidential train.

Roosevelt was under pressure. The Soviets were desperate for the Anglo-Americans to open a second front in 1942, and Churchill was equally desperate to avoid such a step, at least on the continent of Europe in 1942. So adamant was Churchill on this issue that at one point in the Washington talks, an outraged General Marshall threatened to ignore the Atlantic Theater altogether. Caught between the demands, Roosevelt proposed an invasion of Morocco and Algeria, the colonies still held by Vichy, the French collaborationist government.

In doing so, Roosevelt overruled Marshall, who regarded North Africa as a waste of time. But as Marshall later admitted, the "leader in a democracy has to keep the people entertained. That may sound like the wrong word, but it conveys the thought."

Churchill flew back to London on the night of June 25. In keeping America involved in the Atlantic Theater without a 1942 Channel crossing, he had won a concession from Roosevelt. It would be Roosevelt's last significant compromise with the British.

• • •

Two days after Churchill's Boeing Clipper took off, the armored forces of General Rommel crossed the border from Libya into Egypt; by the end of the day, they had raced fifty miles toward the Suez Canal. July 1 found the Germans at El Alamein, forty miles from Alexandria and eighty miles from Cairo.

Even more than before, Churchill was trapped in the role of a dependent. From Cairo, General Sir Claude Auchinleck, commander of the British forces in the Middle East, was pummeling London with demands for reinforcements. The only help available, however, was American. American planes and armored vehicles were starting to reach the delta of the Nile, leaving Churchill with the need to show Roosevelt that Great Britain was not altogether the debtor.

"I feel anxiety about the negative attitude we are adopting towards . . . the American operations in the Pacific," Churchill wrote in a note to Admiral of the Fleet Sir Dudley Pound on July 3. "I promised we would assist by making diversions in any way possible, but of course I did not commit us to any particular operation. We must now show a helpful attitude."

Three days after Churchill penned these words, General Marshall, Admiral King, and Harry Hopkins landed in London. Their instructions from Roosevelt were to reach "immediate agreement" with the British on "joint operational plans" for the rest of 1942. Churchill had been hankering to have a go at Japanese-occupied Burma. Such an offensive might have been what Churchill had in mind by way of a diversion; Burma had been a British colony. But the American delegation overruled him. The joint Anglo-American landing in North Africa was to put all other proposals in abeyance. Great Britain's return to colonial Burma was the least of Roosevelt's concerns.

The greatest of Stalin's concerns was that Washington and London would fail to open a second front to force Hitler to withdraw some of his divisions from the Soviet Union. Roosevelt and Churchill in turn were anxious to keep the Soviets in the war. At the end of July, therefore, Churchill made a huge swing by air, first to inspect the

Egyptian Theater, then on to Moscow to meet "the ogre in his den," to give Stalin assurances that the North African campaign would indeed take place.

Churchill's Liberator landed at Moscow on the afternoon of August 12, 1942. On hand to greet him as he stepped to the runway were Vyacheslav Molotov, the Soviet foreign minister, and Averell Harriman, by that point the U.S. ambassador to the Soviet Union. After inspecting a Red Army honor guard, Churchill and his party were driven to a dacha just outside the Soviet capital. Churchill wrote,

> Everything was prepared with totalitarian lavishness. There was placed at my disposal, as aide-de-camp, an enormous, splendid-looking officer . . . who acted as our host and was a model of courtesy and attention. A number of veteran servants in white jackets and beaming smiles waited on every wish or movement of the guests. A long table in the dining-room and various sideboards were laden with every delicacy and stimulant that supreme power can command. I was conducted through a spacious reception room to a bedroom and bathroom of almost equal size. Blazing, almost dazzling, electric lights displayed the spotless cleanliness. The hot and cold water gushed. I longed for a hot bath after the length and the heat of the journey. All was instantly prepared.

Churchill's talks with Stalin, held between August 12 and 16, 1942, went smoothly enough: Stalin seemed to accept the North African invasion as a substitute, of sorts, for a second front in France. But when Churchill dropped hints of an Anglo-Soviet agreement to divide the Balkans between them at the end of the war, Stalin, significantly, was silent.

The Americans were not. When Churchill returned to London on August 24, he came across what he termed "a [his aides deleted the expletive] bombshell." Remembering Churchill's fiasco at the Dardanelles and suspicious of his desire to expand the British Empire into the Balkans, American representatives made quite clear that Washington would not be caught in a Mediterranean "suction pump." Operation Torch, the North African invasion, would go forward, but it would do nothing to further British ambitions in the Mediterranean.

After two weeks of transatlantic wrangling, Churchill accepted the American version of Torch. "I am," he communicated to Harriman, "the president's loyal lieutenant."

5

The end of summer and the beginning of autumn 1942 brought the promise of change on the battlefronts. The Americans landed successfully on Guadalcanal, at the base of the Solomon Islands above New Guinea. The Germans reached Stalingrad and entered the city, but as the first snows fell, the Soviets started to besiege the Germans. Early in September, so British intelligence concluded from messages decoded from the Western Desert, Rommel was running low on fuel.

October 23 saw the opening of the British counteroffensive against Rommel. Four days later, as Churchill learned by cable from Egypt, Rommel threw all available tanks into the battle but "gained no ground." The Royal Air Force, the message continued, "intervened on a devastating scale. In two and a half hours bomber sorties dropped eighty tons of bombs in [Rommel's] concentration area, measuring three miles by two, and the enemy's attack was deflected before he could even complete his forming up. This was the last occasion on which the enemy attempted to take the initiative."

Rommel was stopped, then forced to retreat. Churchill exulted in a cable to Roosevelt that the victory in the desert was a "good prelude to Torch!"

In a celebratory mood, Churchill on November 6 gave a luncheon at 10 Downing Street. Among the guests was Harold Nicolson, who recorded Churchill's account of the Battle of Egypt: "'The enemy,' he says, 'were stuck to the Alamein position like limpets to a rock.

We cut them off'—at that he makes a gesture of someone cutting a limpet off a rock with a knife—'we detached them utterly. And what happens to a limpet when it loses its rock? It dies a miserable death. Thirst comes to it—aching, inescapable thirst. I should not like our armies to be suffering what the Africa Corps will suffer in these days.

"Brendan Bracken [an aide] then comes in and Winston tells him to arrange for all the bells in England to be tolled on Sunday [November 8, the date scheduled for the start of the North African invasion]."

The next day, Churchill decided to postpone the ringing of the church bells until the landings had succeeded. News of the success reached Churchill at nightfall, and the order for the bell-ringing went forth from 10 Downing Street throughout all Great Britain.

Even so, Churchill was far from being a happy man. The very next day he would give voice to his lament.

6

At one o'clock on the afternoon of November 10, 1942, a squadron of fighter planes began to circle the sky over the city of London, offering protection against any German aircraft that might appear. In that same moment, loudspeakers around the Bank of England announced that Churchill was about to arrive. All along Fleet Street, up on Ludgate Hill, and around the steps of St. Paul's Cathedral, a huge crowd immediately assembled. All around were the skeletons of buildings, craters in the pavement, and rubble piled high along the sidewalks. The day was nasty, cold with a pewter sky and rain clouds scudding in from the English Channel. But the people did not care. They had turned out to see the prime minister, who, at last, could boast of a military success.

Riding in the back of an open car and seated beside his wife, Churchill was beaming, holding up two fingers in the V for victory sign. Then, just below the Bank of England, he got out of the car and entered Mansion House.

Behind its classical façade, Mansion House, the official residence of the lord mayor and in the past the site of elegant banquets, had fallen on hard times: because of the exigencies of the war, its dining facilities had closed almost altogether. On this day, however, a luncheon had been organized and the gold plates were out. The thousand or so guests dined on turtle soup and turkey, and drank sherry and wine.

The luncheon over, Sir John Laurie, the retiring lord mayor, introduced the speaker of the day, Winston Churchill. The prime minister went to the lectern:

"I notice, my Lord Mayor, . . . you have reached the conclusion that news from various fronts has been somewhat better lately," he said. "I have never promised anything but blood, tears, toil, and sweat. Now, however, we have a new experience. We have victory—a remarkable and definite victory. The bright gleam has caught the helmets of our soldiers and warmed and cheered all our hearts."

Paying homage to the various nationalities that were contributing to the North African success—"Indian troops, Fighting French [de Gaulle's Free French], Greeks, representatives of Czechoslovakia, and others"—he went on to praise Roosevelt as the "author of this mighty undertaking."

But then, at the end of his speech, Churchill's tone changed. "Let me . . . make this clear," he asserted. "In case there should be any mistake about it in any quarter: we mean to hold our own. I have not become the king's first minister in order to preside over the liquidation of the British Empire!"

From Robert E. Sherwood, playwright, speechwriter for FDR, and author of *Roosevelt and Hopkins: An Intimate History*, we understand something of why Churchill had used those words: "Churchill had waited a long time for an opportunity to say just that. He had suffered and seethed when Roosevelt urged him to establish an independent India, when Roosevelt proclaimed that the principles of the Atlantic Charter extended . . . to . . . everywhere on earth. . . . But now, with the wine of victory coursing in his veins, he hurled at all and sundry, at friend as well as at foe, the defiance that he never for one instant had abandoned: 'Here we are and here we stand, a veritable rock of salvation in this drifting world.'"

Churchill's rhetoric, however, obscured reality. To Churchill, the romantic and reactionary believer in the British Empire, its colonies, its gunboat diplomacy, its white man's burden, and all that, may have still seemed grand. But the grandeur was fading fast. The British Empire was in swift decline and, as the rest of the war made clear, the United States was consciously and deliberately taking its place.

CHAPTER 13

The Big Three

1

Despite his pessimism, Churchill's Mansion House speech followed directly on two decisive victories along the basin of the Mediterranean. In the Egyptian desert at El Alamein on November 4, 1942, General Bernard Montgomery, who had taken command of the British armored forces around Cairo, had dealt Rommel a grievous defeat. And four days later, not long after midnight, the Allies had landed successfully on the shores of Morocco and Algeria.

Under the leadership of General Dwight D. Eisenhower, Operation Torch had appeared to be a risky business. The largest amphibious venture then in history, the assault had involved more than a hundred thousand men—three-fourths of them American and the rest British—who had set forth from ports as far apart as Portland, Maine, and Loch Ewe in Scotland. Separated into three groups, they had been under orders to land at three widely separated points: Casablanca, which was 600 miles from Oran, which in turn was 250 miles from Algiers. All this had been complicated enough. Adding to the complexity had been Eisenhower's hope of deceiving the Germans as to the locales of the landings. As the Oran and Algiers fleets steamed through the Strait of Gibraltar, where they had come to the attention of German intelligence, they had made a feint toward Libya. But then, on the night of November 7–8, they had turned southward, heading for Oran and Algiers, cities under the control of Vichy France.

Although defeated in the metropole and in Indochina, France was still legally in possession of its colonies in sub-Saharan and North Africa. French authorities in those territories, therefore, were subordinate to the government at Vichy; and Vichy survived only by answering to Hitler. So the major question confronting the Allied planners of the invasion of North Africa had been: how serious would be the French resistance?

The answer turned out to be varied. Landing at Algiers before dawn on November 8, 1942, the Allied force by midafternoon was in the hills overlooking the city; by evening they controlled the streets. Oran, where memories of the British attack on the French fleet at Mers-el-Kébir in 1940 were vivid, anti-Allied sentiment ran high; rumors of the impending invasion had been widespread, and Vichy forces were waiting behind the shoreline. Once landed, Eisenhower's amphibious units had to spend two days taking charge of the city. Casablanca proved the most difficult of all. Anchored in the harbor was the battleship *Jean Bart*. Still under construction at Bordeaux when the Germans invaded France, it had been moved to North Africa for safety. Although in dry dock once again at Casablanca, its four big guns were fully operable, and when Allied ships showed up offshore, they opened with formidable fire. Only when American aircraft pummeled it with bombs was the *Jean Bart* put out of action. Not until November 11, the anniversary of the World War I armistice, did Casablanca fall.

In the middle of November, therefore, Eisenhower was able to begin the drive toward Tunisia. He did so uneasily, for as he later explained, "There still existed the fear that the Germans might thrust air forces down across the Pyrenees into Spain, to attack us from the rear." However, no such attack materialized. But when Eisenhower's armored columns reached Tunisia, they had to fight their way through well-dug-in German defenders. Christmas Day 1942 found Eisenhower's advance stalled about twenty-five miles from Tunis.

Rommel's armored forces nonetheless were being squeezed from east and west, so Roosevelt and Churchill felt confident of ultimate victory in North Africa. As they were aware, furthermore, the

Soviet Union had held the German advance and was at last taking the fight to the enemy. And the Americans were inexorably pushing the Japanese back across the Pacific. Allied victory was not exactly at hand, but it was visible on the horizon.

Yet as the strategic issues had begun to resolve themselves, tactical questions were arising, demanding resolution. Given the emerging Soviet success, just when should the British and the Americans plan to cross the English Channel? Should Eisenhower's army simply stay in North Africa, whence it could protect the Mediterranean sea-lanes? Or should the Allies go north? And if so, where? Was Italy to be the next target? Or should the Allies move farther to the east, to Crete, Greece, and Yugoslavia? All such questions demanded further consultation at the summit.

2

November 25, 1942

Dear Winston;

Our own combined chiefs of staff will, I believe, have a recommendation for us within a few days as to what the next steps should be, but I feel strongly that we have to sit down at the table with the Russians. My notion would be a conference in Cairo or Moscow: that each of us would be represented by a small group meeting secretly: that the conclusions of the conference would of course be approved by the three of us. I would probably send Marshall to head up our group, but I presume that all the services should be represented. . . . Will you let me know as soon as you can what you think of my proposal?

Churchill agreed to Roosevelt's proposal in principle but urged that the heads of government be included. Roosevelt had no objection but he resisted Churchill's suggestion that the military part of the American delegation fly first to Great Britain. "I would question the advisability of Marshall and the others going to England prior to the conference," Roosevelt wrote to Churchill on December 2, "because I do not want to give Stalin the impression that we are settling everything between ourselves before we meet him." In a reference to the historic meeting between Napoleon Bonaparte and the czar of Russia, Roosevelt added that "I prefer a comfortable oasis to the raft at Tilsit."

As it turned out, Stalin would not meet with Roosevelt and Churchill anywhere, not in early 1943; he refused to leave the Soviet Union during the height of hostilities. So the meeting would be down to Roosevelt, Churchill, and their military staffs. But where? "England must be out for me for political reasons," FDR wrote, hinting at the past and present American antipathy toward the British Empire. "My thought is," the president continued, "that if time suits your plans we could meet back of Algiers or back of Casablanca about January fifteenth [1943]."

The thought was as good as a command. The meeting would start in the middle of January and take place at Casablanca.

Late in the evening of Saturday, January 9, 1943, Roosevelt, Hopkins, and a White House aide, along with a group of top-ranking generals and admirals, motored to a secret siding at the Bureau of Engraving and Printing, at the intersection of Fourteenth and C streets, southeast of the White House, and boarded the presidential train. After a Sunday spent passing through the pine forests of the Carolinas and Georgia and the marshes and sandy flatlands of the eastern Florida coastline, the train early Monday morning reached Miami. In the harbor formed by Miami Beach, a Pan American Clipper was ready for takeoff. After Roosevelt and his party were aboard, it left in the direction of Trinidad.

Flying for the first time in a decade, when he made his dramatic trip to the 1932 Democratic nominating convention in Chicago, and proud of being the first president since Lincoln while in office to visit a battle zone (a plaque in Fort Monroe commemorates Lincoln's using the site to survey the scene at Hampton Roads), Roosevelt wanted to see everything. At the president's request, the pilot flew over the Citadel in Haiti; Roosevelt had a clear view of the jungle along the South American littoral, the mouths of the Amazon

River, and the freighters in the water off Belém. Following the northern shore of Brazil, the Clipper set out on the overnight flight to Bathurst, the port of British Gambia on the hump of Africa.

From Bathurst a Douglas C-54 on January lifted the presidential party over the snow-tipped Atlas Mountains and onto the air strip just outside Casablanca. Secret Service agents carried Roosevelt to a waiting armored car; the vehicle raced past the green parks and flower gardens of the Casablanca oasis and up a driveway to the Anfa Hotel, selected as the site of the conference. Surrounded by sentries and barbed wire and protected by antiaircraft guns, the hotel had the look of a military compound; steel shutters guarded its windows. Yet its balconies afforded unimpeded views of the sparkling blue of the Atlantic Ocean. Roosevelt settled into a villa nearby to prepare for his encounter with Churchill.

Stormy weather forced Churchill to leave London not on the evening of January 11, as originally scheduled, but rather later the next day. Flying with him were Lord Moran, Averell Harriman, Colonel Thompson, and the valet Sawyers, among a few others. Nine hours after takeoff, the Liberator bomber touched down at Casablanca. Churchill awaited the arrival of a second airplane, this one bearing Admiral Pound and Generals Sir Alan Brooke and Sir Hastings Ismay. Together they also rode to the Anfa Hotel.

"Conditions most agreeable," Churchill cabled to Clement Attlee, the Labour leader who was second in charge of Great Britain's coalition war cabinet. "I wish I could say the same of the problems. I think at least a fortnight will be required."

The first night in Casablanca was given to the civilities. Before dinner, Churchill went to Roosevelt's villa for drinks; then they and their staffs gathered in the hotel's dining room. Fortified by excellent French wines, the participants were relaxed and merry. At one point in the evening an air-raid siren went off but the men just chattered away, their faces illuminated by the candlelight on the table. They talked of families and mutual friends; of Stalin; and, of course, they conversed about the war.

After dinner Elliott Roosevelt, who was present, wrote, "Father and Churchill sat down on a big, comfortable couch that had been set back by the big windows. The steel shutters were closed. The rest of us pulled up chairs in a semicircle in front of the two on the couch. During the next two or three hours, one after another of the generals and admirals would take his leave, until by midnight only Father, Churchill, Hopkins, Harriman, and I were left."

The conversation continued, but in a desultory way, and the session broke up at some point well after midnight. Roosevelt retired to his bedroom, but asked Elliott to stay.

His thoughts, Elliott wrote, "turned to the problem of the colonies and the colonial markets, the problem which he felt was at the core of all chances for future peace. 'The thing is,' he remarked thoughtfully, replacing a smoked cigarette in his holder with a fresh one, 'the colonial system means war. Exploit the resources of an India, a Burma, a Java; take all the wealth out of those countries but never put anything back into them, things like education, decent standards of living, minimum health requirements.'

"'That look that Churchill gets on his face when you mention India!'

"'India should be made a commonwealth at once. After a certain number of years—five perhaps or ten—she should be able to choose whether she wants to remain in the empire or have complete independence.

"'As a commonwealth, she would be entitled to a modern standard. But how can she have these things when Britain is taking all the wealth of her national resources away from her every year? Every year the Indian people have one thing to look forward to, like death and taxes. Sure as shooting, they have a famine. The season of famine, they call it.'"

In Elliott's account, Roosevelt paused for a moment, thinking. Then he said, "'I must tell Churchill what I found out about his British Gambia today.'"

"'At Bathurst?'" Elliott asked.

"'This morning,' the president went on, 'at about eight-thirty, we drove through Bathurst to the airfield. The natives were just getting to work. In rags . . . glum-looking. . . . They [the British] told us the natives would look happier around noontime, when the sun should have burned off the dew and the chill. I was told the prevailing wage for these men was one and nine. One shilling, ninepence. Less than fifty cents.'"

"'An hour?'" Elliott asked.

"'A day! Fifty cents a day! Besides which, they're given a half cup of rice.'"

Roosevelt had not finished: "'Dirt. Disease. Very high mortality rate. . . . Life expectancy—you'd never guess what it is. Twenty-six years. These people are treated worse than livestock. Their cattle live longer!'"

In Elliott's account, Roosevelt concluded with: "'Churchill may have thought I wasn't serious last time. He'll find out this time.'"

The next morning Elliott went down for breakfast, then joined his father in the villa. Marshall, King, Arnold, Hopkins, and Harriman were all gathered there, discussing the agenda for the Casablanca Conference. Later they gathered in the garden, surrounded by oleanders and bougainvilleas, for luncheon. Then they met with the British and the meeting got under way.

In the course of the next week, the Anglo-American military chieftains, convening fifteen times together and three times with Roosevelt and Churchill, reached agreement on the following points: (1) the first priority would be the destruction of the German submarine fleet in the Atlantic; (2) the United States as quickly as possible would build up its forces in Great Britain; (3) operating out of bases on British soil, American bombers would intensify their raids against Germany, flying even in the daytime; (4) joint planning for a cross-Channel invasion would begin immediately; and (5) as soon as Tunisia was secured, the Anglo-Americans would invade Sicily, eventually relieving some of the German pressure on the Soviet Union.

These were all military decisions, and as such they embodied the primary objectives of the Casablanca Conference. But another purpose, at least that of Roosevelt, became evident when on January 22 he was driven 110 miles to Rabat to visit the sultan of Morocco.

Upon arrival in that sun-baked port city, FDR lunched with soldiers from General Mark Clark's Fifth Army; during a meal of ham and sweet potatoes, musicians played "Alexander's Ragtime Band" and "Deep in the Heart of Texas." The following night, joined by Churchill and Elliott Roosevelt under a huge tent, the president hosted a dinner for the sultan and the sultan's son.

Elliott Roosevelt remembered the dinnertime discussion thus:

The sultan expressed a keen desire to obtain the greatest possible aid in securing for his land modern education and health standards. Father pointed out that, to accomplish this, the sultan should not permit outside interests to obtain concessions which would drain off the country's resources. Churchill attempted to change the subject. The sultan, picking up the thread again, raised the question of what Father's advice would entail, insofar as the French government of the future was concerned. Father, balancing his fork, remarked cheerfully enough that the postwar scene and the prewar scene would, of course, differ sharply, especially as they related to the colonial question. Churchill coughed and again plunged into conversation along different lines. Politely, the sultan inquired more specifically, what did Father mean, "differ sharply"? Father, dropping a remark about the past relationship between French and British financiers combined into self-perpetuating syndicates for the purpose of dredging riches out of colonies, went on to raise the question of possible oil deposits in French Morocco. The sultan eagerly pounced on this; declared himself decidedly in favor of developing any such potentialities, retaining the income therefrom; then sadly shook his head as he deplored the lack of trained scientists and engineers among his countrymen, technicians who would be able to develop such fields unaided. Churchill shifted uneasily in his chair. Father suggested mildly that Moroccan engineers and scientists could of course be educated and trained under some sort of reciprocal education program which, for instance, some of our leading universities in the United States [provided]. The sultan nodded. If it had been etiquette, he would have taken notes, names, and addresses of universities, right there on the spot. Father pursued his point, toying with his water glass. He mentioned that it might easily be practicable for the sultan to engage firms—American firms—to carry out the development program he had in mind, on a fee or percentage basis. Such an arrangement, he urged, would have the advantage of enabling the sovereign government of French Morocco to retain considerable control over its own resources, and, indeed, eventually take them over completely. Churchill snorted and tried not to listen.

[The dinner was] delightful, everybody—with one exception —enjoying himself completely. As we rose from the table, the sultan assured Father that, promptly on the heels of the war's close, he would petition the United States for aid in the development of his country. Glowering, biting at his cigar, Britain's prime minister followed the sultan out of the dining room.

It seems little wonder that Churchill glowered. He had just heard Roosevelt propose the replacement of French and British oil companies with American ones, in Morocco and by implication throughout the world. Back in Casablanca and just before departure, Roosevelt also surprised Churchill by making a unilateral pronouncement: the Allies would settle for nothing less that Germany's and Japan's "unconditional surrender."

3

Roosevelt may have made this pronouncement to make sure that Russia stayed in the war. If so, he need not have worried. Triumphant at Stalingrad, Stalin's armies as early as February 1943 were starting to shut off supply lines to the German forces that for sixteen months had laid siege to Leningrad; liberating Leningrad, the Red Army managed to take three hundred thousand German prisoners of war, including twenty-five generals. At Kursk, and now without the aid of snow and ice, the Soviets defeated the Germans again. Hitler threw two thousand airplanes into the battle but to no avail. By midsummer 1943 about two-thirds of the Russian territory overrun by the Wehrmacht was back in Soviet hands.

The Western Allies, too, were making significant gains. Tunisia finally fell, and the Anglo-Americans in July crossed the Mediterranean, into Sicily. Eisenhower then led them across the Strait of Messina onto the toe of Italy, pushing rapidly up along the lower part of the boot. On September 8, 1943, Italy surrendered.

Soon thereafter, however, eleven German divisions moved down through northern Italy, halting Eisenhower's advance just south of Rome. For the British and the Americans, the setback was worrisome enough. But so was the Soviet advance.

This second worry was critical. On August 22, 1943, a report prepared by the U.S. Joint Chiefs of Staff stated that in the European Theater America subscribed to two "fundamental aims": first, "to destroy the German domination of Europe," and second, "to prevent the domination of Europe in the future by any single power (such as the Soviet Union), or by any group of powers in which we do not have a strong influence. If we do not achieve *both* these aims," the memorandum concluded, "we may consider that we have lost the war."

The following day, August 23, 1943, the British and American military chieftains endorsed Operation Rankin. If Germany appeared to be collapsing too rapidly, the plan proposed—that is, before the Western Allies were prepared to start the cross-Channel invasion—London and Washington would parachute forces into Germany *to prop up the Nazi regime.* Thus by late summer 1943, an American historian has contended, Washington had "realized that the . . . 'second front' across the Channel could be used to aid the Soviets militarily and block their expansion at the same time."

In entering the European side of World War II, Roosevelt and his administration had had in mind two overarching goals: defeating Nazi Germany and dismantling the British Empire. Now, in mid- to late 1943, a third objective was becoming clear: the containment of the military might of the Soviet Union.

In pursuing that third goal, Uncle Sam was clearly replacing John Bull. Throughout much of the Victorian era, Great Britain had played the "Great Game," defining czarist Russia as its principal enemy and seeking to contain the Slavic "peril." Then, under Otto von Bismarck, imperial Germany had emerged as the new danger, or at least the putative one, and so early in the twentieth century London had pigeonholed its differences with St. Petersburg: in a 1907 treaty, the British government had acknowledged a Russian sphere of influence in northern Persia. Now, in 1943, the United States was replaying the earlier British role: Germany was receding, Russia was advancing, and America was assuming the responsibility of containing the Russian menace, real or supposed.

Washington, accordingly, wanted to limit the impending Soviet hegemony in Eastern Europe. So in October 1943, despite his fear of flying, Secretary of State Hull took a plane to Moscow. There he demanded that Stalin accept free trade in the emerging Soviet zone in Eastern Europe. Stalin refused to cooperate. Hull and Roosevelt nonetheless hoped to find a way, short of continued war, of limiting Soviet control of the region.

Roosevelt thus agreed to meet with Stalin and Churchill late in 1943. The place chosen for the first summit of the Big Three was Tehran. First, though, came a stopover in Cairo, where the president took yet another opportunity to needle Churchill about the coming fate of the British Empire.

Official photographs taken during the Cairo Conference show the major participants; Churchill in a white linen suit; Roosevelt in a dark business suit; Chiang Kaishek, the leader of China (whom Roosevelt had ordered to show up in an effort to persuade Chiang actively to pursue the war against the Japanese), in a high-collared khaki uniform; and Madame Chiang, who translated for her husband, in a white silk jacket and a black slit skirt, seated in side-by-side chairs under the Egyptian sunshine. The pictures conveyed a sense of amity.

For Churchill the conference turned out to be anything but amicable. Roosevelt let him know that after the war he intended to include China, along with Great Britain, the Soviet Union, and the

United States, in what he called "the Four Horsemen." Realizing that Roosevelt wanted thereby to dilute British influence in the councils of the victors, Churchill exploded with wrath. He protested that China in general and Chiang Kaishek in particular were weak, corrupt, and attractive to the United States only because America planned after the war to replace Great Britain as the dominant foreign power in China.

Roosevelt ignored Churchill's protest. China, he informed the prime minister, was destined to become America's junior power.

By the time of the Cairo Conference, American military power in the Asian Theater far surpassed that of Great Britain, and Roosevelt intended to use that power to create a postwar Asia that accorded with American, not British, interests. Churchill even feared that Roosevelt would incite Chiang Kaishek to push the British out of colonial Hong Kong.

On November 27, 1943, with the Cairo Conference over, the Chiangs returned to China. Roosevelt and Churchill flew separately to Tehran.

As Roosevelt's airplane, the *Sacred Cow*, took off from Cairo, it crossed the Suez Canal, the Sinai desert, and soon the green valleys of the Tigris and the Euphrates. Following a highway that zigzagged through the mountain passes of Iran, it finally touched down on a field a few miles outside Tehran.

Soviet agents in the city had discovered, or said that they had discovered, a plot among Nazi sympathizers to assassinate the Allied leaders. Stalin therefore had sent word that Roosevelt should stay at the well-guarded Soviet embassy.

Churchill's own arrival seemed fraught with menace. He wrote,

> As we approached the city the road was lined with Persian cavalrymen every fifty yards, for at least three miles. It was clearly shown to any evil people that somebody of consequence was coming, and which way. The men on horseback advertised the route, but could provide no protection at all. A police car driving a hundred yards in advance gave warning of our approach.

The pace was slow. Presently large crowds stood in the spaces between the Persian cavalry, and as far as I could see there were few, if any, foot police. Towards the centre of Tehran these crowds were four or five deep. The people were friendly but non-committal. They pressed to within a few feet of the car. There was no defense at all against two or three determined men with pistols or a bomb. As we reached the turning which led to the [British] legation there was a traffic block, and we remained for three or four minutes stationary amid the crowded throng of gaping Persians. . . . However, nothing happened. . . . In due course we arrived at the British legation, which lay within a strong cordon of British-Indian troops.

The trip from Cairo and the drive to the legation, however, left Churchill exhausted, barely able to speak. For the prime minister, thus, the Tehran Conference got off to a bad start, and it only got worse.

Each of the Big Three—Stalin, Churchill, and Roosevelt—had a different vision of the postwar world. Stalin wanted a security zone around the periphery of the Soviet Union, a buffer that would grant protection against future invasions and that would extend to the very heart of Germany. Churchill longed for the restoration of the British Empire and even its expansion, as into the Balkans. And Roosevelt wanted a world free of zones and empires, a world of open markets in which the United States, with its superior economy, could be the dominant force. American and Soviet goals thus stood in direct contradiction one to the other. But Stalin and Roosevelt recognized that after the war their countries would be the only great powers and that they had better find some way of reaching mutual accommodation. And they agreed on one further point: neither would countenance a resurrection of the British Empire.

So during the first dinner put on for the Big Three, Roosevelt and Stalin virtually ignored Churchill. He returned to the British legation in a black mood: "Stupendous issues are unfolding before our eyes," he blurted out to aides, "and we are only specks of dust that have settled in the night on the map of the world."

On the third day of the conference, Churchill sent Roosevelt a note suggesting that they take lunch together. To the prime minister's dismay, the president declined the invitation, going off to meet privately with Stalin and Molotov. And at dinner that night, a small affair hosted by Stalin at his embassy, the Soviet leader proceeded to taunt Churchill without mercy. The prime minister, Stalin claimed, was soft on Germany: he wanted the kind of peace that would enable the Anglo-American powers to unleash Germany once more against the Soviet Union. Churchill was so outraged that he stalked out of the room; only when Stalin followed him and clapped a hand on his shoulder did the prime minister return.

Churchill's depression, however, did not lighten. On November 30, during a full day of discussion, Stalin smoked, doodled, and made blunt points, items with which Roosevelt did not disagree. Churchill, scowling, realized that the balance had swung inexorably against him, his eastern Mediterranean strategy, and indeed the future of his empire.

Roosevelt in his turn tried all his arts of persuasion to turn Stalin away from his determination to grab and keep most of the countries of Eastern Europe. The president explained away the American opposition to such seizures by alluding to American domestic politics. The United States presidential election was in the offing, he pointed out to the Soviet dictator; and therefore he, Roosevelt, had to cultivate the goodwill of the large numbers of voters of Eastern European, especially Polish, background, for they were certain to look with horror on Soviet control of their ancestral lands. So Roosevelt had to maintain a facade of protest.

It did not work. Stalin was unmoved.

Roosevelt tried another tack, trying to woo Stalin by using Churchill as a foil. Roosevelt later said to Frances Perkins, his secretary of labor,

I began almost as soon as we got into the conference room. I talked privately with Stalin. I didn't say anything that I hadn't said before, but it appeared quite chummy and confidential, enough so that the other Russians joined us to listen. . . .

Then I said, lifting my hand to cover a whisper (which, of course, had to be interpreted), "Winston is cranky this morning, he got up on the wrong side of the bed."

A vague smile passed over Stalin's eyes, and I decided I was on the right track. As soon as I sat down at the conference table, I began to tease Churchill about his Britishness, about John Bull, about his cigars, about his habits. It began to register with Stalin. Winston got red and scowled, and the more he did so, the more Stalin smiled. Finally Stalin broke into a deep, heavy guffaw. . . . I kept it up until Stalin was laughing with me, and it was then that I called him "Uncle Joe."

None of Roosevelt's act had the slightest effect, however, on Stalin's views. Stalin did accept Roosevelt's and Churchill's assurances that they would invade France the following year; and the Tehran Conference did produce agreement on the creation of the United Nations. Beyond such points, though, the meeting served largely to reveal fissures among the Big Three and within what Churchill so fondly called the "Grand Alliance." Churchill's hopes for obtaining support for a Britannic imperial restoration were simply ignored: the restoration of the world order once led by Great Britain was passing fast, under the control of the United States of America. Yet at the same time, a clash between the imperial interests the United States was inheriting from Great Britain and the interests of imperial Russia being inherited by the Soviet Union—a conflict between an open, integrated, worldwide economic and political order and a segregated, walled-off zone of autonomy to the east—was becoming evident.

At the end of the Tehran Conference, the participants presented the press with a picture of trilateral concord. But all they were doing was papering over a gaping crack in the wall. Indeed, throughout the rest of the war, what had been implicit at Tehran became explicit: the Allies were on the road to victory over the Axis powers; and the

United States was not only dismissing Great Britain as an imperial partner but also preparing to challenge the Soviet Union as America's last international rival.

4

After the Tehran Conference, which ended on the first day of December 1943, Roosevelt flew to Sicily. There he formally charged General Eisenhower with the responsibility of commanding the invasion of France, scheduled for June 1944. The Italian campaign was still going slowly, but the Allies were making progress against the German defenders. On the Eastern Front the Soviets were pushing into Romania, Poland, and East Prussia.

Then, in the predawn darkness of June 6, 1944, mile-long convoys of trucks started to move down the roadways of southern England and soon disgorged 2½ million soldiers. The majority of these were Americans, a large minority British and Canadians, and tens of thousands more were Poles, Czechs, Belgians, French, Danes, Norwegians, and others still, all marching onto docks that jutted from the English Channel coast. Waiting to take the men aboard were 900 vessels of war—battleships, cruisers, and PT boats—and 4,000 landing craft. Behind them more than 100 air bases were ready to send up the airplanes that would cover the assault; 120,000 hospital beds were available for the wounded.

Just a few miles above the piers of Portsmouth stood a trailer equipped with lines of communication to 10 Downing Street and the White House: Eisenhower's headquarters. Ensconced there with the top British and American commanders, Eisenhower received a weather report: the forecast was for clouds and high winds over the Channel, hardly ideal for sending the armada across the water. After some moments of agonizing, Eisenhower gave the order. It was "Go."

Thus on D-Day began the Allied invasion of the beaches of Normandy. The Germans, well dug in along the French coastline, fought back hard, inflicting huge casualties among the invaders.

Within a month, though, the sheer weight of American armor and the power of its bombs had proved too much for the defenders. The American industrial machine had come to dwarf that of Nazi Germany, making Hitler's defeat inevitable.

In contrast to the Asian and European economies, almost all of which had been devastated by warfare, American factory production between 1940 and 1944 had shot up by 90 percent; agricultural output had increased by 20 percent; and the gross national product of the United States had risen by an overall 60 percent. But could such growth continue in the postwar world? It would not do so, Secretary Hull believed, if the United States could not freely import and export. Henry Grady, an economist with the Roosevelt administration, agreed: "The capitalist system is essentially an international system," he stated. "If it cannot function internationally, it will break down." Will Clayton, a Texas businessman turned State Department official, agreed, calling for international arrangements that could prevent a return to the "beggar thy neighbor" policies of the 1930s.

To make sure that the world did not revert to those policies, the United States called a conference of forty-five non-Axis nations to meet at Bretton Woods, New Hampshire. The task before the more than seven hundred delegates was the reconstruction of the international economic system along lines designed by the United States. The sessions began on July 1, 1944.

The Bretton Woods Conference took place in an old Victorian hotel that stood in the shadow of Mount Washington, almost at the Canadian border; the long porch of the red-roofed, white-painted hostelry was so chilly that despite the time of year, most of the delegates outfitted themselves in winter suits. Heading the American group, the largest, Treasury Secretary Morgenthau told reporters that he wished he had brought along a pair of woolen socks.

Morgenthau, however, had more serious things to communicate. In an address given in the hotel ballroom following his election as permanent president of the conference, Morgenthau stated that the first item on the agenda was "the formulation of a definite proposal for a stabilization fund of the United States and Associated Nations" and that the second was a plan for "an international bank for postwar reconstruction."

In the back of the thinking of Morgenthau and the rest of the forty-seven-member American delegation was the understanding of how international economics had worked during the reign of Queen Victoria. Covering the Marshall Plan four years later, the American journalist Theodore H. White in his memoirs accurately described the worldview of Morgenthau and the rest of the Americans at the Bretton Woods Conference: in the nineteenth century,

> the entire globe was made one. Europe made it one—and England led Europe. At the beginning of that century London was about to become the capital of the world. . . . By the end of that time the price of bread in Europe was not only what bread actually cost at the bakery, but also a statistical intersection of prices in London, reflecting the wheat yield in Kansas and the Ukraine. In that period, the plantation millionaires of the Amazon had flourished and then passed away as international trade stole the rubber culture from them, and transplanted rubber to Malaya and Sumatra. Cables and telegraph wires linked prices and markets together so that men in London or Liverpool could make fortunes on futures in copper, pepper, cotton, bristles, zinc, or cocoa, and be sure of delivery and payment in recognized standards of quality and money. From the ports of Europe, all oceans, sea lanes, cargo carrying, insurance rates, were interlinked as one. Gold measured all values; London set the price of gold; the phrase "payable by draft on London" meant anyone, anywhere, could buy or sell, secure in London's guarantee to deliver gold.
>
> The stability of the pound, and the globe-girdling authority of the British Navy as it brought the heathen to accounting, set up a rhythm of economic progress never before matched. . . . Only the British understood [the] American dream of restoration. The British had centralized the nineteenth-century world that America was now trying to re-create.

The Americans at Bretton Woods intended to recapture that golden past, only this time under the leadership not of Great Britain but rather of the United States. The "international bank" to which Morgenthau had referred actually became two financial institutions, the International Bank for Reconstruction (the World Bank) and the International Monetary Fund (the IMF—designed to stabilize currencies), both to be headquartered in Washington and capitalized largely by the U.S. government. Imposed on the conference by Secretary Morgenthau, both banks were intended to create just what Cordell Hull had been calling for throughout the preceding decade: an open international marketplace with a minimum of state interference and certainly no high tariffs.

John Maynard Keynes, the brilliant economist who led the British delegation, fought back hard against Morgenthau. He knew, as did Churchill back in London, that the Roosevelt administration was going to use the World Bank and the IMF, along with the almighty dollar, to force the British Empire into opening itself to American trade and investment.

At Bretton Woods, however, Morgenthau simply steamrollered over the British objections. And an even more bitter clash took place when, in September 1944, Roosevelt and Churchill joined at Quebec for their penultimate meeting.

5

On September 12, 1944, the date on which the Quebec Conference commenced, the U.S. First Army crossed the German frontier just west of Aachen. On that same day, the Soviets made an unexpectedly swift entry into Bulgaria. The vise was closing on the remnants of Nazi Germany and its European empire, so the overall question facing the Americans and the British at Quebec was what to do with Hitler's former realms.

Morgenthau certainly knew what he wanted to do with them: level all German industry and turn the country, once it was divided among the occupying armies, into a pasture. Although Churchill was horrified at the idea—he foresaw the use of Germany as a buffer against further Soviet expansion—Roosevelt was attracted to the Morgenthau plan. With the presidential election fewer than two months away, he saw the political advantage of taking a dramatic step of sure and certain appeal to the American Jewish communities.

Then, for reasons known only to Roosevelt, he changed his mind, repudiating the Morgenthau scheme. He did so without consulting Churchill, which only magnified the prime minister's sense of becoming a global irrelevancy.

For as the conferees met in the Château Frontenac, the huge, copper-roofed hotel that stood perched high on the northern bank of the St. Lawrence River, Churchill came to believe that Roosevelt and his advisers, in the words of a modern historian, now thought "of the Soviet Union, and not the collapsing British Empire," as their major postwar partner. Indeed, at Quebec, FDR so rudely scoffed at Churchill's concerns that Churchill finally blurted out, "Do you want me to beg, like Fala [Roosevelt's Scottie]?"

CHAPTER 14

The Road to Yalta

1

The arrival was supposed to be a secret, but when, early on the morning of Armistice Day, November 11, 1944, rumors of the advent spread through the French capital, hundreds of thousands of Parisians gathered along the Champs Élysées. Well before the official cavalcade started its procession up the avenue, dense throngs of people packed the broad sidewalks; more people filled the nearby windows and balconies and crowded the rooftops. Every tree along the route had up to half a dozen youths roosting in its branches. The lampposts were bright with French, British, American, and Soviet flags. The weather was cold and cloudy, but that did not curb the enthusiasm of the French crowds. The scene was reminiscent of the tumultuous greeting with which Paris had welcomed Woodrow Wilson after World War I; for France, this was a moment of national gratitude. The difference was this time the honored visitor was not the American president but rather the British prime minister, Winston S. Churchill.

Then it happened: shortly before eleven o'clock, surrounded by a tight escort of French motorcycle policemen, Churchill, dressed in the blue-gray uniform of an air commodore, appeared seated in the rear of an open automobile. And seated beside him, uniformed in khaki and the *képi* of a French officer, was the tall figure of the general who with Churchill's support had escaped from France four years earlier, and who was now the acknowledged leader of France, Charles de Gaulle.

After his flight from Bordeaux in June 1940, and his appeal over the BBC to his fellow countrymen to continue the fight, de Gaulle's efforts to establish his leadership faced seemingly insurmountable odds. Although the French escapees from Dunkirk rallied to his cause, only a handful of soldiers from postsurrender France set out to join his organization. By late August 1940 his force numbered no more than seven thousand men.

On August 24, 1940, nonetheless, de Gaulle put his tiny army on display at the Aldershot training center south of London. Eve Curie, a journalist, wrote,

> We French who witnessed the ceremony remembered the mag-nificent, endless parade of 50,000 French troops that had been given for King George VI only two years before, in Versailles, amidst the enthusiasm of our people. The contrast between Versailles and Aldershot was something difficult for us to bear. But not for de Gaulle. The tall, somewhat awkward general behaved as proudly on the Aldershot field as if he had been inspecting the mightiest military force in the world. He knew well that he was reviewing one of the most important armies our country ever had—an army which, all alone, was saving the good name of France. People said: "De Gaulle is difficult." He was. He had a defiant, even an arrogant way of being right. But what of it? More-over, when one came to think of it, what he had done in June 1940 could perhaps only have been attempted by a man with a temper.

Soon after the Aldershot parade, de Gaulle spoke again on the BBC: "Frenchmen," he declared, "once more you have a fighting army! . . . Since those whose duty it was to hold high the sword of France have let it fall broken, I have snatched up the stump!"

The actual record of de Gaulle and his small force, however, bor-dered on the insignificant. He attempted a landing at Dakar, in West

Africa, only to be driven off by the resident forces of the Vichy government. Late in 1941, his few naval vessels seized St. Pierre and Miquelon, rainswept islands off the coast of Newfoundland that the British somehow had overlooked during their eighteenth-century conquest of Canada and that had remained legally part of Vichy France. Mere dots in the North Atlantic, they yielded no strategic advantage. His forces did make inroads into Lebanon and Syria, French colonies, but most of the twenty-five thousand Vichy soldiers stationed in the Levant wanted nothing to do with de Gaulle. He had some armored vehicles, and his men inside them fought with distinction against the Germans in North Africa, but the credit for the victory against Rommel at El Alamein went to General Montgomery and the British.

Then de Gaulle had to deal with Roosevelt. At the Casablanca meeting, the question arose as to which Frenchman should hold authority in the North African regions liberated from Vichy. Presiding over the issue, Roosevelt laid hands on Admiral Jean-Francois Darlan, the head of the French navy but a personage with close ties to Vichy. In so choosing, Roosevelt rejected Churchill's nominee, de Gaulle.

"From the time that America went to war," de Gaulle would write in his memoirs of World War II, "Roosevelt made up his mind that the peace had to be an American peace, that it belonged to him to dictate its organization, that the states swept away in the ordeal be submitted to his judgment, and that in particular France had to have him for a savior and arbiter."

The conflict between de Gaulle and Roosevelt only deepened. On July 6, 1944, de Gaulle landed at Washington National Airport, hoping to secure Roosevelt's recognition for his own future as the leader of France. The general stayed at Blair House and, like a dutiful tourist, visited the usual monuments, but he found the idea of his being a suppliant utterly galling. In conference with Roosevelt, de Gaulle was all intransigence, even demanding FDR's acceptance of France as a "Fifth Horseman."

Remembering France's capitulation in 1940, however, Roosevelt dismissed de Gaulle's demand with scorn. Only through the intervention of several administration officials in Washington, and of General Eisenhower on the ground in Europe, did Roosevelt eventually concede de Gaulle's right to head the liberation of Paris in August 1944.

The feud between Roosevelt and de Gaulle, nevertheless, hardly abated, and it was more than personal. "All my life, I have had a certain idea of France," de Gaulle would write in his memoirs. "In brief, to my thinking, France could not be France without grandeur." But Roosevelt, who as the war progressed and victory drew within sight became ever more paternalistic, thought of himself as the overseer of the world. Roosevelt "conceived of international order as being enforced by the wise and mighty, acting as impartial judges," Milton Viorst, journalist and foremost chronicler of the Roosevelt-de Gaulle relationship, has written. "He, of course, thought of the United States and of himself as the wisest, the mightiest, and most impartial. He saw no place for France in his global magistery."

None of this conflict was apparent in Paris on the morning of Armistice Day 1944. As their automobile reached the Étoile, Churchill and de Gaulle walked side by side to the Tomb of the Unknown Soldier beneath the Arc de Triomphe; the band of the Garde Républicaine played the British and French national anthems. After placing their wreaths, the prime minister and the general stood by the tomb, and a single cannon shot marked the start of the traditional moment of silence. At the sound of a second shot, the great crowd assembled along the Champs Élysées exploded with cheers.

De Gaulle and Churchill then walked together along the avenue to a nearby reviewing stand. They took their places, and the victory parade was under way.

Churchill's three-day visit to France gave him and de Gaulle a chance to establish a united front against Roosevelt's postwar designs, which relegated France to the role of a nonentity.

Roosevelt had resisted France's membership in a European Advisory Council. As its title implied, the body was to wield no real power, but de Gaulle saw it as the only forum in which he could press French views of how the war should end. Only after protracted pleas from Downing Street did Roosevelt relent; Churchill was able to relay the news to de Gaulle during the Armistice Day parade. Roosevelt's condescension nonetheless did not render de Gaulle exactly appreciative.

More important, de Gaulle sought an expansion of the size of the French military; he wanted France to be able seriously to contribute to Germany's defeat, thus making certain of its own return to the ranks of the great powers. Upon returning to London, Churchill again pressed de Gaulle's case. He informed Roosevelt,

> I sympathize with the French wish to take over some of the line, to have the best share they can in the fighting or what is left of it—and there may be plenty—and not to have to go into Germany as a so-called conqueror who has not fought. . . . The important thing for France is to have an army prepared . . . to assist in the holding down of parts of Germany later on. . . . The French pressed very strongly to have a share in the occupation of Germany, not merely as subparticipation under British or American command, but as a French command. I expressed my sympathy with this, knowing well that there will be a time not many years distant when the American armies will go home and when the British will have great difficulty in maintaining large forces overseas.

Roosevelt's response left Churchill dumbfounded. He wanted to have France meet its postwar duties, he stated, but he had no authority to provide weapons for a postwar French military force. FDR added: "You know, of course, that after Germany's collapse I must bring American troops home as rapidly as transportation problems permit."

"If the French are to have no postwar army or time to make one, or to give it battle experience," Churchill shot back, "how will it be possible to hold down western Germany beyond the present Russian-occupied line? We certainly could not undertake the task without your aid and that of the French. All would therefore rapidly disintegrate as it did the last time."

Roosevelt's response was weak: perhaps the French, he suggested, could arm themselves with captured German weapons. Churchill kept his contempt to himself.

But the most significant issue over which Churchill and de Gaulle teamed up against Roosevelt was the matter of empire. From the conference at Argentia to the ones at Casablanca, Cairo, and Tehran, Roosevelt had never failed to express his opposition to colonialism, especially that of France and Great Britain. With the defeat of Germany and Japan imminent, however, and with the Soviet armies reaching into Bulgaria, Romania, Poland, the Baltic states, and the Third Reich itself, Roosevelt's attitude was beginning to shift. He still saw himself as the savior of oppressed peoples. Yet he also was making clear that he wanted military control at least over France's prewar possessions in the Pacific and that he intended to keep American rights to the naval bases extracted from Great Britain in the 1940 bases-for-destroyers deal.

That Roosevelt had his eye on an actual takeover of major parts of the British and French colonial empires was not just a matter of Churchill's imagination or of de Gaulle's pride. At about the time of the 1944 Armistice Day celebration in Paris, Lord Halifax, still the British ambassador to the United States, relayed the following account about an encounter with Roosevelt: "One day we had been chatting away about something or other when the president suddenly said that he thought after the war we ought to do this or that about some French colony. What did I think of his idea? I said that I scarcely saw how he could reconcile it with various pledges he had given to . . . General de Gaulle. That he thought was all right. Had I any other objections? I said that I still did not like it for there was nothing to prevent him from waking up one morning and having a similar brainwave about a British colony. At that the president laughed and said that our case was quite different."

The colony in question was Indochina. Earlier in 1944, Roosevelt had indicated to Secretary Hull that he did not want Indochina returned to France; once the Japanese were expelled, he favored some kind of international trusteeship. "As a matter of interest," he had told Hull, "I am wholeheartedly supported in this view by Generalissimo Chiang Kaishek and by Marshal Stalin. I see no reason to play in with the British Foreign Office in this matter. The only reason they seem to oppose it is that they fear the effect it would have on their own possessions. . . . Each case must, of course, stand on its own feet, but the case of Indochina is perfectly clear. France has milked it for one hundred years. The people of Indochina are entitled to something better than that."

The "something better" that Roosevelt was asserting by November 1944 was the idea of an international trusteeship. Who would be responsible for such an arrangement? Not, Roosevelt's remarks made clear, France or Great Britain. Not Chiang Kaishek's China, which, despite his rhetoric, Roosevelt knew was pitiably weak. And not the Soviet Union, which Roosevelt wanted to keep out of most of the Pacific basin. That left the United States—and, indeed, the American takeover of the French colonial role in Indochina commenced only a decade later.

Aware of Roosevelt's views, Churchill hoped to effect another face-to-face conference between the president and de Gaulle, with himself and Stalin present. Late in November 1944 Stalin agreed to participate. Roosevelt, however, would have no part of it. "Any attempt to include de Gaulle in a meeting of the three of us," he let Churchill know on December 16, 1944, "would merely introduce a complicating and undesirable factor."

The Battle of the Bulge, the German counteroffensive that broke out in mid-December 1944 in the Ardennes Forest, presented de Gaulle with an unexpected gift. Desperate for reinforcements, Eisenhower on December 28 pleaded with Washington to allow the re-arming of eight new French divisions, and to his relief he received authorization overnight. France thus was able to share in the victory and, upon the German surrender, acquire its own zone of occupation in the former Third Reich.

The antagonism between Roosevelt and de Gaulle nonetheless remained as bitter as ever. Roosevelt saw de Gaulle as an anachronism, an intransigent representative of the "old Europe." The president looked forward to the creation of a "new Europe," subservient to American demands.

Neither de Gaulle nor Churchill had the power to contest Roosevelt's sense of entitlement. In the presidential election of 1944, Roosevelt had faced a tough fight against New York's governor Thomas E. Dewey. But Roosevelt had won, and had embarked on his unprecedented fourth term as president.

2

Saturday, January 20, 1945, the day of Roosevelt's fourth inaugural, dawned gray and cold in Washington; the wind off the Potomac penetrated the warmest of clothing. Putting up with the elements, though, several thousand persons left their hotel rooms and homes in the area and, because of gasoline rationing, walked to the White House grounds.

Because of the exigencies of the war and his own increasing frailty, Roosevelt had decided to take the oath of office not at the Capitol but rather at the Executive Mansion. So the onlookers gathered on the hard snow that covered the Ellipse and waited.

Shortly before noon, the Marine Corps Band, resplendent in uniforms of red and blue, appeared on the South Portico and played "Hail to the Chief." The doors opened and, supported by a cane and the arm of his son James, Roosevelt emerged. Despite the frigid air, he wore no overcoat or cloak. Lurching forward, he reached a padded chair and was seated. Exactly at noon, James and a Secret Service agent bent over the chair, lifting the president and carrying him ahead until, standing, he could grip the edge of the podium. There he shook hands with Harry S Truman, just sworn in as vice president. Facing Harlan Fiske Stone, the chief justice of the United States, Roosevelt renewed his own oath of office. Then he turned to address the crowd shivering out on the lawn:

"We Americans of today, together with our allies, are passing through a period of supreme test," he began. "It is a test of our courage—of our resolve—of our essential democracy. If we meet that test—successfully and honorably—we shall perform a service of historic importance—of historic importance which men and women and children will honor throughout all time."

As Roosevelt stood on the South Portico of the White House, he was a dying man; he looked gaunt and shrunken, his shirt collar much too big for his neck, for his doctors had diagnosed him with acute hypertension and congestive heart failure. But the United States of America over which he presided was thriving as never before. Financially and commercially, the country stood like a giant among nations. In the nineteenth century, the world had been Europe-centered, Great Britain-protected, and London-financed. Now, by the time of Roosevelt's last inaugural, the world had become North Atlantic-centered, United States-protected, and New York-financed. The British Empire had been replaced by what in effect was the American Empire. Nazi Germany and imperial Japan were nearly finished as great powers. And aside from America, the only remaining great power was the Soviet Union, which had suffered unprecedented destruction and the loss of some 20 million lives.

3

Warsaw had fallen to the Communists three days before, and on the day of the Roosevelt inaugural, Soviet divisions broke out of East Prussia, pushing fast toward Stettin on the Baltic. Yet Stalin viewed the West with the grimmest suspicion.

Josef Stalin, in the words of Milovan Djilas, a Yugoslav Communist, was

> of very small stature and ungainly build. His torso was short and narrow, while his legs and arms were too long. His left arm and shoulder seemed rather stiff. He had quite a large paunch, and his hair was sparse, though his scalp was not completely bald. His face was white, with ruddy cheeks. Later I learned that this

coloration, so characteristic of those who sit long in offices, was known as the 'Kremlin complexion' in high Soviet circles. His teeth were black and irregular, turned inwards. Not even his moustache was thick or firm. Still the head was not a bad one; it had something of the folk, the peasantry, the paterfamilias about it—with those yellow eyes and a mixture of sternness and roguishness.

Stalin's fingers were yellow from the Russian cigarettes he habitually smoked. Foreign magazines and newspapers, to be sure, almost always depicted him as puffing a pipe. He used it as a showpiece, for the one he affected bore the small white dot of an English Dunhill. He may have wanted to convey the impression of being a Westerner at heart.

He was not. He was a Russian (more accurately, an adoptive Russian, for he had been born in neighboring Georgia and had learned Russian as a second language), a brutal dictator but a Russian one at that, bent on defending traditional Russian interests. Throughout his career as a revolutionary in czarist Russia, Stalin always had been an activist, not a theorist, not a Communist in the sense of following Marxist-Leninist preachments of worldwide revolution. He reflected, rather, ancient Russian fears. In *The Cold War as History*, Louis Halle, a historian, held that from "the beginning of the ninth century and even today, the prime driving force in Russia has been fear. Fear, rather than ambition, is the primary reason for the organization and expansion of the Russian society. The Russians as we know them today have experienced ten centuries of constant, mortal fear. This has not been a disarming experience. It has not been an experience calculated to produce a simple, open, innocent, and guileless society." Stretched over an almost endless countryside, Halle went on, the Russian people from generation unto generation found themselves subjected to wave after wave of conquerors, the "Huns, the Bulgars, the Avars, the Khazars, the Magyars, the Pechenegs, and so on—up through the Tartars, the so-called 'Golden Horde' which did not disappear from Europe until the end of the fifteenth century. . . . Lying defenseless on the plain, they were slaughtered and subjugated and humiliated by the invaders time and time again."

The Russian experience of the nineteenth and early twentieth centuries only added to the terrors. And, of course, Hitler had reminded the Russians, as if they needed reminding, of their barrierless frontiers and their ancient vulnerability. So with the end of the war in sight, Stalin's overwhelming determination was to prevent a return to the past.

By the last week of January 1945, five Soviet armies had reached the Oder, preparing to push on toward Berlin. Even then, however, Stalin's goals mirrored those of the czars. The "western frontiers of the Soviet sphere of influence coincide so closely with those Tsarist Russia planned to draw after the defeat of the Central Powers [in World War I]," observed Robert Strausz-Hupé, another historian, "that Tsarist and Soviet policies appear to differ as regards method only. . . . The aggregate of annexed territories, protectorates, alliances, and Pan-Slav affiliations [under Nicholas II] would have extended Russian influence to the Oder River, the Alps, the Adriatic, and the Aegean. The tsarist project, cleansed of the dynastic and social preconceptions of tsardom, took shape in the system of annexed territories, occupation zones, and ideological affiliations which constitute[d] the Soviet sphere of influence in Europe."

One of the British officials who accompanied Churchill to the Yalta meeting, the future prime minister Harold Macmillan, agreed with such interpretations. "All through its history," Macmillan would write in his memoirs, "the landlocked Russian Empire has sought two main objectives: outlet to the warm seas and a defensive ring around its . . . borders. The [Communist] government pursued the same aims as its predecessors." In Macmillan's view, the czars had longed for access to the Mediterranean; Stalin wanted the same. In 1907, Russia's rulers had acquired by dint of a treaty with Great Britain a sphere of influence in northern Iran; Stalin would cite that agreement as justification of a Soviet presence in the same region. The last Romanov, Nicholas II, had dreamed of extending Russian power into northeastern Asia, but the 1904–1905 war with Japan had shattered the hope; now Stalin would revive it.

As the British understood, perhaps better than the Americans, Stalin was far less a Communist than a practitioner of the traditional game of *Realpolitik*. "Everyone imposes his system as far as his army can reach," Stalin had told Djilas. "It cannot be otherwise."

Churchill also had wished to play the game. In October 1944, hoping to bypass Roosevelt, he had flown to Moscow for an eight-day visit with Stalin. During his sojourn, Churchill had jotted down a spheres-of-influence agreement and handed the paper to Stalin. On it the prime minister had written out a series of percentages: after the war, Great Britain would get 90 percent of Greece; the Soviet Union would have 90 percent of Romania and 75 percent of Bulgaria; Hungary and Yugoslavia were to be divided up on a 50-50 basis. Hardly blinking an eye, Stalin had accepted the deal.

And why not? In the end, as Stalin had known quite well, what mattered was not a number on a piece of paper but rather an army in a country. The British forces were making their return to Greece, but they could reach no farther: native Communist guerrillas were taking charge of Yugoslavia, and the Soviet army had planted itself on the ground of most of Eastern Europe. By the time of the Yalta Conference, Churchill's proposed deal amounted to nothing at all.

The collapse of Churchill's Mediterranean ambitions marked the end of his imperial illusions. By the time of Yalta, only two visions of the postwar world mattered: Roosevelt's advocacy of a liberal international system that would serve the interests of the United States; and Stalin's determination to seal off the Soviet Union by projecting Soviet might into the heart of Europe. For Churchill, what was almost poignant was that once Great Britain had run that liberal world order and had maintained a balance of power in the center of Europe. Churchill left for Yalta already a defeated man.

4

January 1945 was a month of almost unmitigated Allied success. In the first week after the New Year, in the Ardennes Forest, the U.S.

First Army recaptured most of the villages lost to the Germans during the Battle of the Bulge; Eisenhower at last was able to move his
forces forward again. The Soviets, too, were on the offensive: mid-
January found the Red Army only forty miles from Cracow, in southern Poland. On January 17 the Soviets entered Warsaw, the next day
recognizing the so-called Lublin Committee (Polish Communists as
opposed to the London Poles, refugees supposedly Western in their
sympathies) as the Polish Provisional Government. On January 20 the
Soviets moved into Silesia. Two days after that, they were 165 miles
from Berlin and still advancing. In five more days the Red Army had
completed the clearing of Lithuania, crossing the Vistula River near
Torun, once one of the westernmost towns of the Russian Empire.

"We are spellbound by your glorious victories over the common
foe," Churchill cabled Stalin on January 27, "and by the mighty
forces you have brought into the line against them. Accept our
warmest thanks and congratulations on historic deeds."

With their armies on the verge of the final victory over Germany, the Big Three met again, this time at the Crimean resort of
Yalta. The conference would be Roosevelt's last.

Stalin, who had the shortest distance to travel, rode by train past the
burned farmhouses and smashed factories of the Soviet Union. If
Roosevelt realized that Russia was rubble, Stalin feared, he might
order the American armies to keep on going, finishing off the Soviet
Union once and for all. Not wishing to reveal the extent of the dev-
astation he could see from the train windows, therefore, Stalin
would tell the president that Russia lacked only "tin, rubber, and
pineapples." Stalin and the rest of the Soviet delegation reached
Yalta on February 4, 1945, and settled into the Koreis Villa, a run-
down dacha that back in the nineteenth century had belonged to
Russian nobility. From there, while awaiting the arrival of his Allied
counterparts, Stalin continued to direct what Churchill called the
Soviet Union's "immense front, now in violent action."

Churchill and his own entourage left Great Britain on January
29, 1945, flying down to British Malta, there to wait for the coming
of Roosevelt. Boarding HMS *Orion*, a British warship stationed in

the harbor at Valletta, Malta's major port, Churchill revealed his fears for the future. "I think you would do well to read it," he wrote to his wife; he had nearly finished a book by Beverley Nichol, *Verdict on India*. He continued,

> It is written with some distinction and a great deal of thought. It certainly shows the Hindu in his true character and the sorry plight to which we have reduced ourselves by losing confidence in our [imperial] mission. Reading about India has depressed me for I see such ugly storms looming up there which . . . may overtake us. I have had for some time a feeling of despair about the British connection with India, and still more about what will happen if it is suddenly broken. Meanwhile we are holding on to this vast empire, from which we get nothing, amid the increasing criticisms and advice of the world and our own people and increasing hatred of the Indian population, who receive constant and deadly propaganda to which we can make no reply. However out of my shadows has come a renewed resolve to go fighting on as long as possible and to make sure the flag is not let down while I am at the wheel.

Roosevelt sailed on January 22, 1945, aboard the cruiser *Quincy* from the Hampton Roads Port of Embarkation, escorted by a fleet of destroyers and heading out across the Atlantic for the Mediterranean. At nine-thirty on the morning of February 2, 1945, the *Quincy* steamed into the harbor at Valletta.

As the cruiser passed close to the *Orion*, Roosevelt and Churchill waved to each other across the water. Two hours later, Churchill rode by launch to the *Quincy*, staying for lunch with the president.

"My friend has arrived in the best of health and spirits," Churchill cabled his wife; everything is going very well. Lovely warm sunshine."

Only Churchill expressed such optimism about Roosevelt's condition. "What a change in the president," one of Churchill's staffers wrote in her diary. "He seems to have lost so much weight, has dark circles under his eyes, looks altogether frail and as if he is hardly in this world at all." Present at the luncheon aboard the *Quincy*, Anthony Eden, the foreign secretary, commented that Roosevelt "looked considerably older since Quebec; he gives the impression of failing powers."

In the evening, some seven hundred British and American officers and diplomats made their way by taxi and jeep to Malta's Luqa airfield, ready for their predawn flights. Their destination in the Soviet Union was the Saki airfield on the Crimean peninsula. Lined up along the tarmac and waiting for the passengers were twenty American Skymasters and five British Yorks. Seeing the size of the air fleet, Sarah Churchill, who was accompanying her father, wondered aloud if the Russians would think they were being invaded.

Throughout much of the night, at ten-minute intervals, the airplanes took off on their fourteen-hundred-mile journey. Flying in a steady stream, they all adhered to the same route: straight east across the Mediterranean; southward in a swing around Crete; then up across Turkey and the Black Sea—making contact with the tower at Saki to indicate that indeed they were not an attacking force—and down on the newly built concrete-block runway.

Once Roosevelt's airplane, the *Sacred Cow*, had landed, and FDR had been carried to the ground, Soviet soldiers lining the runway snapped to attention. The Red Army Band struck up "The Star-Spangled Banner," "God Save the King," and the Communist "Internationale." Lifted then into a jeep, Roosevelt headed off to inspect Stalin's honor guard.

Churchill accompanied the slow-moving vehicle on foot. As Sir Alexander Cadogan, a high-ranking British official, recorded the scene, the "P.M. walked by the side of the president, as in her old age an Indian attendant accompanied Queen Victoria's phaeton."

With the inspection over, the Soviet welcoming committee—principally Foreign Minister Vyacheslav Molotov, his deputy Andrei Vishinsky, and Andrei Gromyko, the ambassador to the United States—led the foreigners into a tent for classic Russian refreshments: hot tea with lemon and sugar, vodka, cognac, champagne, caviar, smoked sturgeon and salmon, white and black bread, fresh butter, cheese, and hard- and soft-boiled eggs. Churchill, being Churchill, indulged himself to the fullest. But Roosevelt, a light eater and drinker, started out almost immediately through the snowy mountains for the ninety-mile ride to Yalta.

Around the Yalta resort, pine-covered mountain slopes ringed the parks and gardens where stood the cedars, magnolias, and olive trees of a Mediterranean-like climate. In their retreat, the Germans had laid waste to many of the buildings, and the red tile roofs and the French windows that once had opened onto balconies, and the seafront promenade below, were largely demolished. The Soviets nonetheless had worked feverishly to restore Livadia, Czar Nicholas II's fifty-room palace: huge numbers of painters, plasterers, and plumbers had come down from Moscow to redo the interior. Trucks had hauled chairs and lamps all the way from hotel rooms in the capital. The results were frumpy and garish.

Roosevelt stayed in Livadia, in a ground-floor bedroom decorated with orange velvet panels; next door, the czar's old billiard room of oak and red velvet served as the president's private dining room. Alone among the American delegation, Roosevelt enjoyed his own bath. On the same floor, Secretary of State Edward Stettinius (a former chairman of the board of U.S. Steel who, after serving four years in the State Department, had succeeded the ailing Cordell Hull) had a two-room suite that overlooked the Black Sea. Others in the American group, including Harry Hopkins; Charles Bohlen, a Russian-speaking official in the State Department; and Alger Hiss, the State Department officer later accused of espionage, were relegated to more cramped quarters upstairs.

Churchill's villa was in a state of considerable disrepair. The British establishment, Cadogan wrote to his wife, was a "big house of indescribable ugliness . . . with all the furnishings of an almost terrifying hideosity." Their rooms, the Britons soon discovered, were infested with bedbugs.

Stalin and Churchill agreed to hold their meetings in the ballroom of the Livadia Palace, on the first story and convenient for Roosevelt in his wheelchair. The room had been built in the grand style, with a handsome molded ceiling, marble columns along its length, tall windows that gave onto an interior courtyard, and a fire-place at one end.

A photograph taken during the week-long conference at Yalta showed the Big Three seated side by side in wooden armchairs. Churchill sat on the left, bareheaded and swathed in a double-breasted, military-style greatcoat. Stalin wore a beaked Soviet mar-shal's cap and a heavy coat with epaulettes. Roosevelt, the palm of his right hand resting on a wasted thigh and the fingers of his left hand holding a cigarette, wore a dark cape. Unsmiling, each appeared to be immersed in his own hopes or fears.

Churchill at Yalta maintained his customs of sleeping late, orating over dinner about anything and at anyone who would listen, and work-ing until two or three in the morning. His daughter Sarah thought him depressed. For years he had suffered from what he called his "black dog," but now he had an especially good reason to be downcast.

On January 21, 1945, the *New York Times* on its front page had run a banner headline: "U.S. AIM FIRM PEACE, CHURCHILL IS TOLD." The following article had gone on to state that American public opinion would not accept the possibility that "a discredited old order [the British and French Empires] rise from the ashes . . . or see the tyranny of Nazi occupation [in Greece] replaced by some cat's-paw totalitarianism masquerading behind a native name [George II, king of the Hellenes, whom the British were seeking to install in Athens, much as the Soviets were seeking to establish the Lublin Poles in Warsaw]." President Roosevelt, the article had stated, believed that "liberated people should choose for themselves."

In keeping with that sentiment, Roosevelt at Yalta, much to Stalin's amusement, teased Churchill mercilessly about the Britannic decline. Churchill said later to Mary, another daughter, that at Yalta he had felt crushed between the American buffalo and the Russian bear.

5

The Yalta Conference brought one issue to a quick resolution: there would be a United Nations with a Security Council and a General

Assembly; the organization would be the first international congress, furthermore, dominated by the United States and the Soviet Union. Other issues, however, soon raised fears and tempers.

Stalin demanded Allied recognition of rule in Poland (already asserted by the Kremlin) by the Communist, anti-German underground fighters, the Lublin Poles. Churchill objected vehemently. He wanted a "more broadly based" Polish government, meaning that authority in Poland should rest in the hands of the Poles who had fled in exile to London and who, presumably, would be pro-Western.

To Churchill, the governance of Poland was an issue of keen importance. Great Britain, after all, had gone to war with Nazi Germany over Poland, and Churchill had no wish to see the Soviet behemoth replace the German one at the center of Europe. For more than a century it had been a fixed idea in British thinking that keeping the bulk of Europe out of the control of any one power was vital to the security of the empire. Churchill was reflecting the thinking of the past.

In response, Stalin, as was his wont, erupted in wrath. Since Nazi Germany had attacked the Soviet Union by crossing the plains of Poland, he fairly screamed, the establishment of Poland as a Communist-run buffer zone was for the Soviet Union a "question of both honor and security." In the end, Stalin did agree to "free elections" in Poland. Neither Roosevelt nor Churchill pressed him for an explanation of the phrase, nor did he offer any.

The Big Three quarreled over the new borders of Germany and over Stalin's demand for $20 billion in reparations from whatever German authorities succeeded Hitler. Churchill wanted Great Britain to share in any wealth that could be extracted from Germany, but he got little of the sort.

Roosevelt brought up a favored State Department proposal, pushed by Stettinius, a Declaration of Liberated Europe. The document would have pledged the Americans, the British, and the Soviets to "act in concert" with regard to Eastern Europe. Such action, the State Department's language went, would enable those peoples freed from the Nazis "to create democratic institutions of their own choice." This, the draft contended, "is a promise of the

Atlantic Charter—the right of all peoples to choose the form of government under which they will live—the restoration of sovereign rights and self-government to those people who have been forcibly deprived of them."

Upon hearing these words, Molotov, who usually sat in silence at meetings, interjected himself into the discussion. The declaration, he stated bluntly, meant an Anglo-American veto over the Soviet Union's right to self-defense. He demanded that "act in concert" be replaced by "mutual consultations." Powerless to impose anything where the Red Army already ruled, Roosevelt yielded, and the Soviets gave the now meaningless declaration their approval.

But what of the areas of the world where the Red Army did not rule? From the study beside his bedroom in the Livadia Palace, Roosevelt, through his interpreter, Charles Bohlen, let Stalin know that the United States and the Soviet Union, like the great powers of old, could cut a deal: they could divide the Eurasian landmass into two gigantic spheres of influence.

At no point, to be sure, did Roosevelt use precisely those words; they smacked of the old-style European imperialism to which Americans regarded themselves as innately superior. Nor did Roosevelt soften his criticism of the Soviet system, fast being transplanted into the soil of Eastern Europe. It was rather with a wink, or even an implied wink, that Roosevelt and Stalin acknowledged each other's suzerainty over the lands where their two armies now stood in Europe: the United States in the west and the Soviet Union in the east.

The tacit European settlement, furthermore, did not conclude the Yalta talks. Roosevelt wanted Stalin to enter the war against Japan. Stalin agreed to do so, on the condition that the Soviet Union get back the territories lost to Japan earlier in the century. Having no objection, Roosevelt conceded that Stalin was entitled to the southern half of Sakhalin and the Kurile chain above Japan proper; Stalin also got the rail line from Siberia down into Manchuria. For his own part, Stalin agreed officially to recognize the government of Chiang Kaishek, Roosevelt's favorite Chinese leader; concomitantly, Stalin pledged to extend no aid to the insurgent Chinese Communists.

In Asia and the Pacific, therefore, Stalin got the farthest extensions of the czarist empire and Roosevelt got the whole of the Pacific and China (so he thought). Korea, the two leaders agreed as they met alone in the Livadia Palace, could serve as a buffer between their two spheres.

In the years to come, but especially in the decade or so after the end of World War II, many in the United States charged that at Yalta Roosevelt had sold out American interests to Stalin. His critics missed the point. Roosevelt had written Eastern Europe off because he could do nothing about the presence of the Red Army there. But in the other half of the world, the Soviet Union had got some barren islands, arid steppes, and a rickety railroad, while the United States had gained the Pacific, the Japanese islands with their promise of future wealth, and access (albeit temporary) to the China market, where at the war's end American businesses were decisively replacing the British. Stalin had won his security zone and the United States had laid claim to most of the rest of the world.

And more: well before the end of World War II, the Roosevelt administration had begun to lay plans for confronting the Soviet Union with a preponderance of American power. In no sense was the United States going to tolerate the Soviet Union as a rival to its own worldwide imperium.

CHAPTER 15

Potsdam

1

On the first page of its issue of Thursday, April 12, 1945, the *Washington Post* reported the latest war news. The battle for Okinawa, only 325 miles south of Japan, had been raging, and while the strongly entrenched Japanese defenders were firing away with small arms, mortar, and even artillery, the U.S. Marines were killing them at a ratio of eleven to one. In Europe, Soviet tanks had just cut one of the last remaining German escape routes from Vienna, while Russian shock troops had stormed across the Danube Canal into the heart of the city. In Germany itself, in a startling advance, armored columns of the U.S. Ninth Army had swept to within 57 miles of Berlin and 114 miles of the Russian front.

Despite the drama of the news reports, the mood in Washington that day was quiet. The morning was cloudy and foggy, with a light drizzle, but the rain cleared away around lunchtime, and a high temperature of only seventy degrees produced a most pleasant spring afternoon. The cherry trees along the Tidal Basin were in full bloom, as were the magnolias on Capitol Hill.

Up in the Capitol, nobody seemed in a mood for work. After voting on a few minor bills, the House of Representatives adjourned early. As the members left their seats, filing out through the rear doors, Speaker Sam Rayburn, a short, bald Texan, stepped down from the rostrum. Leaning over the railing, he invited Lewis

Deschler, the parliamentarian, to join him for a drink in Rayburn's private office, known unofficially as the "Board of Education."

"Make it around five o'clock," Rayburn said. "Harry Truman is coming over."

Born into a farming family in western Missouri, Harry S Truman (since his parents had been unable to agree on a middle name, the *S* was not an abbreviation of anything), by background, appearance, and manner was utterly unlike the aristocratic Roosevelt. Of medium height and build, and afflicted with terrible eyesight that required thick spectacles, Truman had graduated from high school but, aside from a few night law courses, was too poor to go on to college. After working as a clerk in Kansas City, he served in the Army in World War I, rising to the rank of captain of D Battery, 129th Field Artillery, Thirty-fifth Division; to his own amazement, he discovered within himself considerable leadership ability. With the war over, he joined with Eddie Jacobson, an army pal, in opening a Kansas City haberdashery. The nationwide recession of 1921, however, caused the store to fail. Another service friend, Mike Pendergast, came to the rescue, intervening with his uncle, Tom Pendergast, boss of the Kansas City Democratic machine, to get Truman elected as a road commissioner in Jackson County. That was in 1922. Two years later, Truman ran for the job again and lost. At forty years of age, he was out of a job and deeply in debt. Then his father died and Harry had to work the farm.

Nonetheless, Harry Truman was not the type to despair. When he was not out in the fields, he was jaunty in appearance: Margaret, his daughter, would say that he usually looked as if he had just stepped out of a bandbox. He was affable and, in the age-old tradition of American politicians, he was an eager joiner: he belonged to the Masons, the American Legion, and something called the National Old Trails and Roads Association. He was a Baptist, but outside church, his language was profane and salty. He eventually married his childhood sweetheart, Elizabeth Wallace, called Bess, and moved into her mother's house in Independence, but he seemed most comfortable with the "boys," going off to various locales around the town for evening poker games and goodly portions of bourbon.

Yet he was neither an alcoholic nor irresponsible, and during his time of working with the Kansas City political machine, he kept his hands clean. He was a small-town midwesterner to the core, representative of the people around him, and therefore still had political potential.

When in 1934 Boss Pendergast—big, bluff, cheery, and wholly corrupt—needed someone to run for the U.S. Senate, he turned to Truman; throwing machine money into the race, he got Truman elected. Truman thus went off to Washington dubbed the "Senator from Pendergast." But Truman played the Capitol game: as a freshman senator he kept his head down, sought no publicity for himself, and slogged away at the committee work that few others wanted to touch. Proud and ambitious, he ran for the Senate again in 1940, this time on his own: Tom Pendergast was in jail. By dint of driving all over the state of Missouri to give campaign speeches, Truman won again.

Now, out from under the cloud of bossism, Truman sought to make himself a national figure. Hearing reports of war profiteering, he formed the Senate Special Committee to Investigate the National Defense Program, or, as the papers called it, the Truman Committee. One thing is certain about defense spending—there are going to be cost overruns and other abuses—and going from one munitions plant to another in his Dodge, Truman uncovered lots of shady dealings. *Time* put him on its cover. So by the spring of 1944, he had emerged as a possible Democratic vice-presidential candidate.

It was an open secret in Washington in the summer of 1944 that Roosevelt was dying. Without question, as the sitting president he would be renominated and probably reelected, but the vice presidency would be a prize beyond measure. This was especially so since Henry Wallace, the incumbent vice president, had fallen from grace: with the mood in America turning anti-Communist, Roosevelt considered him too left-wing. But who would succeed Wallace? Several old-line New Dealers in Washington floated the name of Supreme Court Associate Justice William O. Douglas: he was a staunch liberal, but arrogant, and lacking in solid judicial accomplishment; among the delegates to the Democratic National Convention, his constituency was almost invisible. The early leading contender was James F. Byrnes of South Carolina. Byrnes had been a representative, a senator, briefly a Supreme Court justice, and during the war America's economic czar. Shrewd and skilled in politics, he had been a major implementer of both the New Deal and Lend-Lease. But he was a southerner and, as such, racist and antiunion. Organized labor, a major force in the Democratic Party, wanted no part of Byrnes.

And then there was Harry Truman. Truman was from Missouri, a border state during the American Civil War. He had been a New Dealer, but never rabidly so. He had criticized malfeasance—always a good vote-getting posture—but in no way the war effort itself. He had made few if any enemies: in the language of professional politicians, he had acquired no negatives. And with Roosevelt indifferent as to his successor, the bosses of the party made the safe choice, Harry Truman. So it came about that on January 20, 1945, in the White House ceremony, the man from Missouri took the oath of office of vice president of the United States.

On the pleasant, lazy afternoon of April 12, 1945, in Washington, in his constitutional role of president of the U.S. Senate, Truman was in his seat above the chamber floor. Bored by a speech being delivered by a senator from Wisconsin, he was writing a letter to his mother and sister back in Missouri: "Turn on your radio tomorrow night at 9:30 your time, and you'll hear Harry make a Jefferson Day address to the nation. I think I'll be on all the networks, so it ought not be hard to get me. It will be followed by the president [Roosevelt had gone to Warm Springs to rest after his trip to Yalta], whom I'll introduce."

While Truman was finishing his note, Lewis Deschler, the House parliamentarian, was opening the door of the Speaker's hideaway office. Rayburn was inside already, pouring himself a drink. Deschler busied himself by laying out glasses, ice, and soda for the other guests, soon to arrive. Soon James M. Barnes, head of the White House congressional office, came in. As he started to fix his own drink, the telephone rang. Rayburn answered.

"Yes, Steve," the Speaker said after a pause. "I'll tell him."

"That was Steve Early [the presidential press secretary] at the White House," Rayburn explained as he hung up. "He wants the vice president to call him right away when he gets here."

A few moments later, Truman ambled in. As usual, he was dressed crisply, with a white shirt, a blue polka-dotted bow tie, and a handkerchief tucked neatly into the upper left pocket of his double-breasted gray suit. On his left hand he wore a gold Masonic ring. He greeted the men gathered in Rayburn's office like old friends. Within moments, bourbon in hand, he was perched on the arm of a black, brass-studded leather chair.

Deschler was in another armchair, facing Truman. "Mr. Speaker," the parliamentarian said to Rayburn, "wasn't the vice president supposed to call the White House?"

"Oh, yeah, Harry," Rayburn said. "Steve Early wants you to call him right away."

While Truman placed the call to the White House, Deschler was watching him closely. Those gathered in the Speaker's room could hear Early's voice come on the other end of the line. As it did so, Truman's face went pale. He hung up, then said, "Jesus Christ and General Jackson!"

"Steve Early wants me at the White House right away," Truman said to Rayburn.

A limousine was waiting for Truman just outside the Capitol. Following Early's instructions, Truman told the driver to go down Pennsylvania Avenue and to enter the White House grounds by the western gate. The grass on the lawn was still wet, and the tulips were flourishing. The limousine stopped under the North Portico. The time of arrival was 5:25 PM.

Ushers inside led Truman to the elevator. He got out on the second story, proceeding as directed to a sitting room. Early was there, as were Anna Roosevelt Boettiger, the Roosevelts' daughter; her husband, Colonel John Boetigger; and Mrs. Roosevelt herself. As Truman entered the room, Mrs. Roosevelt walked forward and, putting a hand on his shoulder, said, "Harry, the president is dead."

An hour later, with Mrs. Truman and Margaret summoned from the vice-presidential suite in the Wardman Tower Hotel, across the bridge on Connecticut Avenue, and in the presence of the assembled members of the cabinet, Truman faced Chief Justice Harlan

Fiske Stone and, raising his right hand, became president of the United States.

Shortly thereafter, Secretary of War Stimson took Truman aside. The United States, he told the new president, would soon test a bomb of unbelievable power.

2

There is something of a legend about Truman and his first weeks in office: that, inexperienced as an administrator and no more knowledgeable in the realm of foreign affairs than any ordinary reader of the newspapers, he felt overwhelmed by the job. Without question, when on the night of April 12, 1945, he finally returned to the family apartment, Margaret found him practically in a state of shock. And after munching a sandwich, he placed several telephone calls, including one to an old Missouri crony, John W. Snyder. "I feel," Truman reportedly said, "like I have been struck by a bolt of lightning."

Yet Truman was a professional politician and, as such, acutely aware of the mood of the American public: already the nation wanted a president who would stand tall against the menace, real or supposed, of the Soviet Union. So on April 23, 1945, only eleven days after he had become president, Truman called Vyacheslav Molotov, the stolid, square-built, gray-faced Soviet foreign minister, who was in Washington and staying at the embassy on Sixteenth Street, in to the White House. Truman was in a fighting mood. In "words of one syllable," he declared later, he warned Molotov that unless Stalin started to behave himself, the United States would see him as the new enemy.

Outraged, the usually unflappable Molotov protested that he had never been talked to like that by anyone in his life. Truman later boasted that he had given Molotov "the straight one-two to the jaw."

The next day, Truman received a letter from Secretary of War Stimson. The message hinted that Truman could do more to the Soviets than just throw a punch:

Dear Mr. President;

    I think it is very important that I should have a talk with you as soon as possible on a highly secret matter. I mentioned it to you shortly after you took office, but have not urged it since on account of the pressure you have been under. It, however, has such a bearing on our present foreign relations and has such an important effect on all my thinking in this field that I think you ought to know about it without much further delay.

Born in 1867, Henry L. Stimson had grown rich as a Wall Street lawyer, then had become the very embodiment of American foreign policy. He had served as secretary of war under President Taft; acted as the U.S. governor-general of the Philippines in the late 1920s; returned to Washington as President Hoover's secretary of state; and in 1940, although a Republican, accepted President Roosevelt's appointment as secretary of war. Had he been a Briton he would have been an earl of the realm, for Woodley, his white-stucco Georgian mansion standing high on a hill behind a row of stately oaks and across Connecticut Avenue from the Washington Zoo, was a symbol of his wealth and influence. By 1945 his close-cut hair had turned white and his once-erect slender frame was somewhat bent, but he had remained mentally acute, and his role was that of elder statesman. And as a leader of the American establishment, he was the foremost exponent of internationalism.

    The word *internationalism*, as opposed to *isolationism*, implied an American commitment to the maintenance of world order, as the British in the era of Queen Victoria had sought to maintain a similar world order. But meaning what? The heart of the British imperial ideology, a view that dated back to Napoleon and even before, had been the principle that no one, not even the archangels themselves, should be allowed to command the resources of Eurasia through economic monopolies, political subversion, or outright military aggression. After Napoleon, the British had fought Russia in the Crimean War and Germany in the two world wars to enforce this principle. Now, with British power receding from view, Stimson wanted the United States to shoulder Great Britain's imperial task. Only this time the threat to world order, in Stimson's view, was no longer Germany and Japan but rather the Soviet Union.

As Stimson realized, the United States was about to possess the ultimate weapon for confronting the Soviet Union. Hence his letter of April 24, 1945, to President Truman and their subsequent conversation in the Oval Office.

3

While Truman was trying to absorb an understanding of the atomic bomb, the news from the European front held out the promise of imminent victory. Soviet forces swept into Berlin, and Hitler, along with Eva Braun, his mistress, committed suicide. On May 7, 1945, Germany formally surrendered. Truman therefore faced the question of how to deal with Stalin.

At Yalta, Roosevelt and Stalin had made a deal or, rather, two deals. First, each had acknowledged tacitly that the other was in control of his side of the European continent; neither had shown much willingness to overturn that state of affairs. Second, in return for authority over the inner and northeastern Asian territories once held by czarist Russia, Stalin had promised that soon after Germany's defeat he would enter the war against Japan *and* extend official recognition to America's ally on the Asian mainland, Nationalist China; Stalin had accepted American power in the Pacific. On the whole, thus, it seems clear (contrary to myth) that Roosevelt had got the better part of the bargain.

After the Yalta Conference, Harry Hopkins visited the Kremlin and became convinced of Stalin's willingness to live up to the accord with Roosevelt. Hopkins's report, delivered to the White House on May 28, 1945, went thus:

> Stalin made categorical statement that he would do everything to promote unification of China under the leadership of Chiang Kaishek. . . . He specifically stated that no Communist leader was

strong enough to unify China. . . . He repeated all his statements made at Yalta, that he wanted a unified and stable China . . . to control . . . Manchuria and Sinkiang [now Xinjiang] and that he would respect Chinese sovereignty in all the areas his troops entered. . . . Stalin stated that he would welcome representatives of the generalissimo [Chiang Kaishek] in order to facilitate the organization of Chinese administration in Manchuria. . . . Stalin agreed with America's "open door" policy and went out of his way to indicate that the United States was the only power with the resources to aid China economically after the war. He observed that Russia would have all it could do to provide for the internal economy of the Soviet Union.

Here, according to Hopkins, was Stalin renouncing any aggressive intent, at least with regard to the East Asian theater. Was he sincere? The question is impossible to answer with complete assurance. Yet what Stalin said made sense: it was in the interest of the Soviet Union to have order, rather than anarchy or revolution, along its eastern frontiers; Stalin had little reason to believe then that Mao Zedong and the Chinese Communists could provide that stability. In accepting America's "open door" policy, Stalin was only recognizing a fait accompli: America was replacing Great Britain as the premier foreign power in the China market. And in stating that "Russia would have all it could do to provide for the internal economy of the Soviet Union," Stalin was simply stating the obvious. So with regard to East Asia, he was prepared to live up to the terms of the Yalta agreement. He certainly lacked the means to do otherwise.

Such indeed was Harry Hopkins's interpretation. We must remember, though, that Hopkins had been Roosevelt's most intimate aide. Truman felt no such bond. So the Hopkins report fell upon the White House like seed upon dry ground, for Truman and other advisers were increasingly prepared to have the United States violate the Yalta terms.

The Yalta accords had implied that there would be no further American force buildup around the periphery of the Soviet Union; they had mentioned no such encirclement. As early as 1943, however, officials in the American War and Navy Departments had begun to think about placing permanent military bases overseas. Rejecting any postwar withdrawal into isolation, planners had insisted that the United States maintain indefinitely the control it had gained over the Atlantic and the Pacific. The Joint Chiefs of Staff had recommended that policy to Roosevelt, and in January 1944 he had given it his approval.

Shortly after Roosevelt's death, the idea of forward bases began to take on specific form. Military and naval planners designated several points in the world as "key base areas." Some of these zones reflected a concern for upholding the Monroe Doctrine: Recife, at the tip of Brazil; the Panama Canal and the nearby Galapagos Islands. Not surprisingly, Pearl Harbor was on the list. But so were Newfoundland and St. Thomas-Antigua, with the facilities taken over from Great Britain in the 1940 destroyer swap, as well as Iceland, the Azores, the Canary Islands, and the Cape Verdes, all of which had fallen into American hands during the Atlantic warfare. In the Pacific, Guadalcanal, the Marianas, and the Bonins, all wrested from Japan, were to be part of the network. So were the Philippines, with Luzon's naval facilities at Subic Bay and with the Clark airfield just outside Manila. All these points in the Pacific were intended to give the United States positions from which it could put down quickly anti-American unrest in northeastern and southeastern Asia, as well as to preserve U.S. access to the raw materials of the region.

Clark airfield raised yet another issue. American military planners wished strongly to link U.S.-controlled air routes across the North Pole with another air route, the terminus of which was to be at Clark. According to the plan, the United States was to acquire military air transit rights along a line that ran from the Philippines to Saigon, Bangkok, Rangoon, Calcutta, Delhi, Karachi, Dhahran (on the Persian Gulf side of the Arabian Peninsula), Cairo, Tripoli, Algiers, and Casablanca. In short, Washington was planning forward bases in the Atlantic and the Pacific, thus to the west and the east of the Soviet Union, along with air routes that would flank the

Soviet Union from both the north and the south. In June 1945 President Truman gave his assent to the full implementation of these plans. Here was the containment policy, being designed well before the supposed onset of the Cold War.

Without question, in the late spring and early summer of 1945, what Churchill would call the "Iron Curtain" was already clanging down around much of Eastern Europe. Yet Stalin also was going ahead with his recognition of Nationalist China. Furthermore, he was giving little if any aid to Tito's Communist forces in Yugoslavia. Outside its immediate environs, the Soviet Union under Stalin was acting with remarkable restraint.

Nonetheless, conscious of America's superior economic and military power, and confident that the atomic bomb test would prove successful, the Truman administration was choosing to regard the Soviet Union as the postwar enemy. Doing so, the president and most of his advisers felt justified in trying to overturn the Yalta arrangements.

With Japan on the verge of collapse, top officials in Washington at the time of the German surrender no longer saw any need to bring the Soviet Union into the Asian side of the war. Many even believed that a Soviet entry would cause political problems. Ambassador Averell Harriman, in Washington on leave from the Soviet Union, was sure that Stalin would support Mao Zedong and the Communists against Chiang Kaishek's Nationalist government. From the embassy in Moscow, moreover, George F. Kennan, the American diplomat who had witnessed the Nazi takeover of Prague and who was now in Russia serving as the chargé d'affaires, reinforced Harriman's fear.

As summarized by the State Department and presented to Truman on April 24, Kennan's warning read:

Kennan . . . calls attention to the fact that words have a different meaning to the Russians. Stalin is prepared to accept the principle of unification of Chinese armed forces and the principle of a united China, since he knows that these conditions are feasible only on terms acceptable to the Chinese Communists. Stalin is also prepared to accept the idea of a free and democratic China, since a free China means to him a China in which there is a minimum of foreign influence other than Russian. Kennan is convinced that Soviet policy will remain a policy aimed at the achievement of maximum power with minimum responsibility and will involve the exertion of pressure in various areas. He recommends that we study with clinical objectivity the real character and implications of Russian Far Eastern aims.

On May 12, 1945, just before his return to Moscow, Harriman reiterated these concerns, presenting the State Department with two questions: "(1) The Yalta agreement: Should it be reexamined? ... (2) How urgent is the necessity for quick Russian participation in the war?" These questions were soon on Truman's desk.

The upshot of these considerations was the growing conviction in the Truman administration that the United States should keep the Soviets out of Manchuria altogether. Truman was at the point of deciding to rescind critical pledges Roosevelt had made at Yalta.

Foremost in pushing Truman in such a direction was the man with whom the president replaced Stettinius as secretary of state. He was James F. Byrnes.

Small, lean, and sharp-faced, Byrnes was renowned in Washington as a wheeler-dealer, the ultimate capital insider. He was shrewd to the point of being slick. Truman had no illusions about Byrnes. "All country politicians are alike," Truman wrote in his diary, referring to Byrnes. "They are sure all other politicians are circuitous in their dealings. When they are told the straight truth, unvarnished, it is never believed—an asset sometimes." A country politician himself, Truman had a special reason to be wary of Byrnes: the South Carolinian had never stopped resenting Truman's beating him out for the 1944 Democratic vice-presidential nomination. Yet Truman had not wanted Stettinius around as the secretary of state—as much as possible, the new president wanted his own people in the top positions—and Byrnes certainly knew his way around Washington. Besides, both were southerners (Truman being descended from a Virginia family and a native of the part of Missouri that once had held slaves), and they understood each other well.

Truman listened carefully to Byrnes's advice. At about the date of Byrnes's appointment, the new secretary told Truman that (these are Truman's words) "in his belief the atomic bomb might well put us in a position to dictate our own terms at the end of the war." Later, in May 1945, during a White House meeting at which the nuclear physicist Leo Szilard was present, Byrnes, according to Szilard, "did not argue that it was necessary to use the bomb against the cities of Japan in order to win the war. Mr. Byrnes' view [was] that our possessing and demonstrating the bomb would make Russia more manageable in Europe."

We have more on Byrnes and the bomb. Szilard wrote of a meeting on May 28, 1945, in the secretary of state's apartment in the Shoreham Hotel, which overlooked Rock Creek,

> Byrnes was concerned about Russia's post-war behavior. Russian troops had moved into Hungary and Romania; Byrnes thought it would be very difficult to persuade Russia to withdraw her troops from these countries, and that Russia might be more manageable if impressed by American military might. I shared Byrnes' concern about Russia's throwing around her weight in the post-war period, but I was completely flabbergasted by the assumption that rattling the bomb might make Russia more manageable. . . .
>
> I was concerned at this point that by demonstrating the bomb and using it in the war against Japan, we might start an atomic arms race between America and Russia which might end with the destruction of both countries. . . .
>
> I was rarely as depressed as when we left Byrnes' [apartment] and walked toward the station.

Secretary of State Byrnes was determined to use some kind of demonstration of the power of the atomic bomb to reverse the

Soviet wartime advances. But did Byrnes, whom Truman considered "conniving," bring the president around to his point of view? The answer is unclear, although many have attributed great influence to Byrnes. Nonetheless, other top officials were giving Truman much the same advice. "I tried to point out [that it] may be necessary to have it out with Russia on her relations to Manchuria and Port Arthur and various other parts of North China, and also the relations of China to us," Secretary of War Stimson counseled Truman in the middle of May. "Over any such tangled weave of problems [the atomic bomb] secret would be dominant and yet we will not know until after that time [of testing] whether this is a weapon in our hands or not. We think it will be shortly afterwards [after a meeting of Truman and Stalin], but it seems a terrible thing to gamble with such big stakes in diplomacy without having your master card in your hand."

In a conversation with John J. McCloy, an assistant secretary of war, Stimson added: "[W]e have got to regain the lead [over the Soviets] and perhaps do it in a pretty rough and realistic way. . . . This [is] a place where we really hold all the cards. I called it a royal straight flush and we mustn't be a fool about the way we play it. They can't get along without our help and industries, and we have coming into action a weapon which will be unique."

In the late spring and early summer of 1945, the United States did not yet have the atomic bomb; the test at Alamogordo would not take place until July. The highest officials around President Truman, however, believed that the bomb would soon be in their possession and that, in addition to hastening the Japanese surrender, its very existence would enable the United States to undo the Yalta accords.

What they did not realize was that Soviet spies had penetrated the research facilities at Los Alamos, New Mexico, and that the Kremlin was aware of the progress that was under way. Nor did they understand that knowledge of the bomb would frighten their Soviet counterparts, making Stalin if anything even more determined than before to preserve the buffer around the Soviet Union.

It is clear all the same that in the summer of 1945 the Truman administration was determined to roll back as far as possible the newly acquired domains of Stalin and the Soviet Union, for the White House had defined the resurrected Russian Empire as America's rival, even its enemy. In agreeing to meet Stalin in July 1945 at Potsdam, just outside Berlin, President Truman hoped to dismantle the Soviet wartime gains.

4

"I am getting ready to go see Stalin and Churchill," Truman wrote to his mother on July 3, 1945, "and it is a chore. I have to take my tuxedo, tails . . . high hat, top hat, and hard hat as well as sundry other things. I have a briefcase all filled up with information on past conferences and suggestions on what I'm to do and say. Wish I didn't have to go but I do and it can't be stopped now."

By the end of May 1945, as part of Washington's new stance on Communist control in Eastern Europe, President Truman had moved five U.S. Army divisions to the Brenner Pass and had shifted part of the Adriatic fleet northward: Truman had not been willing to tolerate a Yugoslav takeover of the port of Trieste. In an effort to weaken Stalin's control, Truman also had withheld diplomatic recognition of the new Soviet-backed governments in Romania and Bulgaria. With 3 million American soldiers still in Europe and with the possibility of extending $1 billion to the Soviet Union in credits, Truman was confident that he could subject Stalin to both the carrot and the stick. All the president lacked as he prepared to go to meet the Soviet dictator was the ultimate stick.

At 6:00 AM on July 7, 1945, Truman stepped off the presidential train from Washington and onto Pier 6, midway along the row of covered railroad docks that jutted down from the Newport News army base into the James River. Crisply dressed with a bow tie, a double-breasted suit, and brown and white summer shoes, he bounded up the gangplank to the main deck of the *Augusta*, the cruiser that had transported Roosevelt to his meeting with Churchill at Argentia. Now, accompanied by a large staff that included Stimson, Byrnes, and the five-star admiral of the fleet and chief of staff, William D. Leahy, Truman was off for his own session with Churchill and, of course, Stalin.

Once the president had been piped aboard, a swarm of friends, advisers, and Secret Service men gathered around, and they all went down to the mess for breakfast. Shortly before seven o'clock, Truman climbed to the bridge. There he asked the captain to get under way: under a clear sky with a warm breeze, the *Augusta* slid through the opening in the blue-buoyed submarine net that guarded the mouth of the river and entered the Atlantic Ocean.

A week later, on July 15, the cruiser steamed into the harbor at Antwerp, docking at a city pier. Truman and his party motored to Brussels, then flew on the waiting *Sacred Cow* to Berlin; from the German capital they rode to Babelsberg, next door to Potsdam, where the last wartime conference was to take place.

Three days before Truman reached Europe, Churchill was vacationing in a château at Hendaye, almost on the border of France and Spain and overlooking the Bay of Biscay. As was his custom when in the south of France, he was engaged in landscape painting. On this occasion, however, he seemed to have lost his inspiration. "I'm very depressed," he said to Lord Moran, his physician. "I don't want to do anything. I have no energy. I wonder if it will come back."

According to Great Britain's unwritten constitution, a prime minister had to call a general election no later than five years after taking office; having ascended to the premiership in May 1940, Churchill had complied with the custom, giving his final campaign speech on June 30. Because ballots had to come in from soldiers scattered around the world, the full tally of votes was not yet available, even in the middle of July.

"I shall be only half a man until the result of the poll," Churchill grumbled. "I shall keep in the background at the [Potsdam] conference."

Even while taking in the warmth of the sunshine, Churchill was exhausted. So was the nation he had led during the long years of war. Between "1938 and 1945 Britain's exports declined from £471 million to £258 million," an American historian has pointed out, "and its imports increased over the same period from £858 million to £1,299 million. . . . By the following year its foreign indebtedness was far greater than that of all Western Europe combined and, excluding debts to the United States, three times larger than that of France. The British [had] virtually dissipated the legacy and power of nineteenth-century imperialism." Churchill's best efforts at maintaining British independence had come to naught: for all practical purposes, Great Britain had become an economic, military, and political appendage of the new American Empire.

For Churchill, such facts of life had been wearing enough. Making them worse had been a visit to Churchill by Joseph E. Davies late in May 1945. The son of Welsh immigrants to the United States, Davies had worked and charmed his way into a successful law practice and for a short time had served in the State Department. Truman had sent him to deliver a message to Churchill.

Davies's ebullience had not concealed the bluntness of what he had to say. At Potsdam, Truman would hardly even bother to see Churchill.

On the morning of July 15, a dispirited Churchill left by car for the three-hour drive to Bordeaux. From there, along with his daughter Mary, he flew to Berlin.

Stalin, whose revolutionary code name meant "Man of Steel," was afraid to fly. For his trip to Germany, therefore, he ordered a special train with eleven coaches, four of which workers had extracted from storage and given a thorough cleansing; the four coaches in question had been those of Czar Nicholas II. So as Stalin passed through the moonscapes of war-leveled Russia, Lithuania, and East Prussia, he was able to look out on his new domains from the cushioned comfort of Russia's imperial past.

As the train wound over the vastness of the territories taken from Germany, Stalin must have experienced a degree of satisfaction. He had outdone even his czarist predecessors. The Red Army had already forged a column of satellite states along Russia's western frontier and now was reaching well into Germany itself. Stalin intended to keep that buffer zone at all possible costs.

But he also must have been worried. What would be the attitude of the new American president, Truman, toward a Soviet presence even beyond Berlin?

Truman and Stalin met for the first time on July 17, while the president was working in the "Berlin White House," an edifice in Babelsberg. "Promptly a few minutes before twelve I looked up from the desk," Truman wrote in his diary, "and there stood Stalin in the doorway. I got to my feet and advanced to meet him. He put out his hand and smiled. I did the same, we shook, I greeted Molotov [who was just behind Stalin], and we sat down. . . . After the usual polite remarks, we got down to business."

On Wednesday, July 18, 1945, the Big Three convened in Potsdam's Cecilienhof, once a rural residence of Kaiser Wilhelm II. Charles Mee, a historian of the Potsdam summit, described the palace thus:

> It was a 176-room ersatz Tudor country home, with swatches of stucco here and there interrupted by mock-Elizabethan windows and stone portals that appeared embarrassed by their lack of moats and drawbridges. Topping it all off was a collection of chimneys, one vaguely Italian in inspiration, some reminiscent of the columns of the *baldachino* of St. Peter's Cathedral, and all of them together resembling nothing so much as the rooftops of nineteenth-century Nottingham.

Into this architectural jumble the Russians had moved furniture scavenged from around the region: faded French carpets, clunky German chairs, and second-rate (at best) Italian paintings of mountains and villas. For private consultations, the three principals and their advisers could retire to outlying rooms. The main conference room was on the ground floor. Surrounded by dark-paneled walls, with French doors that opened onto the lake below and let mosquitoes in, the conferees sat around a circular oak table. There, for two hot weeks, with Truman (as the only head of state there) presiding, the Potsdam Conference commenced.

As he had predicted, Churchill played but a minor part in the discussions. Then his party lost the election to the Labour Party, led by Clement Attlee. Churchill became leader of the Opposition. Unlike the American practice, whereby the loser of a presidential contest remains in office for another two months, when the British prime minister's party loses, he or she is replaced as prime minister, that day. On July 28, Attlee, although poorly versed in foreign affairs, abruptly took Churchill's place at Potsdam. A mousy-looking man anyway, Attlee thereafter was hardly noticeable, although he was made aware, as Churchill had been, of the American progress on the atomic bomb.

5

On Monday, July 16, 1945, the day after the American delegation's arrival in Potsdam, Secretary of War Stimson received a message from Alamogordo, the New Mexico atomic test site: "Operated on this morning. Diagnosis not yet complete but results seem satisfactory and already exceed expectations." Stimson took the report immediately to Byrnes and Truman. Although the wording was cryptic, both were, in Stimson's words, "greatly interested."

Presiding over the conference the next day, Truman was brimming over with confidence. "Seizing this hoped for opportunity to take the offensive," Admiral Leahy wrote in his diary, Truman "presented at once, without permitting any interruption, the . . . proposals for the agenda which we had prepared." Starting off with Eastern Europe, Truman read aloud from a statement drafted by the State Department, a document that demanded:

1. "the immediate reorganization of the present governments in Romania and Bulgaria."
2 "immediate consultations to . . . include representatives of all significant democratic elements."
3. Joint British-American-Soviet help "in the holding of free and unfettered elections."

July 18, 1945, brought a slightly more detailed account of the Alamogordo test: the blast had been visible from as far away as 250 miles. "The president was evidently very re-enforced," Stimson noted in his diary, "and said he was very glad I had come to the meeting."

The next day, Truman continued to press for the democratization of Romania and Bulgaria, adding the charge that the Soviet Union was seeking to intervene in Greece. Appearing incensed, Stalin denied the accusation.

Two days later brought at last the full report from General Leslie R. Groves, the commander of the New Mexico test. "[I]n a remote section of the Alamogordo Air Base," Groves cabled, "the first full-scale test was made of the implosion-type atomic fission bomb. For the first time in history there was a nuclear explosion. . . . The test was successful beyond the most optimistic expectations of anyone. . . . I estimate the energy generated to be in excess of the equivalent of 15,000 to 20,000 tons of TNT and this is a conservative estimate."

The news, which Stimson again relayed to Truman and Byrnes, left the latter two elated. "They were immensely pleased," Stimson wrote. "The president was tremendously pepped up by it and spoke to me of it again and again when I saw him." Stimson concluded, "He said it gives him an entirely new feeling of confidence and he thanked me for having come to the conference and being present to help him in this way."

The reason for Truman's sense almost of omnipotence was straightforward. The possession of the atomic bomb, he believed, would enable him to reverse the Yalta deal and to roll back Soviet control in Eastern Europe. As Secretary of State Byrnes stated succinctly on July 23, "[the atomic bomb] is tying in with what we are doing in all fields."

6

None of this is to say, as some historians have implied, that Truman used the existence of the bomb to threaten Stalin. At Potsdam, the president did mention the bomb to Stalin (who, having received intelligence reports, was not surprised). But Truman nonetheless was unable to dislodge Stalin from Eastern Europe. Indeed, the Potsdam Conference ended by tacitly ratifying the status quo: Soviet domination of Eastern Europe; the East-West dismemberment of Germany; and American influence west of the Rhine. By no means had Truman achieved a rollback in the Soviet satellite states.

The events of the Potsdam Conference and the soon-to-come dropping of the atomic bombs on Hiroshima and Nagasaki nevertheless made three points clear about the ending of World War II. First, the United States alone possessed the ultimate weapon of mass destruction (that monopoly would end in a few years, but America would always have the potential of unleashing more devastating power than any other nation or group of nations). Second, with Germany and Japan gone from the ranks of the great powers, and the British and French Empires fading away, the United States would set its sights on eliminating its last imperial rival, the Soviet Union. And third, like Great Britain after the final defeat of Napoleon Bonaparte in 1815, the United States after the defeat of Nazi Germany and imperial Japan in 1945 bestrode the world like a colossus. The age of the American Empire had now begun.

EPILOGUE

The *Pax Americana*

1

"What kind of peace do we seek?" President John F. Kennedy asked publicly in June 1963. "Not a *Pax Americana* enforced on the world by American weapons of war . . . not merely peace for Americans but peace for all men and women—not merely in our time but peace in all time."

In making that statement, JFK was giving voice to the long-standing and deeply rooted American article of faith that the United States does not lead an empire. Empire is for others—the British, the French, and the Soviets in the time of our memories, and, of course, the Germans and the Japanese and distantly the Ottomans and the Spanish, and even further back in history the Romans and the Athenians. But not Americans!

Yet that claim collides with reality. On May 10, 2003, the *New York Times* headlined a column "American Empire: Not 'If' but 'What Kind'?" So what, let us ask again, is an empire? Stephen Peter Rosen, a professor of government at Harvard, writes that "a political unit that has overwhelming superiority in military power, and that uses that power to influence the internal behavior of other states, is called an empire." Charles S. Maier, also a Harvard professor, considers an empire to be "a major actor in the international system based on the subordination of diverse national elites who— whether under compulsion or from shared convictions—accept the values of those who govern the dominant center or metropole."

Mary Ann Heiss, a professor of history at Kent State University, who delivered the keynote address at the April 2000 convention of the Society for Historians of American Foreign Relations, describes empire as "a situation in which a single state shapes the behavior of others, whether directly or indirectly, partially or completely, by means that can range from the outright use of force through intimidation, dependency, inducement, or even inspiration." In *American Empire*, a book published in 2002, Andrew J. Bacevich, the director of the Center for International Relations at Boston University, takes an empire to be the "ultimate guarantor and enforcer of norms." And writing in the *New York Times Magazine* of January 5, 2003, Michael Ignatieff, the director of the Carr Center at the Kennedy School of Government at Harvard, sees an "imperial power" as "more than being the most powerful nation or just the most hated one. It means enforcing such order as there is in the world and doing so in [its own] interest. It means laying down the rules [it] wants . . . while exempting itself from other rules . . . that go against its interest." By all these indicators—power, influence, scope of interest, and role—between 1914 and 1945 the United States became an empire.

2

The seed time of the American Empire, to be sure, lay well before the two world wars, roughly in the 1880s and 1890s. In that era the United States went from being a second-rate power at best to a nation recognized by the statesmen of Europe as having joined the ranks of the great powers. The United States led the world in the production of wheat, coal, iron, and steel. J. Pierpont Morgan and John D. Rockefeller personified the stupendous rise of American riches. The total capital in American banks exceeded that of any other country, and the total value of American industrial output equaled that of any two competitors.

With wealth came might. The same period saw the construction of big-gun steel warships. Although the American fleet by no means was a challenge to Great Britain's, congressional authorizations brought it abreast of Germany's and ahead of Austria-Hungary's and Italy's.

The emergence of American naval power encouraged business-men to push aggressively into foreign markets. Rockefeller reached out to challenge French, Russian, and Dutch oil firms in the Middle East and Asia, and Andrew Carnegie was beginning to sell steel in Europe itself. Occasional newspaper editors and politicians mused about resuming the old contest with Great Britain and even talked about the conquest of Canada. Nothing came of all that, but the United States did acquire its first territory beyond the water's edge.

Midway through January 1893, a group of armed Americans in Honolulu surrounded the Royal Palace, overthrew Queen Lili-uokalani, the Hawaiian monarch, and installed a new government. At the request of the American minister, Marines from the USS *Boston* went ashore to put down any resistance. Once assuredly in control, the authorities demanded that the United States annex the islands.

In 1898 the United States did so and, during the Spanish-American War of the same year, acquired Puerto Rico, Cuba, Guam, and the Philippines. America now possessed a small, seaborne empire. Soon afterward President Theodore Roosevelt bullied, blus-tered, and bragged his way into the seizure of the Panama Canal Zone, making the United States a power in the Caribbean and the Pacific alike.

A committed imperialist and a consummate showman, Theo-dore Roosevelt climaxed his presidency with a spectacular display of American naval prowess: he sent the sixteen battleships of the Great White Fleet all the way around the world. At the end of 1907, the vessels, anchored in Hampton Roads, at the mouth of the James River, took on provisions, aligned themselves into a single column, and steamed out into the reaches of the Atlantic Ocean. With every detail of the voyage given play in American newspapers, they put in at Rio, Santiago, Los Angeles, San Francisco, Honolulu, Auck-land, Sydney, Tokyo, and then at all the major ports of the Brit-ish Empire, from Hong Kong to Gibraltar. Upon their return to the United States in late February 1909, Theodore Roosevelt was on hand aboard the presidential yacht, positioned off Old Point

Comfort, to salute each ship as it passed by. Steaming past the yacht, each battleship returned the honor by booming out a twenty-one-gun salute. Then, surrounded by American flags and red, white, and blue bunting on every house, bridge, and building of the Virginia waterfront towns, the battleships lowered their anchors again and came to rest.

The journey of the Great White Fleet ended just one week before the end of TR's presidency. In politics as in the theater timing is everything.

But what had the voyage accomplished? Not much, except to advertise the hopes of Theodore Roosevelt and other boosters of an imperial America. William Howard Taft, TR's successor, showed little inclination to implement such dreams.

Such a vision, certainly, had little or nothing to do with ordinary American lives. On a summer Sunday five years after the return of the Great White Fleet, America's mood was anything but imperial. On that Sunday, baseball fans in Baltimore happily read that their new rookie, Babe Ruth, had just pitched the minor-league Orioles to victory over the Buffalo Bisons. Elsewhere in the country, people read the feature stories that ran in all the massive Sunday papers. Then it was time for church, and bells tolled in steeples all across the land. In Muskegee, Oklahoma, the Reverend James K. Thompson preached on the dazzlingly unoriginal topic "Whither Are We Drifting?"

The Sunday in question was June 28, 1914. The next morning's papers carried the news of the assassination in Sarajevo of Archduke Franz Ferdinand, heir to the throne of the Austro-Hungarian Empire. Soon America was no longer drifting.

3

By the end of the period that encompassed the two world wars, America had exceeded even the aspirations of Theodore Roosevelt: by all the definitions cited above, it had become the world's dominant empire. By 1945 the United States enjoyed "overwhelming superiority in military power" and, in the reconstruction of Germany and Japan, it used "that power to influence the internal behavior of other states." All across the Pacific and the Atlantic, "national elites" were subordinated to American values. Outside the Soviet zone of control, the United States preeminently shaped "the behavior of others." And as the *Pax Americana* replaced the *Pax Britannica*, the United States became the "ultimate guarantor and enforcer of norms," imposing the Bretton Woods strictures on the rest of the capitalist world. And as was manifested by the FDR–Ibn Saud oil deal, realized behind Churchill's back, America proved itself perfectly prepared to exempt "itself from other rules" that went "against its interest."

President Kennedy's disclaimer notwithstanding, the emergence of the American Empire was the underlying story of the two world wars. So we must inquire: what have been the consequences of that emergence?

4

On the snowy morning of February 21, 1947, in his office in the State Department—then housed in the architectural hodgepodge now called the Executive Office Building, just west of the White House—then-Undersecretary of State Dean Acheson received a visitor from the British embassy. Entering Acheson's chamber, the caller delivered a "blue piece of paper," diplomatic jargon for a most important message. Perusing the document, Acheson saw that its contents were indeed urgent: Great Britain, the message declared, could no longer afford to keep order at the eastern end of the Mediterranean. His Majesty's government, therefore, was asking the United States to take over Great Britain's traditional imperial responsibilities in that part of the world.

Acheson did not hesitate. Quickly informing Truman of the British plight, he recommended that the president ask Congress for funds to quell the civil war taking place in Greece, once a British protectorate. Truman in turn requested that Acheson make the initial appeal on Capitol Hill. Doing so, Acheson early in March 1947 tes-tified before the Senate Committee on Foreign Relations. If the United States failed to intervene in Greece, he warned, then "like apples in a barrel infected by one rotten one, the corruption of Greece will infect Iran and all to the east." Stunned, Senator Arthur Vandenberg, a Republican of Michigan and chairman of the com-mittee, told Acheson that if the president spoke the same way to the Congress as a whole, he would get all the support he wanted.

On March 12, 1947, Truman did just that. In a speech written by Acheson and his staff, the president divided the world between "free people" and governments that relied on "terror and oppres-sion . . . the suppression of personal freedoms." Truman confined his address to Greece and Turkey, not explicitly mentioning the Soviet Union, but he obtained congressional backing for what came to be called the Truman Doctrine: the American intent to contain the Soviet Union.

In its imperial heyday, Great Britain, too, had sought to contain Russia. Now, with the international changing of the guard, Uncle Sam had taken John Bull's place. The Truman Doctrine represented the culmination of the imperial transition that had been under way since the opening of World War I.

5

The imperial replacement did not end even in 1947. In the Middle East, with President Truman's 1948 official recognition of Israel, the United States assumed the old British role as the guardian of the Jews in Palestine.

In East Asia, American businesses supported by the State Depart-ment sought to drive the British out of one of their pre–World War II bastions, the China market; only the victory of the Communists in 1949 aborted that push. Reversing President Franklin D. Roose-velt's oft-expressed antipathy to European colonialism, Washington by the time of the Korean War was underwriting the French effort to return to power in Vietnam.

In the Middle East again, in the autumn of 1956, after Egypt's General Gamal Abdel Nasser nationalized the Suez Canal, a joint Israeli-French-British military force invaded that Arab country. Not wanting an angered Egypt to join the Soviet bloc, President Dwight D. Eisenhower objected strongly to the attack. Over the transatlantic telephone he reduced Anthony Eden, the British prime minister, to tears, threatening that unless the invaders withdrew, the United States would shut off the supply of oil to Britain. Along with the Israelis and the French, the British withdraw. Eisenhower's threat ended any lingering illusions in London that Great Britain was still an empire and asserted the role of the United States as the guarantor of peace in the Middle East.

Peace in the region, however, was a scarce commodity. The Six-Day War of June 1967 put Israel in possession of the Golan Heights, the West Bank of the Jordan River, and the Sinai Peninsula, conquests that seemed to augment Israel's security but that also further enraged Arab sentiment against the Jews. Many observers believed that trouble lay ahead. Surely enough, the Yom Kippur War, fought in the autumn of 1973, led to another Israeli triumph against the Arab armies but also to the Arab oil embargo against the countries that had supported Israel. That meant primarily the United States. So when in early 1974 the Organization of Petroleum Exporting Countries (OPEC) made the embargo real, enormous sums of money began to flow out of the United States and into the coffers of the Persian Gulf oil producers. Although the West's bankers gladly moved in to help the Arabs invest their new fortunes in Western banks, the danger posed by the Persian Gulf states to the American economy was clear.

The Persian Gulf once had been a British lake: Iran had been a British protectorate; British officials had drawn the borders of Iraq and Kuwait; the sheikdoms along the Arabian side of the gulf had been British dependencies. All that, nonetheless, was about to change.

In an article published in *Harper's* in March 1975, Miles Ignotus (Latin for "unknown soldier" and the pseudonym of a Washington-based professor and defense consultant with intimate links to high-level U.S. policymakers) advocated "seizing Arab oil." What he had in mind was America's replacement of Great Britain as the ruler of the gulf.

The scheme had an obvious drawback: the Soviet Union might have responded to an American invasion with conventional or even nuclear weapons. President Gerald R. Ford, in office when the article appeared, did little or nothing to implement the plan.

Under President Jimmy Carter, however, the United States took two steps toward the mastery of the gulf. First, the United States signed a lease to Diego Garcia, once a Portuguese- and later a British-controlled island in the Indian Ocean, about twenty-seven hundred miles southeast of the Persian Gulf: the British had used Diego Garcia as a coaling station, but for the naval forces of the United States it was useful as a jumping-off point to the gulf. Second, the Carter administration made commitments to the defense of Saudi Arabia and Kuwait (the latter having been a British colony); the arrangement allowed the United States to place military bases along the western littoral of the gulf.

The next step of the march to the gulf occurred early in 1987. Concluding that Iran (which had undergone its revolution and was embroiled in a war with Iraq) was a threat to the oil exports of Kuwait (which sided with Iraq in the Iraqi-Iranian war), President Ronald Reagan ordered the emplacement of American flags aboard Kuwaiti petroleum tankers. Designed as a warning to Iranian gunboats to stay away from the tankers, Reagan's command in effect made Kuwait into a British-style American protectorate.

Two months later, after Americanizing the Kuwaiti fleet, Reagan increased the number of American warships in the Gulf from nine to forty-one. Grave incidents took place. A missile fired from Iraq, which the United States was supporting in its anti-Iran war, struck an American warship, killing thirty-seven sailors. Then in the summer of 1988, an American naval commander mistook an Iranian airliner for an attacking jet and shot it down. Nevertheless, the passageway through the Persian Gulf remained open, and like the Royal Navy before it, the American fleet kept it so.

Once the Soviet Union began visibly to fall apart, Washington no longer feared Moscow as a deterrent to military actions in the gulf. So when, on August 2, 1990, Iraq's dictator, Saddam Hussein, overran Kuwait, President George H. W. Bush vowed to defend Saudi Arabia and to free Kuwait. In doing so, he was defending long-standing British interests, for the Great Britain of Prime Minister Margaret Thatcher depended heavily on investments from Kuwait. In an action that was a souped-up version of Great Britain's old gun-boat diplomacy, on January 16, 1991, American planes and missiles, many launched from ships in the Persian Gulf, attacked Iraq with massive force. Iraq fought back, but feebly and in vain. Kuwait was liberated. Aside from Iran, all that remained to complete the conquest spelled out by Miles Ignotus was Iraq itself.

6

Whatever the motivations that have led to the U.S. invasion of Iraq in 2003, the American occupation of that country is a lineal descendant of the great transformation of international relations that began in 1914. From the anticolonial tone of Woodrow Wilson's Fourteen Points to the similar message of Franklin D. Roosevelt's Atlantic Charter, and finally the reduction of Great Britain to the status of an American dependent, the world witnessed the substitution of the *Pax Americana* for the *Pax Britannica*. In the post–World War II era, the United States again and again entered into power vacuums caused by the collapse of the British and French Empires. Vietnam was a case in point, for there the United States carried on what had been a French colonial war. So was the Persian Gulf, which the British began to vacate in the 1960s.

Just about everywhere post–World War II America has gone, the British, and to a lesser extent the French, had gone before: the Levant; Indochina; and even central Asia, where the British and Russian Empires played out the nineteenth-century Great Game, vying to control access to the rich plains of the Indian subcontinent. Then as now, Afghanistan was a pawn in that struggle.

Around the Persian Gulf, as David Fromkin, the author of *A Peace to End All Peace: The Fall of the Ottoman Empire and the Creation of the Modern Middle East,* has written, the British "created countries, nominated rulers, delineated frontiers, and introduced a state system of the sort that exists everywhere else." Their fatal flaw lay in their failure "to ensure that the dynasties, the states, and the political systems that they established would permanently endure."

President George W. Bush's invasion of Iraq represents a culmination of America's own imperial quest and its takeover of the world from its Britannic forerunner. But ever since the British carved Iraq out of the Ottoman Empire after World War I, the land long known as Mesopotamia has been racked by anarchy and violence. The British eventually despaired of ever being able to quell the troubles. So it is today. Given Churchill's bitterness over being forced to preside over the "liquidation of the British Empire," we might call the unruliness that America faces now in Iraq "Winston's revenge."

Notes

Prologue: Hail, Caesar!

1–3   *the scene aboard the* Quincy: *New York Times,* February 24, 1945.

Chapter 1: The Waltz of War

9–12   *the assassination in Sarajevo:* Dedijer, 10–16.
12   *the scene in Vienna:* Zweig, 200.
13   *"eliminated as a factor of political power":* Nomikos and North, 36.
14–15   *Paléologue's descriptions:* Paléologue, 11–28.
15–16   *the kaiser aboard the ship:* Müller, 1–8.
17   *"discussion had reached":* Churchill, *World Crisis,* 1:204–205.
18   *"state of war":* Nomikos and North, 113.
     "I went down to the beach": Churchill, *World Crisis,* 209.
20   *"Therefore . . . with regard":* Nomikos and North, 138.
     "It was truly France": Poincaré, 4:334.
21   *"The theory that England":* Ferguson, 75.
     "It is no exaggeration": Brock, 138.
     "At the cabinet": Churchill, *World Crisis,* 230.
22   *"Oh! Say there is":* quoted in Young, 103.
23–24   *Grey's speech: Westminster Gazette,* August 4, 1914.
24–25   *"I looked at the excited cheerers":* Asquith, 264.
27   *"Henry looked grave":* ibid.
     "England would be forever contemptible": Hendrick, 1:314.
28   *"suddenly contracted":* Lloyd George, 1:77.

Chapter 2: The Shining City upon the Hill

29   *"looked strangely picturesque": Westminster Gazette,* June 23, 1897.
30   *"was a little, plain": Daily Mail* (London), June 23, 1897.
31   *"Tired of the routine":* Rosecrance, 97.
33   *the Philadelphia scene:* Bowen, 3–5.
34   *"The state of Georgia":* ibid., 32.

35–36   *"[W]e proceeded down the channel"*: DeVoto, 278–279.
39   *"The cup of forbearance"*: McCormac, 414.
41   *"day when not a foot"*: Perkins, 167.
42   *"a short sturdy figure"*: Fremantle, 40.
43   *"a seedy looking old gentleman"*: Shannon, 26–27.
44   *"six impartial jurists"*: LaFeber, 241.
45   *"Chronic wrongdoing"*: ibid., 242.
46   *the Veracruz scene:* Quirk, 78–80.
47   *"Lift your eyes"*: Baker, 275.

Chapter 3: The *Lusitania*

51   *"Are there not other alternatives"*: Baldwin, 57.
         "I've told it many times": Morgenthau, 152–153.
53   *"At the summit true politics"*: Churchill, *World Crisis*, 298.
54   *the shore raid:* Simpson, 29.
         Churchill's escape: Sears, 378.
56–57   *"Livebait Squadron"*: Simpson, 29–30.
57   *description of the* Lusitania: *Times* (London), June 8, 1906.
58   *The* Lusitania's *interior:* Preston, 45–49.
         "some forty British merchant": *Times* (London), March 17, 1914.
60   *"if I bought up the market"*: Preston, 93–94.
         "large number of German sailors": ibid.
         "Sooner or later": Viereck, 64.
62   *"U-30 puts to sea"*: Simpson, 117–118.
63   *"There is always a danger"*: quoted ibid., 116.
65   *"The* Lusitania *was sent"*: Kenworthy and Young, 211.
68   *Schwieger's logbook:* ibid., 154.
69   *"practically all [the* Lusitania's*] cargo"*: ibid., 335–337.

Chapter 4: The Fourteen Points

72   *"You know those Roosevelts"*: quoted in Burns, *Lion and Fox*, 35.
87   *"long and detailed"*: Lansing, 112.
         "had become a partner": Coogan, 193.
88   *"our businessmen ought to"*: quoted in LaFeber, 292;
         "Let us build": quoted in Link, 4:339.
89   *The Fourteen Points:* quoted in Baker, *Woodrow Wilson: Life and Letters*, 7:456.

Chapter 5: The Peace of Paris

91   *"everything was already familiar"*: quoted in Edmund Wilson, 465.
92   *"robber capitalists"*: quoted ibid., 473–474.
92–93   *"All the dark"*: and *"all the objective"*: quoted in Lincoln, 43.
93   *"To pass so quickly"*: quoted ibid., 44.
94   *"black cloud of the east"*: Baker, *Woodrow Wilson and the World Settlement*, 2:64–65.
95   *"in face and figure"*: quoted in Mee, *End of Order*, 17.
96   *"this goat-footed bard"*: quoted ibid., 31.
98   *"very tall"*: Seymour, 36.
99   *"No one ever"*: Bolitho, 346.
100–101   *"If England insists"*: quoted in Macmillan, 21.
101   *"There was no glow"*: Lloyd George, *Truth*, 1:181–182.
102   *"feverish, persistent"*: quoted in Mee, *End of Order*, 35.
                "turned out to be": Seymour, 104.
103   *"have costly paintings"*: Shotwell, 87–88.
106–107   *"coldest man"*: Stoddard, 136; *"merely a pawn"*: Longworth, 279.
109   *"the establishment of an organization"*: quoted in Claude, 97.

Chapter 6: The Washington Conference

113   *"Today"*: quoted in Hecksher, 645.
114   *"at the bottom"*: quoted in Litwack and Jordan, 634.
115   *"I don't like Roosevelt"*: quoted in Burns, *Lion and Fox*, 73.
115–116   *"Mr. President"*: quoted ibid., 74.
116   *"Washington state"*: quoted ibid., 74–75.
117   *"gets the last"*: quoted in Ward, 534.
                "We had a chance": quoted in Burns, *Lion and Fox*, 76.
119   *"I grew up"*: quoted in Sinclair, 7–8.
119–120   *"Like the town"*: *Literary Digest*, July 27, 1920.
120   *"took orders"*: Howe, 173.
121   *"other fellows"*: quoted in Sinclair, 136.
                "an orderly . . . world": Sullivan, October 9, 1920.
122   *"American structure"*: LaFeber, 334, 336.
123   *"measureless shyness"*: quoted in Koskoff, 67.
124–125   *"I am thus"*: Herbert C. Hoover, 2:28.
126   *"establish a* Pax": Hughes, 159.
126–127   *"I thought"*: *Congressional Record*, 4008.
127   the banners: *Washington Post*, November 13, 1921.
129   *"an earnest expression"*: *New York Times*, November 13, 1921.
129   *"I am happy"*: quoted in Pusey, 2:466.

130   *"furnished the most"*: William Allen White, 598.
130–131   *"into an international"*: *Literary Digest*, April 18, 1922.
131   *"Which is going"*: quoted in Fowler, 292.

Chapter 7: Imperial Decline

134   *"the fish to bed"*: Herbert C. Hoover, 2:42.
137   *"The Lord's Prayer was"*: quoted in Morris, 300.
138   *"Irish conscription"*: quoted in Manchester, 716.
139   *"This new Irish murder"*: quoted in Bromage, 62.
139–140   *"Do my darling"*: Clementine Churchill, 270.
140   *"I cannot feel"*: quoted in James, 143.
142   *"The Greeks"*: Aitkin (Beaverbrook), 10.
143   *"in the twinkling"*: *Daily Telegraph* (London), October 24, 1933.
144   *"The [train]"*: Nehru, 43–44.
144–146   *The Amritsar atrocity*: Wallbank, 117.
149   *"I think that"*: quoted in Birkenhead, 303.

Chapter 8: The Resurgence of Roosevelt

154   *"Today"*: *New York Times*, July 22, 1932.
155   *"I have no fears"*: ibid., March 5, 1929.
156   *"Our joint undertaking"*: Herbert C. Hoover, 1:289–296.
           "the men are sitting": Bliven, 89.
156–157   *"feeding fires"*: Schlesinger, *Crisis*, 168.
157   *"leaders of our organization"*: U.S. Senate Committee on Manu-
           facturers, 214.
           "never a good-morning": I. H. Hoover, 180.
167   *"Ours must be a party"*: quoted in Burns, *Lion and Fox*, 139.
169   *"[p]eople began to look"*: Schlesinger, *Crisis*, 429.
           "a contest between": *New York Times*, November 1, 1932.

Chapter 9: The British Declaration of War

174–175   *"looking across under"*: *Washington Daily News*, March 6, 1933.
176   *"handsome"*: Acheson, 30.
           "king of evils": quoted in Dallek, 33.
176–177   *"unhampered trade"*: Hull, 81–82.
177   *"backwoods Tennessean"*: quoted in LaFeber, 373.
178   *"The Reichstag"*: Goebbels, 269–270.
           "we noticed": Papen, 268.
179–180   *"Neither the Kaiser"*: Shirer, 275–276.
180   *"By a unique upheaval"*: Dokumente, 1:20–24.

183	*"entire lower floor"*: Shirer, 392.
184	*"the first soldier"*: quoted in Elson, 184.
186	*Taylor's argument*: Taylor, *Origins*, 132.
187	*"A full blizzard"*: Kennan, 98–99.
188	*"Economic warfare"*: Medlicott, 1:12–24.
	"silver bullets": Newman, 8–52.
	After Munich: Irving, 58–69.
189	*"Chamberlain arrives"*: Nicolson Diáries and Letters, 393–394.

Chapter 10: The Horrible Year

194	*"I'm just a babe"*: New York Times, February 24, 1938.
	"tycoon who": quoted in Davis, 94.
195	*"It is true"*: New York Times, October 20, 1938; *"This is not our fight"*: quoted in Davis, 98.
	"want to be finished": quoted in Whalen, 275; *"the real fact"*: quoted in Davis, 97–98.
196	*"My dear Churchill"*: Loewenheim, Langley, and Jonas, eds., 89.
197	*"Gentlemen"*: Fraser, 78–79.
198	*"For five months"*: quoted in Wernick, 76.
199	*"Only Finland"*: Times (London), January 21, 1940.
	"air of unreality": quoted in Wernick, 79.
201	*Amery's speech*: Times (London), May 8, 1940.
204	*"Although I have changed"*: Loewenheim, Langley, and Jonas, eds., 94.
	"I have just received": ibid., 95.
205	*"In this vast external realm"*: U.S. v. Curtiss-Wright.
	The Dunkirk evacuation: King, 85.
206	*"the greatest British"*: quoted in Ponting, 92.
	"We shall go": Times (London), June 5, 1940.
207	*"We all listened"*: Loewenheim, Langley, and Jonas, eds., 98–99.
208	*"monstrosity of red"*: Spears, 138.
209–210	*British finances*: Ponting, chap. 6.
210	*"Dear Mr. President"*: Loewenheim, Langley, and Jonas, eds., 107.
211	*Fighter plane production*: Ponting, 128.
212–213	*FDR's press conference*: New York Times, September 4, 1940.
213	*"blank cheque"*: Loewenheim, Langley, and Jonas, eds., 113.

Chapter 11: The Atlantic Charter

| 217 | *"There is something"*: Washington Post, January 11, 1941; *"The business we now"*: Birkenhead, 458. |

218	*"I felt as if"*: and *"How far should we"*: quoted ibid., 470.
219	*"Except that it was smooth"*: Halifax Diary, January 21, 1941.
	"receive the president": Birkenhead, 473.
220	*"he put us completely"*: Halifax Diary, January 24, 1941.
	"everything under the sun": ibid.
	pierside at Annapolis: Time, February 3, 1941.
221	*The press conference:* Kimball, *The Most Unsordid Act*, 121.
222	*Lend-Lease:* Perrett, 75.
	"The most unsordid act": Churchill, *Finest Hour,* 569.
222–223	*demands on Britain:* Kimball, *The Most Unsordid Act*, 235.
223	*Taylor's contention:* Taylor, *English History,* 469 and 533; *Hitler's mockery:* Compton, 32.
	"paid vassal": *Auswärtige Amt,* 252.
224	*the ABC Agreement:* Naval Historical Center, Strategic Plans Division, series VII, box 117.
228	*"Hardly were we free"*: Pitt, 47–48.
	"This government proposes": Loewenheim, Langley, and Jonas, eds., 137; *"midway between the"*: Stimson Diary, April 10, 1941.
229	*"In our common interest"*: Loewenheim, Langley, and Jonas, eds., 143–144.
229–230	*"We cordially welcome"*: ibid.
231	*"time to get Hitler"*: quoted in Heinrichs, 138.
232–233	*"How are you, Harry?"*: quoted in Theodore A. Wilson, 82–83.
233	*"The* Prince of Wales": quoted ibid., 84.
234–235	*"None who took part"*: Churchill, *Finest Hour,* 452.
235–236	*Elliott Roosevelt's account:* Roosevelt, 33.
236–237	*the Atlantic Charter: New York Times,* August 13, 1941.

Chapter 12: The Turning of the Tide

238	*"British understandably"*: Theodore A. Wilson, 127.
239	*"[I]t is now clear"*: *New York Times,* September 12, 1942.
239–240	*"I am grieved"*: Loewenheim, Langley, and Jonas, eds., 163.
240	*"When I reached"*: Winant, 197.
241	*"The prime minister"*: Harriman and Abel, 111.
	"I turned on my": quoted in Gilbert, 6:1267.
241–242	*"We looked at one another"*: Winant, 198–199.
242	*"The accession of the United States"*: quoted in Gilbert 6:1274.
244	*"was often quite"*: Pawle, 150.
244–245	*"Whether it be"*: *New York Times,* December 25, 1941.
245	*"dashing through the streets"*: Moran, 15.
246	*"I cannot help"*: *New York Times,* December 27, 1941.
247	*"we have not journeyed"*: ibid., December 31, 1941.

247   *"[F]or the first time"*: Moran, 21.
248   *"balmy after the bitter"*: ibid., 22.
            "This is a shocking tale": quoted in Gilbert, 6:41.
249   *"if the West fails"*: Klymer, 14.
250   *"no hope or help"*: Stein, 78.
251   *"I speak to you"*: *Times* (London), February 16, 1942.
            "His broadcast": Gilbert, 7:59.
252   *"leader in a democracy"*: quoted in Larrabee, 9.
253   *"I feel anxiety"*: quoted in Gilbert, 7:146.
254   *"Everything was prepared"*: quoted in Gilbert, 7:173.
255   *"suction pump"*: quoted in Kimball, *The Most Unsordid Act*, 159;
            "I am the president's": Harriman and Abel, 363.
            "gained no ground": quoted in Gilbert, 7:244.
257   *"I notice, my Lord Mayor"*: *Times* (London), November 11, 1942.
257–258   *"Churchill had waited"*: Sherwood, 656.

Chapter 13: The Big Three

260   *"There still existed"*: quoted in Collier, 149.
261   *"Our own combined"*: Loewenheim, Langley, and Jonas, eds.,
            286.
261–262   *"I would question"*: ibid., 291.
262   *"England must be out"*: ibid., 295.
263   *"Conditions most agreeable"*: quoted in Gilbert, 7:293.
264   *"Father and Churchill"*: Roosevelt, 67.
            "turned to the problem": ibid., 74.
264–265   *"I must tell Churchill"*: ibid., 75–76.
266–267   *"The sultan expressed"*: ibid., 110–111.
268   *"fundamental aims"*: U.S. Joint Chiefs of Staff memorandum,
            August 22, 1943.
            "realized that the": Stoler, 136.
270–271   *"As we approached"*: Churchill, *Closing the Ring*, 303.
271   *"Stupendous issues"*: Burns, *Soldier of Freedom*, 409.
272–273   *"I began almost as soon"*: Perkins, 83–85.
275   *"The capitalist system"*: quoted in Gardner et al., *Creation*, 508.
275–276   *"the formulation"*: *New York Times*, July 2, 1944.
276   *"the entire globe"*: Theodore H. White, 287–288.
278   *"of the Soviet Union"*: Harbutt, 261.

Chapter 14: The Road to Yalta

279   *Paris scene: Le Monde*, November 12, 1944.
280   *"We French"*: quoted in Thompson, 129.
            "Frenchmen": ibid.

281   *"From the time"*: de Gaulle, *L'Unité*, 98.
282   *"All my life"*: de Gaulle, *L'Appel*, 5.
       "conceived of international order": Viorst, 222.
283   *"I sympathize"*: quoted in Feis, 471.
284   *"One day we had"*: quoted in Sherwood, 851.
284–285 *"As a matter of interest"*: quoted ibid., 858–859.
285   *"would merely introduce"*: quoted in Viorst, 227.
286–287 *"We Americans of today"*: *New York Times*, January 21, 1945.
287–288 *"of very small stature"* Djilas, 61.
288   *"the beginning of the ninth"*: Halle, 12.
289   *"western frontiers of the Soviet"*: quoted in Mee, *Meeting*, 61.
290   *"Everyone imposes"*: quoted in Djilas, 114.
291   *"We are spellbound"*: quoted in Gilbert 7:1161.
292   *"I think you would"*: quoted ibid., 1166.
292–293 *"My friend has arrived"* and *"What a change"*: quoted ibid., 1167.
293   *"P.M. walked"*: quoted ibid., 1168.

Chapter 15: Potsdam

300   *"Make it around"*: quoted in Kirkendall, 260.
302   *"Turn on your radio"*: quoted in Harry S Truman, 159.
303   *"Mr. Speaker"*: quoted in Donovan, 4.
       "Harry, the president is dead.": Harry S Truman, 5.
304   *"I feel"*: Margaret Truman, 86.
       "the straight one-two": quoted in Stimson and Bundy, 609.
305   *"Dear Mr. President"*: quoted in Harry S Truman, 85.
306–307 *The Hopkins report*: "The Entry of the Soviet Union," Sherwood, 887.
308   *Roosevelt's approval*: U.S. Joint Chiefs of Staff memorandum, January 7, 1944.
308–309 *base areas and air routes*: drawn from map in Leffler, 57.
309–310 *Kennan report*: *United States Foreign Relations: China*, 97–98.
310   *"The Yalta Agreement"*: Forrestal, 56.
       "All country politicians": Ferrell, 49.
311   *"in his belief"*: Harry S Truman, 87; *"did not argue"*: Szilard, "A Personal History," 14–15.
311   *"was concerned about"*: Szilard, "Reminiscences," 127–128.
312   *"I tried to point out"*: Stimson Diary, May 15, 1945.
       "[W]e have got": ibid., May 14, 1945.
313   *"I am getting ready"*: quoted in Daniels, 265.
314   *"I'm very depressed"*: Moran, 276.
314–315 *"1938 and 1945"*: Kolko, 490.

316   *"It was a 176-room"*: Mee, *Meeting*, 44.
317   *"Operated on this morning."*: Stimson Diary, July 16, 1945.
            "Seizing this hoped for": Leahy Diary, July 17, 1945.
318   *"The president was evidently"*: Stimson Diary, July 18, 1945;
            Stalin's denial: Churchill, *Triumph and Tragedy*, 636.
            "[I]n a remote": Stimson Diary, July 21, 1945.

Epilogue: The *Pax Americana*

321   *"a political unit"*: Rosen, 30–31; *"a major actor"*: Maier, 28.
322   *"a situation in which"*: Heiss, 513.
            "ultimate guarantor": Bacevich, 3; *"imperial power"*: Ignatieff, 24.

Sources

Archives Consulted

Balliol College, Oxford
Borthwick Institute of Historical Research, University of York: Halifax Paper.
Library of Congress, Manuscript Division, Washington, D.C.: Leahy Diary.
National Archives, Washington, D.C.
Naval Historical Center, Navy Yard, Washington, D.C.
Ohio Historical Society, Columbus, Ohio
Public Record Office, London
Franklin D. Roosevelt Presidential Library, Hyde Park, New York.
Yale University, Sterling Library, New Haven, Conn.: Stimson Diary.

Published Papers

Auswärtige Amt. Documents on German Foreign Policy, 1918–1945. 13 vols. Washington, D.C.: U.S. Government Publishing Office, 1949–1964.
Dokumente der deutschen Politik, 1933–1940. Berlin: 1935–1943, I (1935).
Myers, W. S., ed. *Herbert Hoover State Papers.* 2 vols. Garden City, N.Y.: Doubleday, Doran & Company, 1934.
Loewenheim, Francis L., Harold D. Langley, and Manfred Jonas, eds. *Roosevelt and Churchill: Their Secret Wartime Correspondence.* New York: Saturday Review Press, 1975.
U.S. Congress. *Congressional Record.* 67th Cong., 2nd sess., 1922.
U.S. Congress. Senate. Committee on Manufacturers. *Unemployment Relief: Hearings.* 72nd Cong., 1st sess., 1931.
U.S. v. Curtiss-Wright Export Corp. et al. In Garraty, John A., ed. *Quarrels That Have Shaped the Constitution.* New York: Harper & Row, 1962.
U.S. Department of Defense. *The Entry of the Soviet Union and the War against Japan: Military Plans, 1941–1945.* Washington, D.C.: U.S. Government Printing Office, 1955.
U.S. Department of State. *United States Foreign Relations: China, 1944–1949.* Washington, D.C.: U.S. Government Printing Office, 1949.
———. *United States Foreign Relations: Conference of Berlin (Potsdam), 1945.* Washington, D.C.: U.S. Government Printing Office, 1960.

———. *Foreign Relations of the United States, 1950*. vol. 1. Washington, D.C.: U.S. Government Printing Office, 1977.

U.S. Joint Chiefs of Staff. FDR to SecState. Hyde Park, N.Y.: Roosevelt Library, January 7, 1944.

———. Memorandum, August 22, 1943.

Articles and Chapters

Bliven, Bruce. "On the Bowery." *New Republic*, March 19, 1930.

Fraser, Admiral of the Fleet Lord. "Churchill and the Navy." In *Winston S. Churchill: Servant of Crown and Commonwealth*, ed. Sir James Marchant. London: H.M. Stationery Office, 1954.

Hamburger, Philip. "Profiles: Mr. Secretary." *New Yorker*, November 12, 1949.

Harbutt, Fraser. "Churchill, Hopkins, and the 'Other' Americans." *International History Review*, May 1986.

Heiss, Mary Ann. "The Evolution of the Imperial Idea and U.S. National Identity." *Diplomatic History*, Fall 2002.

Ignatieff, Michael. "The Burden." *New York Times Magazine*, January 5, 2003.

Kirkendall, Richard S. "Harry Truman." In *America's Eleven Greatest Presidents*, ed. Morton Borden. Chicago: Rand McNally, 1971.

Klymer, Kenton J. "The U.S. and the Decolonization of Empire in Asia." In *American Studies in Malaysia*, ed. K. S. Nathan. March 1986.

Maier, Charles S. "An American Empire?" *Harvard Magazine*, November–December, 2002.

Rosecrance, Richard. "Why England Slipped." *Wilson Quarterly*, Autumn 1987.

Rosen, Stephen Peter. "The Future of War and the American Military." *Harvard Magazine*, May–June 2002.

Stoler, Mark A. "The 'Second Front' and American Fear of Soviet Expansion, 1941–1945." *Military Affairs*, October 1975.

Sullivan, Mark. "The Stump and the Porch." *Collier's*, October 9, 1920.

Szilard, Leo. "A Personal History of the Bomb." *Roundtable*, September 25, 1949.

———. "Reminiscences." *Perspectives in American History*, 1968.

Books

Biographies and Autobiographies

Acheson, Dean. *Present at the Creation: My Years in the State Department*. New York: W. W. Norton, 1969.

Aitkin, Max (Lord Beaverbrook). *The Decline and Fall of Lloyd George*. New York: Duell, Sloan, & Pearce, 1963.

Asquith, Margot. *An Autobiography*. New York: George H. Doran, 1922.

Baker, Ray Stannard. *Woodrow Wilson: Life and Letters*. 8 vols. Garden City, N.Y.: Doubleday, Page, 1922–1939.

Baker, Ray Stannard. *Woodrow Wilson and the World Settlement.* 3 vols. Garden City, N.Y.: Doubleday, Page, 1933.

Birkenhead, Earl of. *Halifax: The Life of Lord Halifax.* London: Hamish Hamilton, 1965.

Bromage, Mary C. *Churchill and Ireland.* South Bend, Ind.: University of Notre Dame Press, 1964.

Burns, James MacGregor. *Roosevelt: The Lion and the Fox, 1882–1940.* New York: Harcourt, Brace, & World, 1956.

———. *Roosevelt: The Soldier of Freedom.* New York: Harcourt Brace Jovanovich, 1970.

Charmley, John. *Churchill: The End of Glory: A Political Biography.* New York: Harcourt, Brace, 1993.

Churchill, Winston S. *The World Crisis.* 2 vols. New York: Charles Scribner's Sons, 1923.

Dallek, Robert. *Franklin D. Roosevelt and American Foreign Policy, 1932–1945.* New York: Oxford University Press, 1979.

Daniels, Margaret Truman. *Harry S Truman.* London: Hamish Hamilton, 1973.

Davis, John H. *The Kennedys: Dynasty and Disaster, 1848–1984.* New York: Shapolsky, 1985.

De Gaulle, Charles. *L'Appel.* Paris: Plon, 1954.

———. *L'Unité.* Paris: Plon, 1956.

DeVoto, Bernard. *The Journals of Lewis and Clark.* Boston: Houghton Mifflin, 1953.

Donovan, Robert J. *Conflict and Crisis: The Presidency of Harry S Truman, 1945–1948.* New York: W. W. Norton, 1977.

Ferrell, Robert H., ed. Off *the Record: The Private Papers of Harry S Truman.* New York: Harper & Row, 1980.

Forrestal, James. *The Forrestal Diaries,* ed. Walter Millis. New York: Viking, 1951.

Gilbert, Martin. *Winston S. Churchill.* 8 vols. Boston: Houghton Mifflin, 1971–1986.

Goebbels, Josef. *Vom Kaiserhof zur Reichskanzlei.* Munich: Zentral-verlag der NSDAP, 1936.

Harriman, Averell, and Elie Abel. *Special Envoy to Churchill and Stalin.* New York: Random House, 1975.

Hecksher, August. *Woodrow Wilson: A Biography.* New York: Macmillan, 1991.

Hendrick, Burton J. *The Life and Letters of Walter H. Page.* 3 vols. New York: Doubleday, Page, 1922.

Hoover, Herbert C. *Memoirs.* 3 vols. New York: Macmillan, 1951–1953.

Hoover, I. H. *Forty-two Years in the White House.* Boston: Houghton Mifflin, 1934.

Hull, Cordell. *The Memoirs of Cordell Hull.* 2 vols. New York: Macmillan, 1948.

James, Robert Rhodes. *Churchill: A Study in Failure.* New York: World, 1976.

Kennan, George F. *Memoirs: 1925–1950.* Boston: Little, Brown, 1967.

King, Cecil Harmsworth. *With Malice toward None: A War Diary.* Madison, N.J.: Fairleigh Dickinson University Press, 1971.

Koskoff, David E. *The Mellons: The Chronicle of America's Richest Family.* New York: Crowell, 1951.

Lansing, Robert. *War Memoirs of Robert Lansing, Secretary of State.* Indianapolis, Ind.: Bobbs-Merrill, 1935.

Link, Arthur. *Wilson.* 5 vols. Princeton, N.J.: Princeton University Press, 1947–1964.

Lloyd George, David. *War Memoirs.* 5 vols. Boston: Little, Brown, 1933.

Longworth, Alice Roosevelt. *Crowded Hours.* New York: Charles Scribner's Sons, 1933.

Manchester, William. *The Last Lion: Winston Spencer Churchill: Visions of Glory.* Boston: Little, Brown, 1983.

McCormac, Eugene Irving. *James K. Polk: A Political Biography.* Berkeley and Los Angeles: University of California Press, 1922.

Moran, Lord. *Churchill: Taken from the Diaries of Lord Moran.* Boston: Houghton Mifflin, 1966.

Morgenthau, Henry. *Mostly Morgenthaus: A Family History.* New York: Ticknor & Fields, 1991.

Morison, Elting. *Turmoil and Tradition: The Life and Times of Henry L. Stimson.* Boston: Houghton Mifflin, 1960.

Nehru, Jawaharlal. *An Autobiography.* Boston: Beacon Press, 1958.

Nicolson, Harold. *Diaries and Letters.* New York: Atheneum, 1966.

Paléologue, Maurice. *An Ambassador's Memoirs.* New York: George H. Doran, 1923.

Papen, Franz von. *Memoirs.* London: André Deutsch, 1952.

Pawle, Gerald. *The War and Colonel Warden.* New York: Alfred A. Knopf, 1963.

Perkins, Frances. *The Roosevelt I Knew.* New York: Viking, 1946.

Poincaré, Raymond. *Au service de la France.* 10 vols. Paris: Plon-Nourrit, 1926–1934.

Pusey, Merlo J. *Charles Evans Hughes.* 2 vols. New York: Macmillan, 1951.

Roosevelt, Elliott. *As He Saw It.* New York: Duell, Sloan, & Pearce, 1946.

Seymour, Charles. *Letters from the Paris Peace Conference.* New Haven, Conn.: Yale University Press, 1965.

Shannon, David A., ed. Beatrice *Webb: American Diary, 1898.* Madison: University of Wisconsin Press, 1963.

Sherwood, Robert E. *Roosevelt and Hopkins: An Intimate History.* New York: Harper & Brothers, 1950.

Sinclair, Andrew. *The Available Man: The Life Behind the Masks of Warren Gamaliel Harding*. New York: Macmillan, 1965.

Spears, Edward. *Assignment to Catastrophe*. 2 vols. London: Heinemann, 1954.

Stimson, Henry, and McGeorge Bundy. *On Active Service in Peace and War*. New York: Harper & Brothers, 1949.

Truman, Harry S. *Year of Decisions*. New York: Smithmark, 1955.

Truman, Margaret. *Souvenir: Margaret Truman's Own Story*. New York: McGraw-Hill, 1956.

Ward, Geoffrey C. *A First-Class Temperament: The Emergence of Franklin Roosevelt*. New York: Harper & Row, 1989.

Whalen, Richard J. *The Founding Father: The Story of Joseph P. Kennedy*. New York: New American Library, 1964.

White, Theodore H. *In Search of History: A Personal Adventure*. New York: Warner Books, 1979.

White, William Allen. *Autobiography*. New York: Macmillan, 1946.

Winant, John G. *A Letter from Grosvenor Square: An Account of a Stewardship*. Boston: Houghton Mifflin, 1947.

Zweig, Stefan. *Die Welt von Gestern: Erinnerungen eines Europäers*. Berlin: S. Fischer, 1962.

Historical Studies

Adams, Frederick C. *Economic Diplomacy: The Export-Import Bank and American Foreign Policy, 1934–1939*. Columbia: University of Missouri Press, 1976.

Alperovitz, Gar. *Atomic Diplomacy: Hiroshima and Potsdam*. New York: Simon & Schuster, 1965.

Bacevich, Andrew J. *American Empire: The Realities and Consequences of U.S. Diplomacy*. Cambridge, Mass.: Harvard University Press, 2002.

Baldwin, Hanson. *World War I*. New York: Harper & Row, 1962.

Bolitho, William. *Twelve against the Gods: The Story of Adventure*. New York: Simon & Schuster, 1929.

Bowen, Catherine Drinker. *Miracle at Philadelphia: The Story of the Constitutional Convention, May to September 1787*. Boston: Little, Brown, 1966.

Brock, Michael and Eleanor, eds. *H. H. Asquith's Letters to Venetia Stanley*. New York: Oxford University Press, 1982.

Churchill, Winston S. *Closing the Ring*. Boston: Houghton Mifflin, 1951.

———. *The Hinge of Fate*. Boston: Houghton Mifflin, 1950.

———. *Their Finest Hour*. Boston: Houghton Mifflin, 1949.

———. *Triumph and Tragedy*. Boston: Houghton Mifflin, 1953.

Claude, Inis L. Jr. *Power and International Relations*. New York: Random House, 1962.

Cohen, Warren I. *Empire without Tears: America's Foreign Relations, 1921–1933*. Philadelphia: Temple University Press, 1970.

Collier, Richard. *The War in the Desert*. Alexandria, Va.: Time-Life Books, 1977.

Compton, James V. *The Swastika and the Eagle: Hitler, the United States, and the Origins of World War II*. London: Sidney Bodley, 1968.

Coogan, John W. *The End of Neutrality: The U.S., Britain, and Maritime Rights, 1899–1915*. Ithaca, N.Y.: Cornell University Press, 1981.

Dedijer, Vladimir. *The Road to Sarajevo*. New York: Simon & Schuster, 1967.

Divine, Robert A. *Second Chance: The Triumph of Internationalism during World War II*. New York: Atheneum, 1967.

Djilas, Milovan. *Conversations with Stalin*. New York: Harcourt, Brace, & World, 1962.

Elson, Robert T. *Prelude to War*. Alexandria, Va.: Time-Life Books, 1977.

Feis, Herbert. *Churchill, Roosevelt, Stalin: The War They Waged and the Peace They Sought*. Princeton, N.J.: Princeton University Press, 1957.

Ferguson, Niall. The *Pity of War: Explaining World War I*. New York: Basic Books, 1999.

Fitzgerald, Robert, trans. *The Aeneid/Virgil*. New York: Alfred A. Knopf, 1992.

Fowler, Wilton B. *British-American Relations, 1917–18: The Role of Sir William Wiseman*. Princeton, N.J.: Princeton University Press, 1969.

Fremantle, Anne. *This Little Band of Prophets: The British Fabians*. New York: New American Library, 1959.

Gardner, Lloyd et al. *The Creation of the American Empire*, 2nd ed. Chicago: Rand McNally, 1976.

———. *Economic Aspects of New Deal Diplomacy*. Boston: Beacon Press, 1964.

———. *Safe for Democracy*. New York: Oxford University Press, 1984.

Halle, Louis J. *The Cold War as History*. New York: Harper & Row, 1967.

Hartz, Louis. *The Liberal Tradition in America: An Interpretation of American Political Thought since the Revolution*. New York: Harcourt, Brace, 1955.

Heinrichs, Waldo Jr. *Threshold of War: Franklin D. Roosevelt and the American Entry into World War II*. New York: Oxford University Press, 1988.

Hobsbawm, Eric. *The Age of Empire*. New York: Vintage, 1989.

Howe, Frederick C. *The Confessions of a Reformer*. New York: Charles Scribner's Sons, 1925.

Hughes, Charles Evans. *The Pathway to Peace*. New York: Harper & Brothers, 1925.

Hunt, Michael H. *Ideology and U.S. Foreign Policy*. New Haven, Conn.: Yale University Press, 1987.

Irving, David, ed. *Breach of Security: The German Secret Intelligence File of Events Leading to the Second World War*. London: Kimber, 1968.

Kenworthy, Joseph M., and George Young. *The Freedom of the Seas*. New York: Harper & Brothers, 1929.

Kimball, Warren F. *America Unbound: World War II and the Making of a Superpower*. New York: St. Martin's Press, 1992.

Kimball, Warren F. *Forged in War: Roosevelt, Churchill, and the Second World War.* New York: William Morrow, 1987.

———. *The Most Unsordid Act: Lend-Lease, 1939–1941.* Baltimore: Johns Hopkins University Press, 1969.

Knock, Thomas J. *To End All Wars: Woodrow Wilson and the Quest for a New World Order.* Princeton, N.J.: Princeton University Press, 1992.

Kolko, Gabriel. *The Politics of War: The World and United States Foreign Policy.* New York: Random House, 1968.

LaFeber, Walter. *The American Age: U.S. Foreign Policy at Home and Abroad, 1750–the Present.* New York: W. W. Norton, 1994.

Larrabee, Eric. *Commander in Chief: Franklin Delano Roosevelt, His Lieutenants, and Their War.* New York: Simon & Schuster, 1988.

Leffler, Melvyn P. *A Preponderance of Power: National Security, the Truman Administration, and the Cold War.* Stanford, Calif.: Stanford University Press, 1992.

Lincoln, W. Bruce. *Red Victory: A History of the Russian Civil War.* New York: Simon & Schuster, 1989.

Litwack, Leon F. and Winthrop D. Jordan. *The United States: Becoming a World Power.* Redding, Calif.: Northwest Publishing, 2002.

Lloyd George, David. *The Truth about the Peace Treaties.* 2 vols. London: Victor Gollancz, 1938.

Macmillan, Margaret. *Paris 1919: Six Months That Changed the World.* New York: Random House, 2002.

Martin, Kingsley. *The Triumph of Lord Palmerston: A Study of Public Opinion in England before the Crimean War.* London: G. Allen & Unwin, 1924.

Medlicott, W. N. *The Economic Blockade.* 2 vols. London: H.M. Stationery Office, 1952.

Mee, Charles L. *The End of Order: Versailles 1919.* New York: E. P. Dutton, 1980.

———. *Meeting at Potsdam.* New York: Dell, 1975.

Morris, James. *Farewell the Trumpets: An Imperial Retreat.* New York: Harcourt Brace Jovanovich, 1978.

Müller, Georg Alexander von. *The Kaiser and His Court: The Diaries, Notebooks, and Letters of Admiral Georg Alexander von Müller, Chief of the Naval Cabinet, 1914–1918.* New York: Harcourt, Brace, & World, 1961.

Newman, Simon. *March 1939: The British Guarantee to Poland: A Study in the Continuity of British Foreign Policy.* Oxford: Oxford University Press, 1976.

Nomikos, Eugenia V., and Robert C. North. *International Crisis: The Outbreak of World War I.* Montreal: McGill University Press, 1976.

Perkins, Bradford. *The Great Rapprochement: England and the United States, 1895–1914.* New York: Atheneum, 1968.

Perrett, Geoffrey. *Days of Sadness, Years of Triumph: The American People, 1939–1945.* New York: Penguin, 1973.

Pitt, Barrie. *The Battle of the Atlantic.* Alexandria, Va.: Time-Life, 1977.

Ponting, Clive. *1940: Myth and Reality.* Chicago: Ivan R. Dee, 1990.

Preston, Diana. Lusitania: *An Epic Tragedy.* New York: Walker, 2002.

Quirk, Robert E. *An Affair of Honor: Woodrow Wilson and the Occupation of Veracruz.* Lexington: University of Kentucky Press, 1962.

Reynolds, David. *Britannia Overruled: British Policy and World Power in the 20th Century.* London: Longman, 1991.

Schlesinger, Arthur M. Jr. *The Crisis in the Old Order.* Boston: Houghton Mifflin, 1957.

———. *The Imperial Presidency.* Boston: Houghton Mifflin, 1973.

Schumpeter, Joseph. *Imperialism and Social Classes.* Philadelphia: Orion Editions, 1991.

Sears, Stephen W., ed. *The Horizon History of the British Empire.* New York: American Heritage, 1973.

Shirer, William. *The Rise and Fall of the Third Reich.* New York: Fawcett Crest, 1959.

Shotwell, James T. *At the Paris Peace Conference.* New York: Macmillan, 1937.

Simpson, Colin. *The* Lusitania. Boston: Little, Brown, 1972.

Snyder, Jack. *Myths of Empire: Domestic Politics and International Ambition.* Ithaca, N.Y.: Cornell University Press, 1991.

Stein, R. Conrad. *The Fall of Singapore.* Chicago: Children's Press, 1982.

Stoddard, Henry L. *As I Knew Them: Presidents and Politics from Grant to Coolidge.* Port Washington, N.Y.: Kennikat Press, 1927.

Sullivan, Mark. *Our Times: The United States, 1900–1925.* New York: Charles Scribner's Sons, 1935.

Taylor, A. J. P. *English History, 1914–1945.* Oxford, Eng.: Oxford University Press, 1965.

———. *The Origins of the Second World War.* New York: Atheneum, 1962.

Thompson, Robert Smith. *Pledge to Destiny: Charles de Gaulle and the Rise of the Free French.* New York: McGraw-Hill, 1974.

Thornton, A. P. *The Imperial Idea and Its Enemies: A Study in British Power.* New York: St. Martin's Press, 1959.

Viereck, George S. *Spreading Germs of Hate.* New York: H. Liveright, 1930.

Viorst, Milton. *Hostile Allies: FDR and Charles de Gaulle.* New York: Macmillan, 1965.

Wallbank, T. Walter. *India in the New Era.* Chicago: Scott, Foresman, 1951.

Wernick, Robert. *Blitzkrieg.* Alexandria, Va.: Time-Life, 1977.

Wilson, Edmund. *To the Finland Station.* Garden City, N.Y.: Doubleday, 1940.

Wilson, Theodore A. *The First Summit: Roosevelt and Churchill at Placentia Bay, 1941.* Boston: Houghton Mifflin, 1969.

Young, Harry F. *Prince Lichnowsky and the Great War.* Athens: Ohio University Press, 1975.

Index